The Birth of Modern Critical Theory

KLAUS SCHOLDER

The Birth of Modern Critical Theology

*Origins and Problems of Biblical Criticism
in the Seventeenth Century*

SCM PRESS
London

TRINITY PRESS INTERNATIONAL
Philadelphia

Translated by John Bowden from the German
Ursprünge und Probleme der historisch-kritischen Theologie,
first published by Christian Kaiser Verlag 1966.

© Carola Scholder 1966

Translation © John Bowden 1990

First published 1990

SCM Press Ltd   Trinity Press International
26-30 Tottenham Road   3725 Chestnut Street
London N1 4BZ   Philadelphia, Pa. 19104

British Library Cataloguing in Publication Data

Scholder, Klaus, d. 1985
The birth of modern critical theology.
1. Bible. Criticism
I. Title II. Ursprünge und Probleme der
historisch-kritischen Theologie. *English*
220.6

ISBN 0-334-02442-0

Library of Congress Cataloging-in-Publication Data

Scholder, Klaus.
[Ursprünge und Probleme der historisch-
kritischen Theologie. English]
The birth of modern critical theology: origins
and problems of biblical criticism in the
seventeenth century/Klaus Scholder.
p. cm.
Translation of: Ursprünge und Probleme der
historisch-kritischen Theologie.
Includes bibliographical references.
ISBN 0-334-02442-0: $18.95
1. Bible—Criticism, interpretation, etc.—
History—17th century. 2. Theology—
Methodology—History of doctrines—17th century.
3. Religion and science—History—17th century.
4. Authority (Religion)—History of doctrines—
17th century. 5. Theology, Doctrinal—
History—17th century. I. Title.
BS500.S32413 1990
230'.09'032—dc20   90-32534

Phototypeset by Input Typesetting Ltd, London
and printed in Great Britain by
Richard Clay Ltd, Bungay, Suffolk

For my wife

CONTENTS

INTRODUCTION

The Rise of Historical-critical Theology as a Problem for Church History

1

The development of historical-critical theology is without doubt one of the most important events in the history of modern theology. However, up till now it has not been described in context. So there is considerable uncertainty over the question of its origin, relating to both the period of this origin and the circumstances which brought it about.

In his famous article 'New Testament and Theology', Rudolf Bultmann speaks of the time 'thirty or forty years ago' when 'all that has been said so far' – namely about the task of demythologizing – could already have been said 'in a similar way'.[1] Evidently despite his subsequent references to the critical theology of the nineteenth century, he thought that this problem was fully realized only around the turn of the century. H.Liebing associates the concept of historical-critical theology with the name of Ferdinand Christian Baur. In his view, there is 'historical-critical theology in the full sense' only after the great Tübingen scholar.[2] G.Hornig claims Johann Salomo Semler as the starting point,[3] whereas H.-J.Kraus thinks of Richard Simon around a century earlier: 'This is the decisive point at which historical-critical scholarship begins.'[4] Alongside this it is above all Spinoza to whom a priority is assigned in this context. 'With brilliant intuition' he is said to have developed a programme 'which was only implemented by the theology of the nineteenth century. He is the first to practise immanent and thus historical criticism; he is the founder of historical-critical research into the Bible.'[5] Without doubt all these names have a firm place in the history of historical-critical scholarship. And yet there is something haphazard about such a list, because in each instance these figures represent only particular moments of a development which has to be understood and depicted overall as a cultural process.

Ebeling takes the opposite course when, starting from the question of the nature of the historical-critical method, he seeks to define its historical context in a way which is to some degree deductive.[6] The paragraph which is important for us here begins: 'It leads only to obscuring the nature of the problem when the critical historical method is held to be a purely formal scientific technique, entirely free of presuppositions, whose application to the historical objects in the theological realm provokes no conflicts and does no hurt to the dogmatic structure...' For historical criticism is more than 'lively historical interest' such as could be found more or less in the 'early and mediaeval churches' and was given new life by the Renaissance, Humanism and the Reformation. 'And yet all that was merely accompaniment... It was not what we know today as the critical historical method. For the latter is not concerned with the greatest possible refinement of the philological methods, but with subjecting the tradition to critical examination on the basis of new principles of thought.'

So in what does the nature of this modern historical criticism consist? The decisive statements in Ebeling run as follows: 'It [this method] is – not just, say, where it oversteps its legitimate limits, but by its very nature - bound up with criticism of content. In its concern with the past and its interpretation of the sources of the past it cannot simply set aside the understanding of reality as that has been acquired by the modern mind. It is therefore closely coupled with the advance of the sciences and with the development of philosophy.'[7]

Almost a century earlier, Ferdinand Christian Baur had already defined the principle of historical-critical theology in a very similar way. 'But in the end,' he says at one point when arguing with his Jena colleague Karl Hase, 'only that view can prevail which brings unity, connection and rational consistency to our world-view, our understanding of the history of the Gospel, our whole consciousness.'[8]

'Unity, connection and rational consistency': that means, quite simply, honest exegesis – honest to the degree that in principle it must be carried on with a concern for the understanding of reality 'which has been gained by the spirit in modern times'.

The consequence of this thesis for the question of the origin of historical criticism is obvious. If historical-critical theology is characterized by the fact that in principle and in method it takes the modern understanding of reality into account, its beginnings must be bound up with the rise of the new, modern picture of the world. And in fact that is what we also read in Ebeling: 'The critical historical method first arose out of the intellectual revolution of modern times... In order to grasp the nature of the critical historical method it is thus necessary to take account of the intellectual change in the modern world.'[9]

Here, beyond the historically contingent, historical-critical theology is understood as a process which was necessarily sparked off by a particular set of historical circumstances and which was kept in motion by the persistence of these circumstances.

At the same time that indicates the direction that the question of the origin of historical criticism should take. It must begin where the modern understanding of reality takes shape; where – to begin with, only in individual instances – the old unity of scripture, world-view and faith becomes questionable; where the Copernican system can no longer be overlooked and where the triumphant voice of awakening philosophical self-awareness can no longer be missed.

The first attempts at historical criticism with which historical-critical theology takes its beginnings emerge in the controversy with the new understanding of reality which emerges increasingly more decisively from the first decades of the seventeenth century. This understanding more and more clearly clashes with the biblical picture of the world and humankind as handed down in tradition, and endorses this contradiction with increasingly irrefutable evidence.

The following account is devoted to these first attempts.

2

If we look at more recent German literature on the history of theology in the seventeenth century, while we see a series of often admirable investigations of the spirit and history of old Protestant orthodoxy,[10] by contrast there is only one major account which expressly seeks to understand the theology of this period 'in connection with the general movements of European thought'. This is

E. Hirsch's large-scale history of modern theology. But one has to express some reservations, particularly over the first volume of this account, which is concerned above all with our period.

Initially, on closer inspection, some details in the second volume seem to be in need of correction, but that can hardly be surprising, given the almost complete lack of preliminary studies.

Another hesitation is more important. Even in Hirsch's work, which gives a far greater place than usual to developments in Western Europe, the real division in the cultural forces in seventeenth-century Europe does not become completely clear.

It is just one symptom of this cultural balance that of the great figures of this century which may claim European fame, after the death of Johann Kepler in 1630 there is only one German name, that of Gottfried Wilhelm Leibniz, and it is surely no coincidence that he predominantly sought conversation partners from outside Germany. When he died in 1716, he had no worthy obituary in his homeland. It was the French Academy which took on 'the honouring of the greatest German of our time' with a memorial speech by Bernard Fontenelle.[11]

In fact, from the Thirty Years' War until well into the eighteenth century, we can observe that Germany was closed to the great questions of the time in a remarkable way.[12]

We do not have to investigate the reason for that here. The great riddle of 'the German Spirit and Western Europe' – which was put like this for the first time by E. Troeltsch – the wider setting for this complex, still lacks a solution.

The most important thing to begin with is the facts. And in general, it does not seem to have been sufficiently noted that the reception of modern ideas in Germany came almost a complete century later. Whereas around the middle of the seventeenth century orthodoxy had been forced on the defensive in all the other countries of Western Europe, in Germany its 'classical period' was just beginning – in the generation after 1648.[13] So we shall look in vain for important German contributions to the development of the critical position at this time. Where there was no encounter with the modern spirit, there was no need to reflect on the problem theologically. Up to the second half of the eighteenth century the question of modernity had hardly touched German theology and philosophy in any serious way. At all events, the contribution of Germany to the development of historical-critical theology does not relate to its critical components. Perhaps that is one of the reasons why this whole development has so far been so little treated in accounts of the history of theology.

The fact that Lutheran orthodoxy reigned supreme for so long in its homeland – and here we come to another aspect of the problem – has occasionally led to an overestimation of its general significance. A characteristic example of this is the major and influential account of the 'morphology of Lutheranism' by Werner Elert.[14] From a series of passages it can be demonstrated that in particular when it comes to questions of world-view, Elert arrives at conclusions which simply cannot be verified historically. Certainly the development of the great orthodox doctrinal systems is a fascinating scene. Seldom has theology been done with such earnestness, vigour and perspicacity as here. But against the background of the development of the European spirit, from which theology is not dispensed, after the middle of the century – with due respect to the doctors of the church – it played hardly any further part.

Here I am also concerned simply with the dimensions of the questions which were discussed inside and outside Germany in these decisive decades. Orthodoxy had only polemic to oppose to that spirit of self-confident control of the world which was alive in Galileo, Descartes, Herbert of Cherbury, Hobbes or Spinoza, or in their pupils – that spirit which discussed the foundations of the physical and moral world and which put in question the basic positions of traditional faith. It could not see in this spirit more than arrogance, ignorance or atheism. And while it was still working on the development of its doctrine of scripture, it was unaware that the very character of scripture as revelation was in dispute.

It is not completely clear how in the face of this phenomenon, which in essence he nowhere disputes, Elert can see 'almost incalculable' effects radiating from Luther's doctrine of the eucharist 'on the whole development of the modern world-view'. From a historical perspective, at any rate, on this question Lutheranism is almost completely out of the picture.[15]

But is not theology generally out of the picture here? Indeed one can say with some justification that the beginnings of biblical criticism are initially far more a philosophical than a theological problem – philosophy here being understood, as it will be throughout the rest of this book, as it was at the time: as the sum of all natural knowledge, including scientific knowledge. The reason for this, at least initially, is less that theologians utterly repudiated the new ideas than that the problems arose in the sphere of philosophy, so that philosophers were the first to become aware of them.

That suggests that in dealing with these questions the church historian comes upon a situation which is basically different from the problems, say, of the time of the Reformation. Whereas at the Reformation it was faith which forced an answer out of theology, here it is philosophical knowledge; whereas at the Reformation theologians were to some degree fighting on their own ground, here they became entangled in controversies which were alien to them and for which they were not equipped. The church historian finds himself or herself transported into the largely uncharted area which lies between philosophy and theology; he or she must attempt to see the theological positions of the time with the eyes of philosophers and note how they appeared on the basis of the new presuppositions. And conversely, church historians must examine the criticism of philosophical positions from the perspective of the theological possibilities available at the time. But this intermediary position is unavoidable if Ebeling's demand is taken seriously: 'to give an account of the cultural shift to modern times' as the presupposition of 'understanding the nature of the critical historical method'.[16]

3

Any set of questions sheds a particular light on the historical terrain to which these questions are applied. In its rays some contours emerge more sharply, and others, to which the historical approach is accustomed, remain in darkness. That is naturally also true of this account. It leaves completely on one side the question of the development of doctrine, which largely dominates theological literature on the history of orthodoxy. Instead it brings another problem into the centre: the controversy over the authority of scripture.

People are fond of calling the century of the Wars of Religion the confessional age. And without doubt the clash between confessions preoccupied contemporaries to a great degree. Its effects on the position of scripture generally should not be overlooked, and the details of them will concern us later.

However, it seems more important to make another point. In the face of the controversies over the validity of the biblical picture of the world and humankind, confessional differences fade almost completely into the background. Here parties which are otherwise deadly enemies suddenly prove to have an amazing amount in commmon. Whether the issue is the Socinians, the Copernicans or La Peyrère's *Pre-Adamites*, Roman Catholic, Lutheran and Reformed theologians from all the countries of Europe show a strange unanimity as they vie in disputing the theses with which they are presented. For example, almost as though by prior arrangement, in the 1630s, all over the continent, theological opposition to Copernicanism begins, though this question could be regarded as an open one for almost seventy years. As things are, we have no historical justification for making the Roman church principally responsible here.[17] While it may have differed from the Protestant churches in the way it went about things, it certainly did not differ in essentials.

Differentiations are only to be noted from around the middle of the century. Whereas around this period, Germany is clearly becoming increasingly closed, in the Reformed orthodoxy of the Netherlands the great controversy with and over Cartesianism is beginning. Confronted at an earlier period with the critical tendencies of a new time and its self-conscious optimism, here orthodoxy – still unbroken and in full possession of its powers – was the first to take up the battle and – in this as a representative of the whole of continental Protestantism – was to fight alone for more than half a century. However, it seems that the reasons for this were less intrinsically theological than related to the general situation in the Netherlands, which made it essential for theology to fight here.

Be this as it may, in the battle over the unrestricted authority and truth of scripture, a new battleground was being prepared on which the parties measured their strength; to begin with almost unnoticed by contemporaries.

When the beginnings of biblical criticism are mentioned, one usually thinks of names like Hugo Grotius, Johannes Clericus or Richard Simon, who by their philological and historical work were the first pioneers in biblical criticism. And indeed we owe a wealth of critical observations to them. However, the process which I have in mind here extends far beyond these items of detailed criticism. They contributed a good deal to it. But on the whole they played only a subordinate role. They are the symptom, not the cause.

What I am concerned with here is not a series of individual critical observations. It is an intellectual process which ended with the dethroning of the Bible as the authoritative source of all human knowledge and understanding. My investigation is meant to describe, at least in excerpt, the causes and the first results of this incalculably important development.

I am sadly aware of the names and areas which are missing here. Thus for example developments in England have been largely left out, because to some degree they are a special case, although of course they are an indispensable part of an overall account. Moreover concentration on Cartesianism meant that I had to omit any discussion of the political and social sphere, which beyond question played an important role in the whole process. The name of Pascal, who had sharp and wise insights into the question, is missing. To discuss him would have meant extending this book to cover the history of French Catholicism in the seventeenth century, and that would have broken up its framework. However, I hope that despite these limitations, my account gives an adequate historical reflection of the forces and tendencies as a whole.

ONE

The Norm of Faith in Controversies between Catholics and Protestants

1

When does confidence in the truth of the Bible cease to be taken for granted? It is difficult to give an answer to this question. For it is not so much individual critical attacks which begin to shatter this confidence; rather, there is a flood of questions in which the first doubts make themselves felt. These questions become increasingly impossible to ward off as time goes on, because they have their foundation in changes in the world which anyone can see. That is the difference between the sixteenth and seventeenth centuries: Martin Luther's critical principle had still been derived from scripture itself; the questions which now arise and require an explanation are dictated from outside.

Moreover, to begin with they often seem to have nothing directly to do with scripture. However, on close inspection it very soon proves that they almost all come together on one point: the question of the possible ways of understanding scripture and the validity and limits of scriptural authority.

These questions were asked in the first half of the seventeenth century. For the most part they were not yet formulated critically. But they contributed to criticism because they drew attention to the problems with which criticism would soon have to cope. And we have to recognize them in order to understood what suddenly broke over theology, very quickly and very surprisingly, in the second half of the century.

To begin with I shall attempt to investigate some of these questions in detail.

2

'Let it be a Christian, universal and everlasting peace and true and
sincere friendship between the holy imperial majesty... on the one
hand and the holy imperial majesty and kingdom of Sweden... on
the other; and let this [peace] be maintained and fostered honestly
and seriously in such a way that each side furthers the utility,
honour and advantage of the other and that in every respect trust,
neighbourliness and a sure concern for peace and friendship be
revived and again flourish between the entire Roman empire and
the kingdom of Sweden and between the kingdom of Sweden and
the Roman empire.'[1]

The solemn language of the first article of the peace treaty of
Osnabrück[2] matches the significance of the event. It had proved
possible to end a thirty-years' war by a reasonable compromise and
give the empire a new order. This compromise was reasonable
because it took account of the facts. Article V finally declared that
both confessions in the empire had equal rights and prohibited any
change to the confessional situation by force. It was expressly stated
that the treaty should remain valid 'until an understanding has been
achieved about religion by God's grace' (Art.V.1). In connection
with spiritual possessions which belonged directly to the empire it
was further added: 'But if (which God forbid) a gracious agreement
cannot be arrived at because of the division of faith, this treaty shall
nevertheless be perpetually valid and peace shall last for ever'
(Art.V.14). On this basis, and only on this basis, which expressly
left the whole theological problem on one side, it was in fact possible
to think of a new 'trust and neighbourliness' and a 'sure concern for
peace and friendship' between the states of Europe and the structure
of the empire.

In this way the problem of divided Christianity was in principle
given a political solution. As no union could any longer be hoped
for from the confessions, in future political agreements had to be
made which left out any theological problems inherent in them. As
things were, this was the only way, and it was taken more and more
decisively.

Theologically, matters were far more difficult, although, as we
shall see, a solution also offered itself here which was comparable
to the political solution.

The first obvious fact was that the indivisible truth was divided.

Two parties were making the same claim, namely to be the true church of Jesus Christ, and neither had succeeded in winning a decisive victory over the other. The real, deep terror at this only set in at the beginning of the seventeenth century. So far everything had been so much in flux that both parties could hope that at the end of the controversies there would once again be the one church. But the first decades of the new century brought increasing consolidation in the institutional churches along with the outbreak of the Thirty Years' War: two indications that a theological decision was disappearing further and further into the distance. And the more it became clear that from now on there would be two Christian churches in the West, the more disruption and uncertainty grew. Faith was something which could not be conceived of without certainty. But where was this certainty, if two churches which appealed to the same Lord, the same holy scripture, the same early Christian tradition, were making fundamentally different statements about the way to salvation? It was no coincidence that the problem of certainty now increasingly stood at the centre of inter-confessional problems; it was simply an expression of what had increasingly begun to concern the age.[3]

There is, moreover, no more convincing example of this passionate search for certainty which became one of the great, dominant ideas around the middle of the century than the work of Descartes. The purpose of the *Meditations* was to provide proofs for the existence of God which equalled or even surpassed geometrical proofs in certainty and self-evidence.[4] Descartes' whole philosophy was motivated by the question of the possibility of certain knowledge, and its success would be incomprehensible had this not also been the question of his time. But the details of this will have to concern us later.

Here my reference to Descartes is simply meant to recall that less than a decade separates the appearance of his first *Tractate On Method* (1637) from the work that will now occupy us in rather more detail.

3

The literature which is concerned with the problem of 'criteria in controversies' and the 'norm of faith' – usually within the controversy between Catholics and Protestants - is one of the characteristic phenomena of the first half of our century. Christoph Matthäus Pfaff, who notes a whole series of relevant titles in his inestimable *Introductio in historiam theologiae literariam*, keeps noting that of course he can only mention a few of them.[5] That is hardly surprising, for the question of an authority which could decide on the problems under dispute had arisen out of the situation.

So the question itself is less illuminating than the way in which it was discussed. I shall attempt to describe that by means of a work which was very well known and vigorously discussed at the time, the *De acatholicorum credendi regula iudicium* by Valerianus Magni.[6] The author, who nowadays is almost forgotten, was by no means unknown at that time. In the *Dictionnaire de Théologie Catholique*, Édouard d'Alençon describes him, certainly with justification, as 'one of the striking figures in the religious history of the various countries which made up the Holy Empire in the first half of the seventeenth century'.[7] Born in Milan in 1586, he entered the Capuchin order at the early age of sixteen, and made a name for himself as a preacher in Vienna. In 1616 he helped Sigismund III to establish the order in Poland, and after various diplomatic missions became confessor and adviser to the Archbishop of Prague, the later Cardinal Harrach; finally, in 1624, he became Provincial of his order for Bohemia, Austria and Moravia. But only two years later, at the wish of the newly founded Propaganda, he took over the leadership of the newly-founded Counter-Reformation in Bohemia. It was in this connection that the *Iudicium de acatholicorum credenti* came into being; the notorious Juan Caramuel von Lobkowitz thought of it that 'anyone who reads it cannot be either a Lutheran or a Calvinist'.[8] The year 1630 again saw Pater Valerianus on diplomatic missions, including one to the Electoral Conference in Regensburg. Here Emperor Ferdinand II is said to have remarked of his adviser: 'Narrow though his cowl was, he could get six electors' hats into it.'[9] However, there is no doubt that he achieved his greatest successes in work for the Propaganda. The conversion of Bartholomaeus Nigrinus, who had originally been a Lutheran, then became a Reformed preacher in Danzig, and after his conversion was appointed confidential secretary to Ladislav IV, was certainly a result of his influence, and it strengthened the Catholic party in Poland. But above all his reputation was consolidated by the conversion of Landgraf Ernst von Hessen-Rheinfels, who along with his wife publicly abjured the Protestant faith in Cologne

Cathedral at Epiphany 1652.[10] Moreover, it is interesting to see that the arguments used by the Landgraf to justify his conversion corresponded precisely with the argument of the *Iudicium* of 1628.[11]

The last decade of Magni's life was dominated by his controversy with the Jesuits. An *Apologia contra imposturas Jesuitarum*[12] ('called after Jesus, though they should be called after Baal') brought upon him the hatred of the powerful order. They arranged with the Curia that he should be arrested in Vienna and sought to put him on trial in Rome.[13] However, before it came to that, on 29 July 1661 Valerianus Magni died.

Above all these last controversies cast doubts on the character of this extraordinary man. In fact the Catholic judgment on him is strikingly restrained: 'His history has not been written,' writes d'Alençon, 'and the task would be delicate, because of his well-known disputes with members of the Society of Jesus...',[14] while H.G.Bloth supposes that the reason for the amazing lack of knowledge about him even today is to be attributed to the fact that 'his name tends to be studiously suppressed on the Jesuit side'.[15]

We do not have to decide here how much of this is true. What is beyond all doubt is the European significance of this man, who must be counted one of the best controversial theologians of his century on the Catholic side. That is already indicated by the long list of his Protestant opponents. Direct responses were made to the *Iudicium* by the Lutheran Johannes Major of Jena, a friend of Johann Gerhard and a fellow member of his faculty;[16] Jacob Martini of Wittenberg, author of the *Mirror of Reason* (1618), an important work in the Hofmann dispute;[17] Johannes Botsack (Botsaccus), later a friend and ally of Abraham Calov in Danzig and a participant in the Thorn religious conversation;[18] an 'anonymous author', the cloak for the Socinian Joachim Stegman Sr;[19] and finally Conrad Bergius, from 1629 teacher at the Gymnasium illustre in Bremen.[20]

To each of these writings Valerianus Magni devoted a refutation, and these appeared along with the *Iudicium* in Vienna in 1641.[21] But that was only the beginning. In 1644 and 1645 Johann Amos Comenius entered the dispute with two writings under the pseudonym Ulrich von Neufeld, and a lengthy debate developed out of them.[22] Johann Conrad Dannhauer wrote from Strasbourg,[23] and Hermann Conring, the famous polymath historian, from Helmstedt. Valerianus Magni had responded to his *Fundamentorum fidei pontificia concussio*[24] with a *Concussio fundamentorum ecclesiae catholi-*

cae, iactata ab H.Coringio, examinata et retorta in acatholicos,[25]
which Conring again disputed that same year.[26] It is not surprising
that Samuel Maresius also composed a polemical work against
the Capuchin, given the well-known passion for polemics of this
orthodox figure,[27] who has been called 'a Reformed counterpart to
Calov'.[28] In addition, one must take into account the extensive
controversial literature which was produced in connection with
the previous conversations on religion and the conversion of the
Landgraf of Hessen-Rheinfels.[29] Even if one takes into account the
unusual delight people had during the century in writing polemic,
this gives us a picture of the status of this man, which also raised his
works above the mass of ephemeral polemic.[30] In this respect, pace
the Jesuits, we may assign him to that wing of the Counter-
Reformation which sought to win not by compulsion and outward
force but by the force of better arguments. His not inconsiderable
success here, which we have seen, must, however, be attributed not
only to his method, which he himself thought to be infallible, but
also to his personal dexterity.

4

What did the Catholic argument look like? The very first sentence
of the *Iudicium*, in which Valerianus Magni defines the term *regula*,
rule, is remarkably characteristic of the spirit of the whole work. 'A
rule is an instrument with the aid of which lines which one draws
necessarily come out straight; accordingly that norm which those
who follow do not err in believing is called the rule of believing.'[31]
    The transfer of such an evident process as the drawing of a straight
line with a ruler to the matters of faith is no chance: if it is to be of
any help, the 'rule of believing' must exclude any error in matters
of faith in the same self-evident way. Therefore Magni can immediately go on to say that if this rule were given reliable definition here,
it would necessarily lead to the union of all Christians in one true
faith. The necessity mentioned here has the same character as that
of a mathematical proof; namely, it is unconvincing only to those
who deny the foundations of mathematics altogether. So Magni is
only being consistent in first securing these foundations and asserting
what is common to all Christians – whether Catholics or not. He
formulates it in five sentences:

1. There is agrement that the written word of God is certain and infallible.[32]

2. One may not obey any human being, even Paul, nor even an angel from heaven, 'if he puts forward a doctrine contrary to the written word of God, i.e. against the sacred letters'.[33]

3. No one can with certainty understand the true sense of Holy Scripture 'unless he is illuminated within and led by the Holy Spirit'.

4. It is for each and everyone to believe undoubtingly in matters of faith if they are in accord with the word of God.

5. 'No one can be at odds with the word of God who has inner illumination and is guided by the Holy Spirit' (p.3).

It is clear where these five statements are leading, namely to the question who is in possession of the Holy Spirit, and thus is in accord with scripture and therefore in possession of infallible truth. Magni puts the question thus: 'But to whom is the Holy Spirit present infallibly in such a way that they do not err in expounding the true sense of the sacred scriptures?' (4).

This opens up the way for the distinction that he wants to make between the two basic convictions among Christians: those who certainly and undoubtingly believe that it is the church which offers Christianity the true meaning of Holy Scripture, and the others, where individuals ask the Holy Spirit for advice from scripture and then decide what doctrine accords with scripture and what does not: 'These are always called heretics by Catholics and are regarded as such' (4).

There follows a brief account of these two positions which ends up with what Magni believes to be the decisive question:

'The question is therefore whether the Holy Spirit infallibly distinguishes true from false teaching in scripture through the pastors of the church assembled for a general council or through individual Christians who each call on the Holy Spirit for themselves and ask his counsel from the Holy Scriptures' (p.8).

In this way the problem is formulated, and the subsequent passage simply goes on to draw the right conclusions from the given presuppositions.

The most important thing here seems to be the predominant role played by terms like necessary, certain, indubitably, infallibly in the short exposition which is barely eight pages long. In fact the whole controversy is fundamentally concerned only with the question 'Where is more certainty?', 'Which authority can guarantee it more reliably?'. But behind this we can trace the deep uncertainty which arises everywhere because of the split in the church. The theology upon both sides may seem little affected, but these arguments betray the hidden anxieties of the time.

Only against the background of this uncertainty do the purpose and significance of the *Iudicium* become completely clear. Magni avoids all polemic. Rather, he only wants to pursue the consequences of the presuppositions of the *Biblistae*, as he calls them. Here the leading perspective is always the degree of certainty that can be derived from them. Again the starting point consists in five propositions which, as he thinks, convey the presuppositions of the Protestants:

1. Individual Christians can err in matters of faith.

2. All councils, even general councils, can err in decrees of faith.

3. If they have invoked the Holy Spirit, individual Christians can reliably examine from scripture the doctrinal view of any individual and that of general councils.

4. There is no other method of certainly coming to know the truth in matters of faith than, after prayer, asking the Holy Spirit for counsel from scripture.

5. Christian faith excludes any doubt, as it is certain and infallible (p.9).

Magni begins from these five presuppositions. What conclusions does he draw from them? Here is a characteristic series in context.

All Christians, even general councils, can err. Therefore they could also err 'in decrees on the canon of the sacred books'. Therefore the church could have erred when in 494, at a Council in Rome, it issued the decree on the canon and excluded the Apocrypha.[34] Therefore no Christian can be certain that all the books of the Bible were composed by the Holy Spirit unless he asks the Holy Spirit for counsel from the very books which are put in question. The fact that there is general agreement over some of the books does not go against this, 'since all of them can err'. So as no one has certainty here, each individual Christian must decide this difficult question for himself, 'on pain of eternal death'. Therefore each individual must read through all the books of both Testaments, examine most carefully the different editions and translations, and finally come to a decision about the best. All this is necessary in order to decide in which books the Word of God is contained, and because the Holy Spirit, as the arbiter in all questions of faith, can only be recognized 'from the written word of God' (Ch.III, *consequentiae* IV-VII, pp.12-16).

The same is, of course, also true of the articles of faith; the completeness of each one has to be tested by scripture. So each Christian must himself decide on the theological controversies about the marks of the true church, ecclesiastical jurisdiction, the primacy of the Roman pontiff, etc., on the basis of the sacred writings, and it is certainly not enough merely to listen to preaching or the catechism, or read the Augsburg Confession or the *Institutions*; for Luther, Calvin, the preachers, can all err (17f.). All without exception, men, women and young people, learned and unlearned, must themselves examine all the teaching, since that is the only way of knowing for certain whether or not it accords with the written word of God (18f.)

It is clear where the argument is leading: the Protestant scriptural principle is being developed *ad absurdum*. But interestingly enough, the focus is not on the approach, but on the consequences. If there is no authority outside scripture which can give a binding decision in matters of faith, then each individual, on pain of eternal death, must necessarily get certainty from scripture. But as things are, that is impossible, simply given the presuppositions. Or it would be possible only if scripture were clear. This brings Magni to the second main point of his argument, the problem of the *clarity* of scripture.

If the certainty of faith rests on three supports – prayer, the Holy Spirit and scripture – in such a way that the Holy Spirit is the supreme authority in disputed questions; if scripture is the norm without which we cannot come to know his decision and prayer the condition without which he does not act, then all understanding necessarily depends on the 'illumination of the mind' or the 'divine and supernatural motions which the Holy Spirit brings about in the mind of the *Biblistae*' (Ch.IV, *consequentiae* I and II, 20ff.).[35] For although the certainty of faith is grounded in the authority of the revealed God, the pure word of God and true interpretation can be recognized only by the testimony of Holy Scripture. Nor is that contradicted by the claim that the text is clear in itself or can be made clear by a parallel text. It is obviously ridiculous to claim such clarity when for more than fifteen hundred years the true meaning of scripture has been discussed throughout the world – 'and if it has been so discussed, it will go on being discussed until the day of judgment' (pp.21f.).

So in fact each individual must trust the testimony of the Holy Spirit more than the pastors of the whole church of Christ assembled at general councils: 'So the *Biblistae* hope all too much from the Holy Spirit' (p.23). That is rather primitive, but for anyone who has accepted the argument so far, it is impressively supported by a comparison between the presuppositions and possibilities of the individual and the council.

'This *Biblista* is a person. The fathers of the council can be any number. This *Biblista* is a sheep... the fathers of the council are pastors and bishops. This *Biblista* prays by himself. The fathers of the council pray for all who are present at the council, indeed for the whole Christian world... This *Biblista* may be an uneducated woman. They... are the most learned men in the Christian world' (p.27).

This argument, too, finally leads to the demonstration that the Protestant scriptural principle is absurd, because no one can reasonably hold his or her own conviction to be true over against that of Christendom.

The third point that Magni cites as a proof relates to the problem of jurisdiction. We can sum it up briefly here, because it is not particularly related to the question of scripture. What Magni attempts to demonstrate is again thought out consistently in terms of his approach. Denial of ecclesiastical jurisdiction delivers the whole church over to the whim and misunderstanding of individual Christians and their appeal to the Holy Spirit. The best proof of this is the contradictions among the Protestants themselves: there is no *Biblista* who does not condemn numerous other *Biblistae* as heretics (Ch.V, *consequentia* VI, p.33). 'Therefore the church of Christ, assembled in one man by such a rule of faith, necessarily becomes a confused heap of enthusiasts, where no order prevails, but continual terror' (*consequentia* VII, p.34). Finally, church history also demonstrates that the existence of the church is inconceivable without ecclesiastical jurisdiction (*caput* V). In a short personal 'Conclusion of the Author', which once again goes into the question of certainty, Magni comes to his conclusion: 'We must either return to the church or cut ourselves off from Christ' (p.42).

5

The *Iudicium* of the disputatious Capuchin is certainly neither
particularly original nor particularly acute. The arguments are not
new, and one can hardly call them a deep understanding of his
opponents' position – quite the contrary. And yet this brief work
has two features which set it far above the mass of controversialist
literature. First, it is worth noting the almost complete renunciation
of polemic. Anyone who is familiar with the tone of contemporary
controversies, the flood of reciprocal insults,[36] which even people
like Kortholt and Dannhauer did not avoid, will be surprised at
Magni's relative matter-of-factness. The way in which he argues,
coming to meet his opponent as far as possible – though only so as
to be able to convict him of error all the more irrefutably – is by no
means the rule. However, another aspect is more important and
much more far-reaching. With his *Iudicium*, Magni puts the problems of theological controversy in a new light. As is clear from his
answers to Johann Major and Jakob Martini, he is not concerned
with individual opinions on doctrine but with its presupposition as
he understands it: with an absolutely certain, undisputed and
indisputable authority which vouches for it. 'If we assume,' he
remarks at the end of his work, 'that I had denied the authority of
the church, I would be of the opinion that it had fallen victim to
heresies and I would therefore not have subscribed to your view
were it assured to me by you or were I inwardly instructed by the
Holy Spirit. Even in this case, I would doubt whether Scripture is
holy or not, for so far I have not regarded it as holy unless moved
by the authority of the church on it' (p.42). Anyone who argues in
this way and anyone who follows this argument is living on the
frontier of doubt. Are we in error, or is it possible to trace in this
passionate longing for certainty something of the problems with
which the split in the church burdened Western Christianity? And
is it a coincidence that the ancient church understood that earlier
than the later?

  Johann Gerhard can speak on this question confidently and as a
matter of course. 'All those who are in the church recognize quite
automatically the divine authority of scripture, and they think that
they themselves are automatically made credible through it. For
how could the sons of the church doubt the truth of the foundation
on which the church rests? How could they ask about the authority

of the word of God which is contained in scripture, who trace and recognize the power and effectiveness of this word in their own hearts, so that they are reborn through the word to eternal life?'[37]

Here certainty is no problem. Nor is it for Johann Major, Gerhard's friend, and Jacob Martini of Wittenberg, who wrote the first texts against Magni's *Iudicium*. But at the same time that means that a discussion is impossible in principle: Major and Martini could not understand Magni's questions any more than he could understand their answers; and when Magni begins his retort to Major with the sentence 'You have not understood my intent or have deliberately ignored it' (p.46), that is doubtless also true of his own answers.

The discussion, characteristically, keeps going back to the clarity and transparency of the sacred text. Major and Martini both attempt to defend this concept of clarity against Magni's objections. Thus Martini writes: 'Holy Scripture is clear and transparent enough; the reason why many people do not see this clarity and transparent truth is that they approach the reading of scripture with false presuppositions.'[38] If one understands the doctrine of scripture in terms of justification, this explanation is adequate. For in that case scripture is taken up into the action of God; with its understanding and misunderstanding it is itself an expression of God's grace and wrath. It is indeed a principle of knowledge and an arbiter in controversies; never, however, in itself, but always only in the act of faith.[39] However, the incorporation of the doctrine of scripture as a scheme with a potentially metaphysical basis into orthodox dogmatics encourages misunderstanding – even if the dogmatic theologians have taken trouble 'so to open up the statements on scripture and on God to one another that beyond all the divergency of theological objectifications God and his word appear in accordance with their status as a dogmatic unity'.[40] If scripture is understood in this way, then the false opinions which prevent many people from seeing the clarity of scripture are the consequence of alienation from the life of God and thus have a theological quality. By contrast, Magni can understand all this only in psychological terms. So he asks, 'What Christian has no prejudices?' (p.144), to assert shortly afterwards: 'Take from them (the *Biblistae*) the clarity and trans-parency of the sacred text, and the giant edifice of their doctrines collapses of its own accord' (p.145).

Here at the latest we can see the unbridgable difference between the two standpoints. Anyone who, like Magni, develops a theology so rationally, so logically, so much from the human side, can only understand the Lutheran scripture principle in philosophical or psychological terms and thus misunderstand it. Luther's approach, beginning from the incomprehensibility of God, which saw scripture, Word of God and God himself as one, must have seemed to him to be the depths of absurdity, even in the systematized form of orthodoxy. However, this was an absurdity which had split the foundation of the one church and thus severely endangered the only objective and objectifiable guarantee of faith in the world. So Magni keeps repeating his arguments, which must have seemed to him to be quite irrefutable. 'The lowest and most important foundation of the whole of your teaching is that the holy Scripture is clear for each and every individual in respect of the foundations of faith, and that each adult is unconditionally bound by it. Against this foundation I cite as witness the Christian world since Christ's birth over sixteen centuries... As witnesses against you I could cite the sacred text itself, which makes its obscurity evident' (pp.170f.).[41]

But the Lutheran theologians also repeat with the same certainty what Hafenreffer, for example, puts like this: 'Holy Scripture is sufficient and perfect for the definition and determination of all that is necessary to us for the true knowledge of God and his will, for the observance of worship and for the attainment of eternal life.'[42]

Magni simply has no grasp of this withdrawal of scripture from the security of the institution into the freedom of God who proclaims himself in his Word. In it he sees only arbitrariness, which hands over interpretation and thus faith to chance and every whim. He is a realist, and therefore can give his opponent Bergius something to think about in connection with his plans for union: 'Consider the large number of these heretical teachings, the divisions and mutual rivalries, the political interests, and how often attempts are vainly made to bring about harmony between them and (what is most important) the old and new forms of the church, and I do not doubt that you will laugh at yourself, not because you want union but because you hope for it...' (p.319). Because he sees that, the recognition of the authority of the church seems to him to be a command not only of faith, but also of reason; moreover, he is also convinced that Protestants are not apostatizing just from scripture but also from natural reason (p.332). The confidence of faith which relies on the Word of God that bears witness to itself is, as I have said, quite alien to him.

Conversely, however, his Lutheran opponents have no sense of the oppressive burden of that question which underlies Magni's arguments: how can there be certainty of faith when there are two confessions and countless sects? Can one discuss with atheism and scepticism at all (a problem which begins increasingly to become a preoccupation as time goes on: *Responsio ad Jacobum Martini*, pp.172ff.)? To what may one refer doubters, if the authority of the church is shattered? And what will become of Christianity if none of its authorities can give the final decision in a binding way any longer?

That these questions were not just theoretical became evident as the century went on. A clear sign of this came when the confessional standpoints were neutralized in the Peace of Westphalia and began to go their own ways, because the confessions were threatening to prevent any political union. Reformed and Lutheran churches may at first have paid little attention to these questions, but there were people who noted them very clearly and had their own thoughts on the matter. Like the politicians, they looked for a third way.

6

There is an interesting reference in Gisbert Voët's disputation *De ratione humana in rebus fidei* of 1636. He speaks of an anonymous author who in Holland in 1633 had published a book which contained an 'examination of the books of the papist Valerius (sic!) Magnus on the rule of believing for non-catholics: in which the view of the Papists and our own view about the arbiter in matters of dispute are rejected and natural human reason is set up as the judge and norm of faith'.[43] This is a work to which Magni also produced a refutation,[44] evidently also without knowing the author.

Joachim Stegman Sr, the author of the *Brevis disquisitio an et quomodo vulgo dicti Evangelici Pontificios, ac nominatim Val. Magni de Acatholicorum credendi regula iudicium solide atque evidenter refutare queant*,[45] was a Socinian.[46] Originally a Lutheran preacher in the Mark of Brandenburg, in 1626 he was dismissed for his Socinian tendencies, and after that served for a short time as a Reformed minister in Danzig. When he was no longer tolerated there either, he took up the office of rector at the school in Rakow.

Here he remained, at the centre of European Socinianism until the catastrophe of 1638, until in 1631 he was called as a minister to Klausenburg in Siebenbürgen, where he died two years later.[47]

The description of the *Brevis disquisitio* by Voët is apt. As we shall be looking at Socinianism more closely in the next chapter, here I shall limit myself to its contribution to the problem of norm and certainty.

Although the title gives the impression that Stegman is advocating the cause of the evangelical party, in fact he stands outside the two confessions. What binds him to Protestantism is the scriptural principle. But he wants it to be applied much more consistently. For he thinks that one cannot dispute the infallibility of tradition on the one hand and on the other continue to endorse the authority of the first councils without losing credibility – all the more so when here to some degree the Protestant principle is stood on its head: 'For they do not accept the church fathers because these correspond with scripture, but they think that they must understand scripture in a particular way because the church fathers interpret it so' (p.7). More important is his question about the epistemological significance of the inner testimony of the Holy Spirit. Here his question is very similar to that of Magni: 'Who are those who have been taught by the Holy Spirit about the true meaning? And further, if they reply that these are indiviual pious worshippers, the question then arises, who are those who pray as piously as they should? They do not dare to say "all", nor to identify particular people' (p.10). Now if things are like this, no kind of objective certainty can be based on them. That is also and quite especially the case on the presupposition of belief in predestination. Here Stegman points to the circular argument which for him is proof of false and inadequate thinking: 'My question is: "How do you know that you are predestined?" "From the Holy Spirit." "But how do you know that you truly have the Holy Spirit?" "Because I am predestined. In the end those who are predestined cannot err." Who cannot see the shameful circular argument here? For the presence of the Holy Spirit is demonstrated from predestination, and predestination in turn from the presence of the Holy Spirit' (11f.).

No certainty may be arrived at in this way. In that case should one go the way of Rome? But the Roman church similarly falls into a circular argument when it bases the authority of the Pope and the councils on the presupposition that they are guided by the spirit of

Christ, yet claims that the Spirit of Christ is known only in the exegesis of scripture by the Pope and councils (pp.20f.).

'Therefore the view is to be rejected that one can arrive with certainty at the true meaning of the Holy Scriptures only if one is inwardly illuminated and taught by the Holy Spirit' (p.15).

The moment the 'inner testimony of the Holy Spirit' in some way becomes a constituent part of the process of knowledge and exegesis, an element of uncertainty comes into play which Stegman finds quite intolerable. It is intolerable, because with the division of the church the question of certainty has ceased to be a personal problem. Nor is it any longer a purely theological problem, but it is an open question and will remain so as long as the Bible is taken with complete seriousness. For on the other hand it is quite remarkable that the authority of the Bible itself remains undisputed in all three positions, indeed that without this presupposition the argument is utterly inconceivable. The question is not the authority of the Bible itself but only its true meaning. On the borders of the confessions the certainty or uncertainty of faith becomes the problem of hermeneutics.

Stegman wants certainty. And he sees only one way of guaranteeing it. 'So it must be asserted that sound human understanding is sufficient for any man to decide ... not just about all that is absolutely necessary for salvation, but also about many useful things which are not so necessary' (pp.15f.). This is in no way to deny the activity of the Holy Spirit; on the contrary, no matter who interprets a passage of scripture, 'whether it is [the exegesis] of the Holy Spirit or not can be decided only by the judgment of sound understanding' (p.17). For the gift of the Spirit does not abolish reason; rather, it makes use of it as its instrument: 'Just as it [the Spirit] makes use of my eyes to see and my ears to hear, so it certainly uses my understanding to understand and judge, as the only instrument of understanding and judging' (p.17). This is a refutation of Magni. For it now no longer seems ridiculous for someone to trust his reason more than tradition and the fathers, for reason provides absolute certainty. Then Stegman is one of the first to resort to an argument which more than any other reflects the spirit and hope of his time, and which was to be cited countless times more in the course of the century: 'Is there then no certainty at all? Are you, for example, uncertain whether twice two is four? Or whether the three angles of a triangle are equal to two right angles? Whether cause comes before effect? Whether the whole is greater than a part?...' In all these cases there is no doubt, for reason can give clear and unexceptionable proof. 'Why do we not say the same of divine things? Thus there will be one church. There will also be sufficient certainty' (p.19). An exegesis which follows reason must arrive at results which in certainty and general validity are equivalent to mathematical and logical statements. And no one will any longer be able to speak, like the monk, of uncertainty, diversity and confusion as the consequences of such an interpretation. For everything will have been stated and proved: 'It will be certain that God exists and that he is to be shown due worship. The authority of the Holy Scriptures will be certain. Will it be certain whether the papal church is the true church? Whether the pope cannot err? Whether he is Christ's representative or his enemy?' (pp.21f.).

Why not? Why should reason not be able to decide on that?

It is easy to accuse Stegman and his many successors in the seventeenth century of a complete failure to understand what faith means by truth and certainty. But we can do this only at the cost of abandoning the underlying question. Only when we recollect that the confessional differences had already brought Europe to the edge of anarchy and occasionally even beyond will we do justice to this attempt. For there is no doubt that the question of certainty and the indications of it had now been put in a new and unmistakable way. From now on it was to live on in the Christian consciousness – even if the confessions themselves were evidently prepared to pay very little attention to it.[48]

TWO

The Relationship between Reason, Scripture and Dogma among the Socinians

1

Among the problems which seventeenth-century theologians them-selves felt to be critical, Socinianism without doubt occupies first place. Otherwise it is impossible to explain the coherence and vehemence of the anti-Socinian polemic. Lutherans, Reformed and Catholics; Germans, Swiss, Dutch, English, French and Poles; all the confessions and nationalities of Europe unanimously joined in challenging and refuting the Socinian heresy.

E.M.Wilbur gives us some idea of the extent of this polemic among the German Lutherans. From the years between 1595 and 1797 (sic!) he found more than 700 printed dissertations which were concerned to dispute Socinian theses, and thought 'the list must be far from complete'.[1] In fact one important name is missing from among the combatants. A famous example is Abraham Calov, whose anti-Socinian writings amount to around 2000 pages.[2] His 'Reformed counterpart', Samuel Maresius, does not fall far short of him with his *Hydra Socinianismi expugnata*.[3] Also remarkable is the collection of 156 dissertations in Johann Adam Scherzer's *Collegium anti-Socinianum*,[4] or a similar collection by Josua Steg-man who, because of the identity of his name with the two Socinians, was continually suspected of heresy and was particularly prominent in polemic.[5] However, it is not only in an immeasurable flood of individual works but also in the exegetical material of the time that the Socinians are 'a constant, permanent object of dispute... among the Lutheran Orthodox... A look at Gerhard's commentaries,

Hackspan's *Exercitationes*, or the *Illustrated Bible* of Abraham Calov, will convince anyone of this...'[6]

Pfaff already has a clear idea of the European dimension of this controversy when he explains the incompleteness of his bibliography with the remark that anyone who wanted to discuss the matter properly would have to give a complete list of 'Arian and Socinian authors from Spain, Italy, Poland, Germany, Transylvania, Belgium, England and France, and their writings'. Then there would be their opponents 'from the Papists, Lutherans, Reformed, Remonstrants, and so on, and to list them by nation, writers from Germany, Gaul, Batavia, England and Poland could be introduced on to the scene.'[7]

These few references may be enough to make clear how significant the Socinian heresies were for theological Europe in the seventeenth century. The amazing thing here is that at no time did Socinianism represent a real force. Simply in numerical terms its adherents were a tiny little group in comparison to the great confessions;[8] their havens in Poland and Siebenbürgen were far from the centres of the European spirit, and politically they had no support, but rather were despised and persecuted almost throughout Europe. Especially after their expulsion from Poland in 1658, they were without a homeland, without protection and without friends.

When we consider all this, the extraodinary unrest that they caused must lead to the conclusion that here questions were being discussed which touched on the nerve of orthodoxy: questions which evidently had such critical significance for that time that all the polemic power and perspicacity of which orthodoxy was capable were needed to challenge and refute them.

At first glance, however, the Socinians – the term was already being used in the first decades of the seventeenth century – appeared merely as the revivers of old, long-forgotten heresies. And the terms Arian, Photinian or Ebionite which contemporaries liked to use alongside the term Socinian also sought to demonstrate this. 'Still,' F.C.Baur already observed, 'however much the teaching of the Socinians coincided in substance with the conceptions of the old Unitarians, this parallel can only be regarded as a coincidence, and their main characteristic remains that it was only as a consequence of the general shift in consciousness which took place at the time of the Reformation that they could be led to their doctrine of God, which was completely opposed to the trinitarian doctrine of the church.'[9] In fact the controversies over christology and the Trinity in the first centuries cannot in any respect be compared with the questions with which the church saw itself confronted by Socinianism. For Socinian criticism was aimed less at the content of dogma than at its presuppositions. And to the degree that the alteration to these presuppositions penetrated consciousness generally, the danger and influence of Socinian ideas increased.

This is the only explanation of a remarkable phenomenon which is usually noted far too infrequently. The external and internal histories of Socinianism are a very bad match. If we follow Wilbur's account, the views of the anti-trinitarians essentially developed in Poland between 1556 and 1567. 'In 1567 the basic theological positions were staked out, and in Rakow the new church found a significant home which after 1600 became its decisive centre, while in Siebenbürgen – originally their only haven outside Poland – a first public manifesto of anti-trinitarianism could appear: "On the false and true knowledge of the one God by authors who are ministers of the consenting churches in Sarmatia and Transylvania"'.[10] Fausto Sozzini, who came to Poland in 1570, did not change these basic positions substantially, 'but clarified them, consolidated them and defended then ... against a number of opponents.'[11] Around this time Europe had still not taken any notice of the new heresy, and Wilbur can rightly state: 'The Socinian movement in Poland... was fairly well developed before theologians in other lands became much concerned about it.'[12] The famous Rakow Catechism appeared in Rakow in Polish in 1605; in 1608 there was a German translation dedicated to the University of Wittenberg,[13] and in 1609 the well-known and widely circulated Latin version.[14] But the University of Wittenberg took eleven years to produce a refutation; only in 1619 did there appear here the 'Detailed and Thorough Refutation of the German Arian Catechism' by Friedrich Balduin. In 1609 and 1611 the Wittenberg writer Wolfgang Franz produced theses against the Socinians, which were rejected in 1614 in a refutation by the Socinian Valentin Schmalz.

This marked the beginning of literary controversies on a larger scale. It was, though, almost half a century after the rise of the *Ecclesia minor* in Poland that Socinianism became a European problem.[15] And there was also a similar time-lag over the end of the movement. In 1638 Rakow and all its institutions was destroyed at the instigation of the Jesuits. The history of the *Ecclesia minor* ended twenty years later with its expulsion from Poland. From this time, however, there were still small Socinian groups in various places in Germany, Holland and England which, despite a temporary strengthening by the Polish exiles, generally eked out only a very modest existence. When one reflects that nevertheless anti-Socinian polemic lasted until well into the eighteenth century, the incongruity between the external and the internal history of the movement becomes clear; even after the *Ecclesia minor* had long since been destroyed, Socinianism lived on, to become at the end of the century the origin and embodiment of all the modernist heresies.

It is difficult to find any explanation for this other than that here from Poland ideas were put into circulation[16] which in a quite unusual way represented particular tendencies of the time, tendencies which, while only evident at the end of the sixteenth century, made their presence felt increasingly strongly during the course of the seventeenth. But that again brings us to the question what there was about these ideas which made them so extrarodinarily disturbing and influential.

2

Very different answers have been given to this question in discussions of the Socinian doctrinal system in the larger historical accounts.[17] F.C.Baur, who devoted a long chapter to the Socinians in his history of the doctrine of the Trinity, sees their system as a peculiar consequence of the Protestant principle. Both begin from the 'self-consciousness of the Spirit',[18] but differ in that, in contrast to Protestantism, Socinianism excludes any 'objective mediation of the relationship between God and man' and thus arrives at a 'dualistic conflict between the divine and the human'.[19] The denial of the doctrines of the two natures and of the Trinity are merely the consequences of a particular conception of God in which finite and infinite come into direct opposition in the interest of the freedom of God and human freedom.[20] In locating the mediation in feeling and the will, Socinianism succumbs to its decisive deception: for 'God is essentially neither feeling nor will; he is only thought, or the thinking spirit, and as spirit is made up of a union of the finite and the infinite spirit'.[21] These formulations basically tell us more about

Baur than about Socinianism. And remarkably, that is also true of
Adolf von Harnack.

At first sight it is surprising that Harnack thinks that Socinianism
represents 'that destruction of Catholicism which was attempted on
the basis of the contribution of Scholasticism and the Renaissance
– under the secondary influence of Luther's Reformation, without
essentially deepening or enlivening religion'.[22] But here it is evident
that an approach primarily from the perspective of the history of
dogma, where Socinianism can of course only be understood as a
departure from dogma,[23] will not do justice to the phenomenon. In
general the various derivations of Socinianism from the humanistic
and Scholastic traditions disguise its character. Hans Emil Weber
rightly drew attention to this when after a few short historical
observations he wrote: 'But almost more notable is the foreshadow-
ing of what is to come, which can so easily be overlooked by historical
explanation.'[24]

Harnack sees Socinianism as essentially none other 'than humanis-
tic-nominalistic doctrine taken to the logical conclusion of its principles';[25] throughout there is therefore a 'basic Catholic mood',[26]
and as a whole this is a regression in the history of religion.[27] It is
somewhat inconsistent for Socinianism at the same time to be said
to represent a 'powerful', albeit indirect 'progress in the history of
religion'.[28] The contradiction can be explained by a change in criteria
and demonstrates the difficulties which even a historian of the status
of Harnack can find himself in if he uses concepts like regression
and progress which are so problematical for church history and the
history of dogma.[29] Dilthey's account is very much clearer because
it is not hindered by any concern for the 'religious value'[30] of
Socinianism.[31] He can evaluate it in the context of the cultural
history of the seventeenth century as an event which represents 'an
epoch in theology'.[32] For the first time here 'the intrinsic connection
between the dogmas of Christianity was investigated before the
forum of a reason which had had a historical-critical training and at
the same time had been psychologically and morally refined by an
enormous literature about man and the human condition. The
dogmatic criticism of the Arminians and Socinians is the expression
of the coming-of-age of human reason, which is preparing itself to
subject all traditions to examination.'[33] The great achievement of
this criticism was 'that it once and for all annihilated the arrogant
claim of these dogmas to absolute validity'.[34] It is clear that Dilthey

sees the Socinian criticism of dogma as one of the great achievements of the seventeenth century, introducing a process which was as far-reaching as it was irreversible.

Whereas Harnack attempts to understand Socinianism in the context of the history of dogma, and Dilthey stresses its significance for the beginning of the modern spirit, Weber compares it directly with the Reformation theology of the seventeenth century. It seems that the sharpest formulation of the problem would be here. 'The Socinian concept affects everything,' namely the heart of faith, reconciliation and satisfaction through Christ. 'They dream that Christ cannot and need not have made satisfaction, far less actually have done so.' Weber quotes this statement from the *Systema theologicum* of Johann Adam Scherzer.[35] This is the central doctrine of the Socinians, from which everything else can be derived. For if the need for satisfaction is denied, the whole structure of the old Protestant dogmatics collapses. Its place is taken by a moral religion for which Jesus serves as the model and guarantor of the will and promises of God – a perspective to the modernity of which Weber rightly often refers.[36] Orthodoxy indeed felt 'very superior to this Socinian evacuation of dogma since it felt that it was in possession of the truth. But it was certainly visibly disturbed by it.'[37] And rightly so. For its own rationalization 'made things easy for rational criticism'.[38]

The significance of Socinianism lies in the fact that it presents a clear either-or. 'Either the dissolution must continue further to the new deletions made by later rationalism, to the point of modern Jesuanism... Or theological reflection must go back again, i.e. it must press beyond the orthodox rationalization of dogma, a challenge with which Socianism posed the task of struggling once again for the depths of intutition.'[39]

This formulation, too, tells us almost more about the place of the author in systematic theology than about the historical significance of Socinianism.

But that is the remarkable thing about these descriptions. Their authors see themselves directly or indirectly compelled to give an account of their own positions in the face of Socinianism. And it seems that in this form something of the critical force of Socinian ideas which caused so much disturbance in the seventeenth century is still at work.[40]

This force emanates from a single question that Socinianism put quite unceremoniously but with great acuteness and precision for the first time in the modern sense: the question of the relationship between scripture, doctrine and reason.

3

Chief among the accusations made against Socinianism in the seventeenth century was that it denied the central dogmas of the Trinity and the two natures of Christ and thus God himself. But we can hardly see this alone as the reason for such far-reaching and energetic polemic. In the end that is what Jews and Muhammadans also did. What disturbed people so much was rather that this denial was made in the name of the two main authorities of the period, scripture and reason. Anyone who appealed to them might be certain of gaining a hearing. And the Socinians did not weary in doing that.

In fact the significance of Socinianism lies in its attempt to allow both authorities, reason and scripture, to stand side by side without any restrictions. The preface to the third edition of the famous Rakow catechism begins with the statement: 'We offer the public a catechism or instruction in the Christian religion as our church confesses it, drawn from the Holy Scriptures.' In a formal respect, few other catechisms could more justifiably assert that they were 'drawn from the holy Scriptures'.[41]

Other confessional writings are recalled in the preface, writings which are said to have become the occasion for infinite dispute, because they have bound the conscience and laid on Christians the yoke 'of swearing to human words and opinions and establishing these as the norm of faith'.[42]

It is not expressly said, though it is clear, that the Socinian catechism sets out to oppose the word of God to the pernicious 'swearing to the words and opinions of men' and the freedom of faith to the 'establishing them as the norm of faith' which binds the conscience. But this has two presuppositions: open listening to scripture, free from all prejudice, as the place where God's word and will has alone found expression; and the establishment of a criterion by which the freedom of faith can be distinguished from the whims of enthusiasm: 'Therefore we press for that freedom which lies midway between total libertinism and the rule of force, and so that it does not degenerate into libertinism, we wish it to be circumscribed by honesty and pure reason.'[43] So this criterion is provided by 'honesty' and 'pure reason', and the decisive question will of course be who is to decide in matters of doubt.

The Socinians are convinced that they are putting forward the Protestant principle of scripture as the sole consistent principle.[44] The Protestants indeed claim that for them the only norm of faith is the word of God. In reality, however, as for example Stegman Sr argues in the *Brevis disquisitio*, they diverge from this norm: 'Namely they preserve in such a way, in union with the Papists, doctrines which cannot be proved either from the Holy Scriptures or from natural principles, and indeed even contradict both.'[45] The principle of scripture, used uncompromisingly, excludes everything that cannot be directly inferred from scripture or is incomprehensible. We leave the problem of this 'or' undiscussed here for the moment. In fact one can say that in the Socinian system the Bible is accorded a central place.

This is clear from the doctrine of scripture put forward in the Rakow catechism. According to it, scripture is the only way to the knowledge of revealed salvation. Therefore the earlier catechism is quite consistent in beginning: 'What is the Christian religion? The Christian religion is the way revealed by God of attaining eternal life. But where is it revealed? In the Holy Scriptures, above all the New Testament. Are there then also other Holy Scriptures outside those of the New Testament? Certainly. What are these? The writings of the Old Testament.'[46] The gradation in the evaluation of Old and New Testaments which is evident here is generally characteristic of the whole system.

So the Christian religion is a religion of revelation in the strict sense. God has revealed the way to salvation only in scripture, especially in the New Testament, and nowhere else. Corresponding to this is the rejection of any natural knowledge of God which is emphatically advocated by the earlier generation of Socinians. Fausto Sozzini argues here, partly with passages from scripture and partly – this is highly significant – with news that has been brought to him from 'Brazil' and 'India', that there are not only individuals but whole peoples who are said to have no knowledge of any kind of deity.[47] The catechism is also clear here: 'Therefore because man by nature has nothing in common with immortality, he cannot by any means by himself find the way which leads to immortality.'[48]

The other-worldly nature of revelation, grounded in the qualitative difference between creator and creature, is thus firmly maintained.[49]

Since in this way scripture is elevated to the sole source of revelation, the basis for its authority becomes urgent, and so it is not by chance that this is the first of the questions in the catechism. The problem is discussed under the three well-known aspects of certainty, sufficiency and transparency; the form is not dissimilar to old Protestant dogmatics, but now there are decisive differences in content. We have seen[50] how intolerable to Stegman Sr was the orthodox grounding of certainty in the inner testimony of the Holy Spirit. The element of freedom and subjectivity which came into play as a result seemed to him to be quite inadmissible in so serious a question. On the other hand the Roman way, which guaranteed the authority of scripture by the authority of the church, seemed to be excluded as 'swearing to human words and opinions'. What were needed were generally understandable and convincing proofs of the credibility of scripture, and the Socinians spared no effort in producing them.

Here the catechism distinguishes between negative and positive arguments. The former relate to reasons which could cast doubt on the credibility of scripture, like uncertainty about the author, credible counter-writings and the like. This negative proof can be produced relatively easily in view of the unity of all confessions from the beginning of the church. The positive proof was, of course, harder. For if an attempt was made to demonstrate the credibility of scripture from the truth of the Christian religion, as was done in the catechism,[51] this again happened only by a circular argument, unless that proof could be objectified. This is what the catechism attempts to do with the following series of conclusions.

Who tells us that scripture is credible? 'The truth of the Christian religion.' How do we know that the Christian religion is true? 'First from its divine author.' How do we know that this author was divine? 'From the truly divine miracles.' Why are the miracles credible? 'It is clear that he did miracles because not only those who believed in him but also his declared enemies, the Jews, accepted this.' Confirmation of the divine nature of the miracles is also provided by the resurrection from the dead. This in turn can be proved by the assertions of those who saw him as the risen Lord and stood by this despite all tribulations. For it is contrary to common sense that anyone should expose themselves to such tribulations for an untruth, just as it is quite incredible that a religion which gives its followers so little glory and praise would have been accepted by so many nations had Jesus not authenticated his rule in heaven by his resurrection and the miracles which were done in his name.[52]

There is another interesting argument which appears as an addition to the 1680 edition. No one will reasonably dispute that in the past – 'before our existence, when we were not there' – events took place of which we can know only through testimonies and reports. But if any historical report merits faith, it is certainly that about Jesus and his disciples: 'Which has been uninterruptedly confirmed down to our times firmly and unanimously by so many and such significant witnesses from different peoples dispersed widely over the earth, who differ in language, customs and views.'[53]

However, all this is not just argument from probability. Sozzini had already pointed out that absolute proof for the credibility of scripture would be in contradiction to the nature of religion; it would remove its character as a criterion which makes it seem sufficient to the good and insufficient to the bad.[54] An argument of compelling necessity – as one might put Sozzini's views in modern terminology – removes the freedom of human moral decision and thus contradicts the nature of God.

Nevertheless, the probability is so great that anyone who examines things without prejudice and goodwill will clearly be convinced of the divine origin and content of scripture.

In addition to the credibility which this demonstrates, there is the sufficiency of scripture. The first edition of the catechism has an almost terse statement on this. Scripture is quite sufficient: 'because faith in the Lord Jesus Christ and obedience to his commandments is quite adequately handed down and described in those writings of the New Testament'.[55] All the traditions of the Roman church are therefore not only unnecessary, but they endanger faith, because they make people depart from the divine truth and lead them astray into lying human works.

The additions made to the 1680 edition on this question are extremely characteristic of the course followed by Socinianism from the beginning of the century.

First of all there are some more arguments about probability, like the argument that it would be quite incredible if in such an extensive writing, which God intended for the knowledge of 'saving matters', he had not set these saving matters down and written them out completely.

There then follows, almost directly, the question: 'Then is there any use of true reason in things which pertain to salvation?' The answer given is: 'Yes, certainly, since without it neither can the authority of the holy scriptures certainly be grasped nor can what is contained in them be understood... nor can it ultimately be used in practice.' The objection which this part of the catechism is meant to refute is evidently aimed at the impossibility of reconciling sufficiency and true reason in the sense of a new authority which establishes itself outside the scriptures.

This objection is part of the standard arguments of Protestant polemic.[56] It was all the more necessary to refute it, as it threatened to remove the foundation of Socinian doctrine, namely its absolute scriptural principle. The logical conclusion was: 'We therefore in no way exclude true reason when we declare that scripture is adequate for salvation, but include it altogether.' True reason is not something alien to scripture, to some degree a profane authority, but is the instrument of perception. So reason does not conflict with the concept of sufficiency, but is rather the condition of its possibility: only through reason do we recognize the completeness of the statements about salvation. The consequence of this approach becomes clear in the preface, which distinguishes between doctrines necessary to salvation and merely useful doctrines, in such a way that the criterion of necessity is clarity and transparency: 'So what is not clear in this sense we declare as being not necessary for salvation.'[57] In this way reason now becomes independent again; the instrument becomes the principle of knowing.

The same observation can also be made on the discussion of transparency. As the catechism puts it: 'And if certain difficulties appear in it (i.e. in Holy Scripture)... nevertheless what is necessary for salvation is so transparently handed down in other passages of scripture that they can be understood by anyone.'[58]

Of course Socinianism has to argue that scripture is clear in principle. The first reason produces another of the 'it is quite impossible' arguments with which we are already familiar: as God handed down scripture with the intent of making his will known through it, it is utterly improbable that this will could not fact be clearly recognized from it by all. Moreover the apostles addressed their letters containing the mysteries of the Christian religion to quite simple people.

The earlier edition of the catechism was essentially content with this argument. It makes the dulled, prejudiced or ignorant temperament of the reader repsonsible for the difficulties and inconsistencies of the various interpretations. The later edition, however, sees itself compelled to draw some extremely interesting distinctions, which above all relate to the interpretation of passages of scripture which seem obscure and circumstantial. Four points are made here:

1. It is necessary to note carefully the aim and the other circumstances of a passage, as is also necessary in the interpretation of all other writers.

2. A careful comparison should be made with similar and clearer expressions and ideas.

3. The interpretation of obscure pasages is in principle to be made by means of passages where the meaning of scripture is completely clear. Nothing is to be allowed which deviates from that.

4. Nothing may be asserted which contradicts sound reason or contains a contradiction in itself.[59]

There is no doubt that these four points represent a canon of critical scriptural exegesis which in principle is still valid today. The remarkable and significant thing about them is that the idea of scriptural criticism was originally far from the minds of the Socinians. Rather, the standpoint of the catechism of 1609 is that of an extreme biblical positivism. In fact the whole series of 'it is quite incredible' arguments makes sense only where the Word of God and holy scripture are understood to be identical, and there is not the slightest doubt about the authenticity of scripture.

Scripture is complete because it is the word of God. It is comprehensible for the same reason. No other possibility is conceivable nor acceptable. Socinian criticism of scripture begins from these presuppositions. Its confidence in them is so great that it moves from them to criticism without any hesitation. If scripture is sufficient, then anything that is not directly contained in it and said there with clear words must be deleted. However old and important dogmatic traditions may be, on the basis of scripture the Socinians are quite prepared to deny them. The consequences of this principle, however, only become evident in the question of transparency. If scripture is clear – and nothing else is conceivable for the word of

God – then anything which is not clearly comprehensible may be deleted as not being necessary for salvation. The decision on what is comprehensible or incomprehensible can only be made by sound reason: 'In the end lest anything is presupposed which is in conflict with sound reason or contains a contradiction within itself.'[60] In this way reason has again become the instrument for the knowledge of principles. The understanding of scripture is in future determined by the content of sound reason.

It cannot be denied that there is considerable consistency in this argument. Certainly, nothing can be traced here of the depth of what Luther describes as the *iustificatio impii*. For the Socinians, the consolation of the conscience under attack provided by faith in Jesus Christ, the heart of the Reformation, clearly has neither reality nor life. Nevertheless we should perhaps not over-hastily deny them any understanding of revelation. Perhaps they felt assailed elsewhere – where people in the seventeenth century could really be assailed: on the question of the substance of Christianity in the face of so many Christian parties, each of which bitterly defended every single point of its doctrine. One can see this persistence from within, in the light of the development of doctrine; and it certainly has a distinctive grandeur of its own. But it can also be seen from outside, in which case it appears merely as an ocean of rectitude, polemics and dispute. That was the perspective of the Socinians. They looked for a new, clear and generally understandable way of clarifying the word and will of God, and in so doing came upon that authority which was a rising star on the horizon of the century: reason.

4

In connection with the four hermeneutical rules I have spoken of a canon of critical exegesis of scripture which in principle is still valid today. By virtue of this canon, despite their defective scholarly equipment the Socinians arrived at the correct or almost correct explanation of many hundreds of passages, 'the interpretation of which today is as obvious as it is unobjectionable'.[61]

The presupposition for an unprejudiced exegesis was the removal of the dogmatic norms which compelled orthodoxy to such unheard-of and often such tortuous exegetical efforts. The question was, however, how this new norm, sound reason, would work out. What did it mean in practice and in detail for no exegetical judgment to contradict reason or contain contradictions?

Of decisive importance is the distinction which the Socinians – here in the footsteps of Scholasticism – made in this connection and which would continue to be significant until the end of the eighteenth century: the distinction between statements which are against reason and those which are above reason. That certain mysteries of the faith can be above reason is the necessary consequence of maintaining the other-worldliness of revelation. The mysteries of God are above all reason, but in principle they are not against reason. Rather, they can be understood and recognized after they have been revealed: 'Although human reason does not find a way to the mysteries of the Christian faith, it recognizes and affirms it, since these mysteries are revealed as being true by God through Christ.'[62]

This distinction is the attempt, continually repeated at a later stage, to find a logically unassailable way out of the dilemma in which any theology working with reason as its principle undeniably finds itself, even if at the same time it is resolved to maintain the transcendence of revelation. At all events, what is interesting here is the question of what can be counted as above reason and what against reason. It is less interesting, however, in connection with the mysteries of faith than in connection with the content of the reason which is expressed in this decision. Fock sees here among the Socinians only 'the greatest arbitrariness, which by the nature of things cannot be otherwise'.[63] On closer inspection, however, it transpires that the definition of what is above and what is against reason is far from arbitrary. Rather, this definition is made precisely in accordance with what for the first half of the seventeenth century may be regarded as 'the modern understanding of reality'.

The categories of this understanding of reality are already very evident from an enumeration of the most important principles which according to Stegman Sr must be used for exegesis.[64] First of all follows a complex of logical statements: 'Certain (statements) are of a metaphysical kind, such as: cause is later than effect; the whole is more than a part; something is or is not; and other similar statements. Of this nature are also logical statements: there is a sequence from the general to the particular.' Then follow physical and mathematical statements: 'Others are called physical: for example, the eye is an instrument for seeing, the ear for hearing, the understanding for knowing. Others belong to mathematics: for

example, one does not equal three.' Then follows the sphere of the
'humanities': 'Others concern the nature of the moral and the
immoral; these include ethics, politics and economics. Finally,
others rest on the testimony of others: like belief which is now
attested by reports, now by honourable and serious men and also
generally.' Now the point of this enumeration is: 'It must be noted
that these and similar statements, which are not unknown to anyone,
are for sound reasons the foundations of our knowledge, also of the
authority of the Holy Scriptures and their true meaning. Anyone
who is instructed... in them will therefore also recognize from these
very principles that scripture itself is holy and decide without
difficulty from the scriptures what is necessary for salvation.'[65] The
requirement that no interpretation may contradict sound reason
simply means that the 'foundations of our knowledge' have to decide
on the possibility of particular theological statements. Now in the
sphere of these foundations – as a look at Stegman's catalogue shows
– there is fundamentally only one logical figure: the principle of
contradiction. There are no categories for all the other complexes.
Only what does not match up with this principle could be excluded
with reference to sound reason. Remarkable as it might sound even
to the seventeenth century, anything else was in principle acceptable
as being 'above reason'.

That explains why the main attack of the Socinians was directed
against the dogma of the Trinity.[66] For here was a case where a
theological statement not only contradicted the laws of logic but
also was not explicitly formulated in scripture. So here Socinianism
could rely fully on both scripture and reason. The question as
to which proof has priority in this context is a false one. The
presupposition that nothing unreasonable (and here that means
illogical) can be contained in scripture was founded on the nature
of scripture as the word of God, and to some degree it was taken
for granted that the doctrine of the Trinity did not find any support
in it.

It could not be very difficult to prove that the doctrine of the
Trinity is contradictory in itself and thus contrary to reason: 'The
argument is first of all directed in general against the foundation of
the church's doctrine of the Trinity, the remarkable relationship
between the unity of substance and the difference of persons. Three
persons in one substance is – as Socinianism never tired of repeating
– an impossibility; either one must accept one substance and

accordingly also one person and one God, or three persons and accordingly also three substances and three gods.'[67] The Socinians ere convinced that there was no possibility of resolving these contradictions logically, and the final argument, the incomprehensibility of the divine nature, was impermissible because it could ultimately be used to paper over any absurdity and contradiction.[68] Therefore the catechism stressed as being 'extremely useful' in connection with the nature of God: 'The most important thing is that we do not fall into the general error of asserting with a manifest contradiction that God has one substance but not one person, but three persons.'[69] But the proof is given on a logical level: 'This is in fact already clear from the fact that God's nature is one not in form but in number. Therefore a plurality of persons simply cannot be in him, as a person is none other than an individual thinking being.'[70]

From here the catechism makes the transition to the scriptural proof: ' "Who is this one divine person?" He is the Father of our Lord Jesus Christ. "How do you make that clear?" Through the most manifest testimony of scripture...' The passages which are mentioned first here as being most important are John 17.3; I Cor.8.6; Eph.4.6. Then follows a brief account of church teaching and its most important proof-texts, like Matt.28.19; I Cor.12.4ff. and of course the 'Johannine comma' (I John 5.7). These passages are then refuted one after another with a good deal of perspicacity and knowledge. Thus, for example, the questionable tradition of the 'Johannine comma' is singled out. The value of this verse as a proof is shattered with reference to the Greek, Syriac, Arabic, Ethiopian and Old Latin versions, from which it is missing, and modern celebrities like the Louvain theologians,[71] Erasmus, Beza and even Luther and Bugenhagen, who rejected the passage as unsound. Generally and in detail, as Harnack rightly notes, the argument is in fact 'largely irrefutable'.[72]

It is an event of extraordinary significance for the history of theology that the Socinian approach was so convincingly supported by scripture at the central point which it attacked, namely the doctrine of the Trinity. Once the norm of dogma had fallen and the original meaning of a wealth of scriptural passages became clear, the exegetical foundation of orthodoxy inevitably became more and more incredible. Everything – the will of God, scripture and sound reason – seemed to fit together once one left the dogmatic tradition on one side. And it was natural to go on from this to argue not so much for the problems of the tradition, but – and this was far more important – for the correctness of the Socinian approach. But what applied to the doctrine of the Trinity did not necessarily apply to the doctrine of justification. Doubtless the idea of vicarious satisfaction was full of logical and moral contradictions. Equally certainly, however, it was nevertheless put forward by New Testament writers. If Socinianism here acted in accordance with its schema, then scripture had to fall by the wayside. In fact christology was Socinianism's weakest contribution.

The dogmatic criticism of the Socinians rested on their consistent application of the principle of contradiction. Here the range of philosophical and theological statements which in their view went against the principle of contradiction was considerably extended. 'The anti-trinitarians declared a wealth of judgments to be logically impossible which after centuries of the most careful examination had been acknowledged to be without contradiction, even if their positive possibility could not be proved.'[73] This concerned above all the definitions of essence, nature and person which in detail they regarded as 'aimless, pedantic and sophistical'. But the question now is whether this was merely 'a lack of accuracy and criticism', as Dunin-Borkowski conjectures,[74] or whether here there was not rather an underlying feeling that scholastic terminology could no longer provide any answers because its presuppositions no longer existed. For the distinctive feature of the Socinian approach was that a 'careful examination lasting for centuries' no longer offered any guarantee, but reason felt free to make its own decision.

On the other hand the Socinians had no hesitations in acknowledging the biblical miracles. Certainly we find the first beginnings of rational attempts at explanation, but in principle it is thought possible that God himself is the direct author of miraculous events. Thus the famous passage in Josh.10.12f. about the sun and moon standing still for Gibeon and in the valley of Aijalon is explained like this: 'Just as the watchmaker, if he so wishes, can stop the hand or move it backwards, so too God, as the one who made this great world machine, can either stop the sphere of the sun and direct it backwards, or, which is still more probable, can work on the mobile sphere of the earth in such a way that it seems to men as if the sun were standing still or going backwards.'[75] This passage, which in the second half of the century became the shibboleth of the parties arguing for the old picture of the world or for the new, cannot yet be interpreted here in a completely open way. This is an indication that the Socinian system came into being *before* the great philosophical and mathematical movement of the seventeenth century. Only with that movement did miracles become problematical; for the Socinians, the interruption of the causal sequence was above, but not yet in principle against, reason.

5

I have attempted at least to indicate the development which took place within Socinian ideas over the course of a century. That is important for the question of the significance of these ideas in the seventeenth century.

F.C.Baur had already found two different standpoints in Socinianism, 'one of which subordinated scripture to reason and the other reason to scripture'.[76] In earlier Socinianism as represented, say, by the 1609 catechism, the two points were to some degree in equilibrium. But to the degree that the Socinians felt themselves compelled by orthodox polemic to reflect on their theology and make it more precise, the rational element can be seen increasingly strongly to prevail. This can be shown perhaps most impressively by the change in attitudes to natural theology. The moment that sound reason was accepted – and this acceptance already began with Volkelius and Crell[77] – it had to become the first and ultimately the only authority in matters of faith. Kühler rightly observes: 'The natural course of things is that revealed religion is increasingly suppressed by natural religion and that where the two do not coincide, reason must exercise its rights most powerfully... That is the great transition to which the inner development inevitably had to bring Socinianism.'[78] In fact the Socinian approach had almost of necessity to lead to a radical rationalism, all the more so, the more powerfully the rule of reason developed and extended its sway. It is true that at no point did Socinianism succeed in making a real breach in the closed ranks of orthodoxy. But the reason for this was not so much the strength of the orthodox posiion as the weakness of the Socinians. This weakness was that their approach was in advance of its methodological possibilities.

As for the approach, Socinianism had for the first time seriously set Holy Scripture over against what one might now call a 'modern understanding of reality'. It was convinced that it could maintain the authority of scripture and the authority of reason to the full if it sacrificed the dogmatic tradition. This unmistakably posed the question of the relationship between scripture, doctrine and reason – and here reason became a new entity with an independent claim.

However, until the middle of the century – and this was the weak point of Socinianism – the new factor could essentially base its claims only on logic. And in the discussion of logical problems orthodoxy was quite equal to the Socinians. While the Socinian approach was new, the methodological possibilities were essentially still the old ones.

What was inherent in this approach only became clear when as a result of the enormous broadening of perspectives and the sphere of experience in the first half of the century, along with a systematic-philosophical conception, reason could again lay the foundation for its claim to independence, this time irrefutably.

Socianinism had initially drawn attention to the fact that in the sphere of scripture and doctrine which hitherto had in a variety of relationships to regulate Christian doctrine, reason had become an equal and – as soon was to emerge – highly dangerous partner. And at the same time it demonstrated that given this new partner it could not get on without restrictions: restrictions on dogma and restrictions on scripture. In the question of restrictions on dogma Socinianism was both radical and successful. Here, at any rate as far as the doctrine of the Trinity was concerned, it in fact had scripture and reason on its side, and Dilthey was right in saying that 'after the Socinian criticism no honest and clear thinker' attempted to renew these dogmas 'in a literal sense'.[79]

The Socinians resolutely refused to allow restrictions on scripture. Rather, they believed that they were the first to put forward the Protestant principle of scripture really consistently. Nevertheless they could not prevent reason making itself increasingly independent of scripture. The more formally the scripture principle was used on the one side, and the greater the self-awareness of reason on the other, the more inexorably conflict developed which by the nature of things necessarily led to criticism of scripture. The full extent of the conflict still remained hidden from the Socinians, because their philosophical presuppositions were limited. But the whole of the second half of the century in Western Europe is full of bold or even desperate attempts to avoid this conflict in some way.

Only German theology contributed virtually nothing to the solution of this problem, despite its great polemical work. One must assume that it had not even seen the problem. This is the only explanation of what Gensichen demonstrates at length: that the notions and ideas of the Socinians still had an effect far into the eighteenth century, whereas the Lutheran and especially the Wittenberg polemic of the seventeenth century 'was increasingly forgotten'.[80]

THREE

The Credibility of the Biblical Picture of the World: I. Copernicus and the Consequences

1

While theologians reacted vigorously to the dogmatic criticism of the Socinians, the danger of which was obvious, they took far longer to understand the challenge posed by the development of the new picture of the world. That does not mean that this challenge was less dangerous, but it was harder to recognize and its consequences were almost beyond comprehending. Once these consequences also became clear to theologians, polemic immediately began, and was then carried on with all the passion of which the time was capable. The stubbornness with which theology continued to maintain the biblical picture of the world was not just bigotry. For in this controversy the credibility of scripture and thus of the authority of God himself was at stake. Only if we remember that will we understand its importance and significance. The charge which is often made, that from the beginning theology should have distinguished between a picture of the world and faith in scripture, is quite unhistorical. For it presupposes that modern relationship to scripture which could only be the result of this process. That will become clear in due course, as I attempt to demonstrate the development during which a mathematical and astronomical problem became a theological problem.[1]

2

The relationship of the Reformers to Copernicus and the new picture of the world has been the subject of widespread scholarly

controversy.[2] The extreme positions are represented on the one
hand by some older Catholic authors who criticized the fanatical
hostility of the Wittenbergers to the new view of the world,[3] and on
the other hand by Elert, who sees 'almost incalculable' effects 'for
the whole development of the modern picture of the world' stemming
from Luther's theology, especially his eucharistic doctrine.[4] What
was the real situation?

As is well known, from Luther himself we have only one statement
on this question, an extract from his table-talk of 4 June 1539. In it
we read: 'A certain new astrologer was mentioned who sought to
demonstrate that the earth moves and not the heaven, the sun and
the moon, as if someone travelling in a carriage or a ship were to
believe that he was standing still and the earth and trees were
moving.' [B: + Martin Luther replies]. 'But the position is that he
who would be wise should not allow himself to be pleased by the
estimation of others. He must make up his own mind, as does he
who seeks to overthrow the whole of astrology. But even if it is
completely confused – nevertheless I believe Holy Scripture, since
Joshua commanded the sun to stand still and not the earth.'[5]

Heinrich Bornkamm is surely right in supposing that this is a
purely chance remark from which we cannot in any way infer that
Luther was a resolute opponent of the Copernican system.[6]

This is also indicated by the fact that apart from this remark, in
Luther's writings and table-talk there are no further observations
on this question: that is an almost certain sign that he was just not
interested in it.

However, in his rejection of the idea Luther refers to Joshua 10,
and that is not without importance, since, as I have already indicated,
for later generations this passage became the shibboleth of the
parties disputing over the picture of the world. If it did not yet have
this significance for Luther, that was certainly not because the
question was not seriously a pressing one. Still, this already indicates
the direction of later anti-Copernican polemic.

Elert attempts to associate Luther with the modern picture of the
world by means of eucharistic doctrine. In connection with this
doctrine, which called for the omnipresence of Christ, Elert thinks
that Luther broke with the spatial conceptions of heaven in the
Bible and thus paved the way for the new picture of the world. This
conception is said to have been 'of the utmost significance for the
history of our view of the world'[7] and to have had 'an almost

liberating effect'.[8] This brilliant thesis is certainly false, at any rate as far as historical influences are concerned. Nor is there the slightest indication that at any time in the seventeenth century a Lutheran theologian sided with the Copernicans on the basis of this position. On the contrary: Elert himself observes at this time a general withdrawal of Lutheran preachers from this position.[9] Unfortunately the most important Lutheran witness in this question, namely Kepler, was a resolute opponent of the doctrine of ubiquity and a supporter of the Reformed understanding of the eucharist.[10]

So we would do best to leave Luther completely out of account here: while he cannot have been a fanatical opponent of the new picture of the world, he cannot be made a secret protagonist of it either. He was neither the one nor the other, because he did not have any of the necessary presuppositions for seeing the significance of this question.

Things are not very different with Philipp Melanchthon. However, he did go more closely into the problem in his *Initia doctrinae physicae* of 1539. But here too one finds remarkably restrained argumentation compared with the extent and passion of the later controversies.[11] Melanchthon bases his rejection of Copernican views on the one hand on scriptural grounds and on the other on the traditional arguments from physics. Elert concludes from this twofold argument in which the arguments from physics are much more prominent that only the latter were crucial for Melanchthon. 'Had he wanted to decide the question of Copernicus theologically, he would have had to do so on biblical grounds.'[12] There is no basis whatsoever for this conclusion. Quite the contrary; it is the 'divine testimonies' which finally tip the balance for him. Although Melanchthon does not put too great weight on them, this becomes quite clear from his argument.

'Although there are people who mock a physicist who appeals to divine evidence, we nevertheless regard it as appropriate to apply philosophy to the divine communications and in such great darkness of the human mind ask the divine authority for counsel wherever we can.' These are the words with which the decisive section in the *Initia* begins. There follow references to individual passages of scripture: 'The psalm confirms most clearly that the sun moves... (Ps.19.5b-7). We are content with this clear testimony about the sun. Another psalm speaks about the earth... (Ps.78.69). And the preacher says in the first chapter... (Ecclesiastes 1.15). It is also related among the miracles that God willed the sun to stand still, and indeed to go backwards (Josh. 10.12,13; Isa.38.8).' Melanchthon ends with the statement: 'Strengthened by these divine testimonies, we hold fast to the truth and do not allow ourselves to be led astray from it by the blind works of those who think it the glory of the intellect to confuse the free arts.'[13]

The parallel between this statement and Luther's view is striking, and more than a coincidence. In fact here we have a preparation for all the anti-Copernican arguments of the seventeenth century, even down to details; they only need development. The reason why Melanchthon did not undertake this development himself is the same as that for Luther's silence on this point: at this time the question was simply not thought to be in any way a burning one.

Neither Luther nor Melanchthon had the mathematical grounding they would have needed to test Copernicus' theory. Quite apart from that, however, in the middle of the sixteenth century there were no reasons for such a test: to begin with, there was no indication that this theory had to be taken any more seriously than any of the numerous other astrological speculations of the time. The words 'Although there are people who mock a physicist who appeals to divine evidence, we nevertheless regard it as appropriate' convey the certainty of someone who knows that the truth is on his side and means to maintain it against all 'glory' and 'confusion'.

However, things looked rather different for Andreas Osiander. His mathematical and astronomical interests are well known. He was so versed in mathematics and astronomy that along with a mathematician, Johann Schoner, he could supervise the printing of Copernicus' *De revolutionibus orbium caelestium*,[14] 'which truly presupposes no little knowledge of astronomy'.[15]

So in contrast to Luther and Melanchthon, he had the necessary knowledge to be able to judge Copernican theory both for its mathematical probability and its consequences for a world-view. The result of this was the highly controversial preface which he attached to Copernicus' work against the wishes of the author.[16]

This preface is the first sign of the coming storm, and therefore is particularly interesting in this context.

Osiander's starting point is that the true causes of the heavenly movements are in principle unknowable. Therefore in explaining them one has to resort to hypotheses, the truth or falsehood of which depends on the degree to which they correspond with our observations. Here Copernicus has performed an outstanding service. However, truth in the sense of spatial reality need not necessarily correspond with these hypotheses: 'For it is not necessary for these hypotheses to be true or even for them to be probable; it is already enough if they provide a calculation which agrees with the observations.'

The purpose of this theory of hypotheses is clear. Osiander himself speaks of 'certain educated people' who, because they are very disturbed by the new theory, think that 'one should not confuse the free sciences, which have already long been been set in the right direction'. Here we should think of people like Melanchthon, who a few years later felt it necessary to issue a specific warning against 'disturbing the arts'. Osiander is evidently concerned to soothe these people by pointing out that Copernicus's assertion has only a hypothetical character. That, moreover, is already the view of Gassendi, who first indicated that Osiander was the author of the *Praefatiuncula*. The reason he gave was this: 'His intention here was to exculpate Copernicus, although the latter had regarded the movement of the earth not just as a hypothesis but as the true view, and to quieten things down because of those who protested later, as though he [Copernicus] had not accepted such a movement as certain theory but only as a hypothesis.'[17]

While the intention of the preface is clear, it is difficult to assess it. Hirsch already pointed out that those who are fond of ingenious parallels can 'find extremely modern theories of science anticipated by Osiander'.[18] E.J.Dijksterhuis has recently taken this view up again quite seriously: 'The view of the aim and scope of a mathematical and physical theory which underlies his [Osiander's] approach is quite tenable; in fact with good reason one can hold the view that such a theory fulfils the expectations which one may have for it if it succeeds in constructing a mathematical system of thought the results of which correspond with measurements that have already been made and are confirmed by new observations.'[19]

This argument fails to note that Osiander's scepticism about real statements stems from the scholastic tradition and is to some degree pre-scientific, whereas its modern version has a post-scientific character, understanding science here in the sense of a positivistic natural science.

The decisive question in this context is a different one, namely whether Osiander himself was convinced by his theory of hypotheses or whether it was purely a tactic that he adopted. The sentence in the *Praefatiuncula* which allows us to decide on this question runs: 'But as sometimes different hypotheses are offered for one[20] and the same movement (like eccentric and epicyclical hypotheses for the movement of the sun), the astronomer will primarily hold to those which are the simplest to understand, while the philosopher will perhaps seek more probability; however, neither will have or give certain knowledge, because it has not been revealed by God.' In other words, the astronomer will seek the explanation which best fits his observations and calculations; by contrast, the philosopher will prefer the one which comes closest to the truth (which truth? probably that of the biblical and Aristotelian picture of the world); but neither of them can claim ultimate certainty here, because the truth is only with God. If Bornkamm is right that the last sentence 'does not refer to revelation in Holy Scripture but to the impossible possibility of a special communication from God',[21] then here Osiander is not only stating the relativity of all scientific knowledge, but in addition is asserting that a principle which is correct in astronomy can be false in philosophy, and vice versa.

Remarkably enough, it has often been often overlooked that the hypothetical character of scientific explanations was a widespread assumption from the fourteenth century on.[22] So here Osiander was not saying anything new. On the contrary, he was in agreement with the tradition of natural philosophy in late Scholasticism, where it was governed by nominalism. The only new development was the use he made of this assumption and the consequences he drew from it. In connection with Copernican theory the theoretical scientific premises of the scholastics took on an apologetic and ideological character and compelled the claim of a double truth.

So Osiander was adopting a problematical position, even if it was conceivable in this historical period; and as things were, it was the only way in which he could avoid a conflict of authorities. Whereas in this conflict Melanchthon recognized scripture as the ultimate authority, by a theory of double truth Osiander attempted to avoid the difficulties in which he seemed to be landed by his assent to Copernican theories on the one hand and his conviction of the truth of the old biblical-Aristotelian view of the world on the other. From this perspective the last sentence of his preface takes on an almost pleading character: 'No one may expect any certainty about astronomy from the hypotheses, as they cannot offer anything of the kind, so that if he takes that which is devised for another purpose as the truth, he goes away from this discipline more foolish than when he came.'

The influence of the theory of hypotheses can be traced well into the seventeenth century. In 1615, in a letter to the Carmelite Foscarini, who had asserted the reality of the twofold movement of the earth, Cardinal Bellarmine advised him and Galileo to treat the Copernican system *ex suppositione*, i.e. as hypothetical.[23] We shall see in due course why Galileo could not accept this. The Curia also made use of this theory when in 1620, four years after *De revolutionibus* was suspended by the Congregation of Rites, it published a list of necessary improvements. 'They amounted to turning the theses of Copernicus into hypotheses,' a demand which, as is well known, the Catholic Church maintained until 1822.[24] On the Protestant side things did not look very different. Thus as late as 1670 Maresius, a Reformed theologian at the University of Groningen and a controversial advocate of orthodoxy, would allow the Cartesians only a hypothetical use of Copernican theory: '....although because of our modest understanding we cannot see what greater certainty for daily use, whether on sea or on land, can derive from this hypothesis than from the Ptolemaean, all the less since artificial spheres, astrolabes or rings or astronomical quadrants, or heavenly and earthly globes, and similar mathematical instruments, can be fashioned in accordance with that hypothesis...'

There is an express warning against the assumption of any 'truth' and 'necessity': 'But we see, not without indignation, that some learned theologians devote all their acumen to demonstrating the truth and necessity of this theory. In this way they have made a wax nose for Holy Scripture, which they saw as being everywhere rejected by this theory.'[25]

At the same time, it becomes clear at this point how much more acute the problem has become in the meantime: where Osiander could still plead quite openly that the old and the new hypotheses should be allowed to stand side by side because the truth of neither can be demonstrated, Maresius is concerned with the authority and credibility of scripture. In view of this, however, allowing the hypothetical use of the new doctrine seems to be a painful expedient. But we shall have to discuss that later.

Moreover, Osiander's preface is in its way a sign that the consequences of the Copernican shift were not in fact obvious even to experts during the sixteenth century. How otherwise could we explain the fact that its effects 'were initially barely perceptible and only began to take on a clear form half a century after his [Copernicus'] death'? 'One can very soon find astronomers in various countries who declare that they are his supporters, but alongside them others continue to reject his system without being any worse scientists than their opponents.'[26] So in practice there was the same juxtaposition of old and new opinions as in Osiander's theory: an indication that his position was in fact plausible.

After the investigations by Elert and Bornkamm, the claim of the earlier Catholic literature that the Wittenbergers opposed the new picture of the world with fanatic enmity no longer needs to be refuted.[27] A fanatical hostility of this kind presupposes an awareness of the problem which certainly escaped the Reformers.

But the solemnity with which Elert seeks to claim young Lutheranism for the new Copernican picture of the world is equally mistaken. From his comments that 'no historian... can conceal the fact that a Lutheran prince supported the publication of his work, that a Lutheran theologian saw to its printing, and a Lutheran mathematician supervised it,'[28] we may conclude only that the real significance of the whole question escaped all those involved. In this respect the rejection by Luther and Melanchthon and the assent by Osiander, Theticus and Cruciger are in principle on the same level.[29]

3

Until the thirties of the seventeenth century, the situation remained essentially unchanged. However, the trial of Galileo in 1633 then suddenly made clear the whole range of difficulties that Copernicus' discovery was to present to Christian theology.

We must be careful not to blame the decision arrived at in this trial on a specifically Catholic intolerance.[30] Significantly, around this time theological condemnation of this new doctrine also began in the Protestant confessions. The first anti-Copernican monograph to appear in the Lutheran sphere was that of the Danish mathematician and theologian Peter Bartolinus, which was published in 1632. And among the Reformed, Gisbert Voët opened the battle against the new picture of the world when he became professor in Utrecht in 1634. Up to this point, as Hooykaas points out, here too the whole question was still theologically open.[31] It is interesting that the conflict finally broke out over Galileo and not Kepler, although both were of the same opinion on the decisive point, namely in affirming the reality of the Copernican theory.[32] A look at the most important early writings by the two scholars on this question will serve as a demonstration. Kepler's *Prodromus dissertationum cosmographicarum, continens mysterium cosmographicum de admirabili proportione orbium coelestium...*, which appeared in Tübingen in 1596,[33] offers a series of mathematical proofs for the Copernican system which basically could only be understood by experts like Maestlin. Galileo's *Sidereus nuncius*, on the other hand, reported direct observations: 'revealing great and most marvellous phenomena', as the Latin title has it, 'for everyone, and particularly for philosophers and astronomers... which have been observed by Galileo Galilei with the telescope that he has recently invented... and which, previously unknown to all, the author was the first to discover'.[34]

Whereas Copernicus, as he expressly states in the dedication to Pope Paul, intended his work only for specialists,[35] a notion also cherished by Kepler,[36] Galileo spoke to everyone. In fact the *Sidereus nuncius* circulated amazingly quickly, and caused a very great sensation everywhere.[37] Not all the observations were new. Some had already been conjectured in antiquity, but, as Dijksterhuis rightly points out, 'to report that one has really seen these things is rather different from accepting them in speculative fashion'.[38] Even if these observations, above all of the famous moons of Jupiter, had, strictly speaking, demonstrated only the possibility and not the reality of the heliocentric system, to outsiders the proof they that offered was much stronger than Kepler's mathematical arguments. If need be, the latter could always be understood hypothetically, whereas the former finally seemed to be closed to this expedient. It was essentially the greater accessibility and ease of understanding of Galileo's proofs that brought them into the centre of the great argument, quite apart from particular historical circumstances, which naturally played their part.

On the basis of their works, neither Kepler nor Galileo had the slightest doubt about the reality of the world-system that they described.

Kepler made that unmistakably clear in the motto of his *Astronomia nova*.[39] After a quotation from Peter Ramus, in which the latter attacks the 'most absurd fable that the truth of natural things can be demonstrated by false causes', Kepler states: 'In my view it is quite nonsensical to affirm that one could prove natural phenomena by false reasons. But Copernicus has nothing to do with this assertion, since he regards his hypotheses as true; as evidence for this I cite this work.' As the inventor of this 'most absurd fable' Kepler explicity names Andreas Osiander, who gave the work its famous foreword: 'After the death of Copernicus or at least without his knowledge.'[40]

So both Kepler and Galileo faced the same situation. For quite compelling reasons they were convinced of the new system. And at the same time they saw that scripture and church contradicted this truth. So both were compelled to find a way of doing justice to their conviction and their belief.

This is one of the basic situations of biblical criticism, which will be repeated countless times in the centuries to come.

However, at the beginning of the seventeenth century everyone still had to find a solution for himself. Kepler and Galileo found it in their own, highly characteristic, ways. Kepler summed up his ideas on this question in the introduction to the *Astronomia nova*.[41] 'But far greater is the number of those who are led by reverence towards God not to agree with Copernicus. They fear lest the Holy Spirit which speaks in the Holy Scriptures may be burdened with a lie if we say that the earth moves and the sun stands still.' To state the problem clearly: the fear of having to suggest that the Holy Spirit is lying is the cause of the hostility of theology and church to the new picture of the world.

Kepler now attempts to demonstrate that – 'as we experience most, and indeed most important, things through sight' – we often describe how things appear to us, even if we know that they are in fact different. 'There is an example in that verse of Virgil: "We left the harbour, and lands and cities retreated."' So there can be no question of a lie here. Kepler supports his argument with the accommodation theory, which was later so famous and so hotly disputed. In fact the following sentence facilitated the interpretation of particular passages of scripture for generations of theologians, down to the beginning of the nineteenth century:

'But the Holy Scriptures already speak with men of ordinary things (about which it is not their intention to teach them) in a human way so that they may be understood by men; they use what is indubitable among them in order to communicate higher and divine things.'[42]

Scripture speaks with men and women in human fashion, and it is not instituted to give information about 'ordinary matters': these are the two main arguments of progressive biblical criticism in the seventeenth century, around which a bitter controversy was later to break out.

That is already evident from a letter of Matthias Hafenreffer, Kepler's teacher in Tübingen, dated 12 April 1598, in which for all his admiration for the works of his pupil he virtually begs him to maintain the hypothetical character of the Copernican system: 'Therefore if, as I confidently hope, you follow my brotherly council, you will continue to work on the proof of such theses purely as a mathematician, undisturbed as to whether they really correspond to nature or not. I think that the mathematician has achieved his aim when he produces hypotheses to which the phenomena correspond as closely as possible...' As we have seen, this is a correct rendering of Osiander's theory. We have already noted what Kepler thought about it. However, for Hafenreffer, everything depended on whether Kepler would really act in this way. His letter continues: 'If you follow my admonitions and work purely as a mathematician, I have no doubt that your considerations will have the most desirable future. But if you undertake – which may the great and gracious God forbid – to bring those hypotheses publicly into accord with scripture and to defend them, I fear that this matter will certainly lead to the most vigorous controversies. In that case I would wish that I had never cast eyes on your considerations, splendid and admirable though they may be in themselves and from a mathematical point of view.'[43]

Hafenreffer failed to understand Kepler's situation. Kepler *had to* reconcile 'those hypotheses' with scripture, i.e. with the ground of his faith. It is to his credit that he sought to do this in the only way possible to a Lutheran theologian: by a careful new exegesis of the biblical passages in question. And here he showed more skill than many famous theologians of his time. Joshua, as he says, for example, in his interpretation of the famous ch.10, at this moment put his request to God in terms of what he actually saw: 'since at this moment it would have been highly inappropriate to reflect on astronomy and the errors of sight'. And if anyone had reminded him that he had not formulated his request correctly, 'Would not

Joshua have exclaimed that he was merely asking for an extension
to the day, no matter how this might happen?' This is simply a
question of prayer and being heard: 'God understood Joshua's wish
without difficulty from his words and fulfilled it by stopping the
movement of the earth, so that to Joshua the sun seemed to stand
still.'[44] An exegesis which thus aims at the theological nucleus is
clearly not compelled to take refuge in optical miracles, but can
seek to understand what the text means to say.

That can also be recognized from, say, Kepler's discussion of
Psalm 104, which in his day was still regarded as a kind of compendium of physics: 'But the Psalter is far removed from the contemplation of physical causes.' It seeks, rather, to show something else:
'The whole Psalter is based on the exaltation of God, who has
created all this and sings a song of praise to God the creator...'[45] If
one reflects on this rightly, this psalm is a commentary on the
creation story, and it becomes clear that Kepler also wants to see it
in principle as a theological statement.[46] So in a comparison between
the Psalm and the Hexaemeron, he says on Gen.1.6: 'He does not
seek to teach what human beings do not know but to remind them
of things about which they had not thought: the exaltation and
power of God in the creation of a giant structure on such firm
and unshakable foundations.' The distinction between simple not-
knowing and deliberate culpable negligence shows what Kepler
firmly believes this text to be about: it is solely about the relationship
of human beings to God. That has nothing whatsoever to do with
astronomy: 'So that it is quite clear,' he remarks on the work of the
fourth day, 'that it is not concerned here with astronomy. For in
that case it would not have forgotten to mention the five planets.
Nothing is more wonderful, nothing finer than their movement;
nothing attests the creator's wisdom more clearly to those who
understand it.' Scripture is not a textbook of astronomy, but – and
this is Kepler's deepest conviction – astronomy can be a textbook
of God, from which we can learn his wisdom and greatness.

Only at the end, in the last sentence of the treatise, do we learn
something about that self-awareness of reason which compelled
this exegesis. In a magnificent formula Kepler here describes the
principle that from now on will govern modern times: 'But to the
teaching of the saints on these natural matters I would reply in a
word: in theology the authorities have decisive importance, but in
philosophy the decisive importance attaches to calculations.' And

he continues, taking up a saying of Aristotle: 'So Lactantius is holy, who disputed that the earth is round;[47] Augustine is holy, who allowed that it is round but denied the antipodes; holy, too, is obedience to contemporaries who concede the smallness of the earth but dispute its movement. But holier to me is the truth which I demonstrate from philosophy, regardless of the doctors of the church, that the earth is round and inhabited at the antipodes, that it is quite insignificant and small, and finally that it rushes through the stars.'

Here we really can trace something of the emancipation of science (and the scientist), who regardless of the doctors of the church feels bound only by truth which can be objectively demonstrated and proved.

In September 1597 Kepler wrote to Maestlin from Graz: 'I recently sent two copies of my book [the *Prodromus*] to Italy... which were received, as he wrote, with great gratitude and joy by a mathematician from Padua named Galileo Galilei. He has been a supporter of the Copernican heresy for many years.'[48] The brief correspondence which is attached to it shows how similar the two of them felt their situation to be at that time. In his reply of 4 August to which Kepler referred in his letter to Maestlin, Galileo complained about the misunderstanding and enmity that the new theory was encountering on every side. '"I would venture to publish my considerations," he writes, "if there were more people of your kind. But as that is not the case, I will spare myself such trouble."'[49] Kepler wrote back as early as 1 September that the situation was also difficult in Germany, but that he was confident in the power of truth: 'Be confident, Galileo, and press on. If I am right, only a few of the most distinguished mathematicians of Europe will part company with us: so great is the power of the truth.'[50]

How justified Galileo's fears had been emerged from the difficulties in which he found himself immediately after the publication of the *Sidereus nuntius*. They were the occasion of an open letter to Christina of Lorraine, widow of the Grand Duke of Tuscany and mother of his patron, Cosimo II Medici. In it he defended himself against the attacks of his opponents and at the same time set out his thoughts on the relationship between scientific and theological statements.[51] Similarly, in 1615 there appeared a letter from the Carmelite Provincial Paolo Antonio Foscarini to the General of his order, Sebastiano Fantoni, on the same theme and in the same tone.[52] Only the unmistakable theological claim which was made here by representatives of the Copernican system of the world led to the intervention of the Curia and to the suspension of *De revolutionibus* in March 1616. As things were, this consequence was almost inevitable.

The letter to Christina of Lorraine is one of the most remarkable documents in the history of biblical criticism. First Galileo formulates the problem. It is that in the view of his opponents, scripture at many points states that the sun moves and that the earth is stationary. Now as scripture knows neither error nor deception, it necessarily follows from this that the Copernican theory is 'erroneous and to be condemned' (315).[53]

From this Galileo proceeds to the following argument: scripture is indubitably free from error, but only on the presupposition 'that we have penetrated to its true meaning' (ibid.). Now this true meaning is by no means always identical with the wording, as for example the Old Testament anthropomorphisms show. Here the biblical writers speak 'accommodating themselves to the capacity of the people', and skilful exegetes are needed to discover the true meaning of these passages. From this fact, recognized by all theologians, Galileo draws the conclusion that scripture also proceeds similarly in scientific questions, and that therefore its statements cannot be made binding.

'In these circumstances it seems to me,' Galileo continues at this point,[54] 'in discussions of problems of nature we should not begin with the authority of the biblical texts but with the experience of the senses and compelling proofs. For Holy Scripture and nature similarly begin from the word of God: the former as dictated by the Holy Spirit, the latter as the obedient agent of his laws. And as scripture seeks to be universally understood, it is possible to say some things which deviate from absolute truth in the pure meaning of the word: by contrast, nature inexorably and immutably never transcends the boundaries which are allotted to it... so it seems clear that natural effects which either arise out of what we see with our eyes or are confirmed by compelling proofs can in no way be doubted on the basis of scriptural texts which probably meant something quite different. For not every expression of scripture is bound to such strict conditions as are all events in nature; and God reveals himself no less splendidly in these events than in the words of Holy Scripture...' (316f.).

So the authority of the Bible may no longer be asserted in scientific questions. On this point its answers are no longer binding. But the reverse now suddenly becomes conceivable: that the results of the exact sciences are binding on the exegesis of scripture:

'We may not conclude from this that the words of Holy Scripture are not due the highest respect. But if we have gained certain and exact knowledge about particular natural events, we must apply it as the most appropriate means for the right interpretation of Holy Scripture and the investigation of that meaning which is necessarily contained in it, because they are utterly true and correspond with the truth as demonstrated' (317).

The consequence of this new standpoint is obvious, and Galileo draws it immediately: 'Therefore I think that the authority of Holy Scripture is directed mainly towards convincing men of such conceptions and principles which, because they transcend all human thought, cannot find belief through any science or any means other than through the revelation of the Holy Spirit' (317).

It is, as Galileo later says with a witty play on words attributed to Cardinal Baronio, the aim of the Holy Spirit to teach us how to go to heaven, not how the heavens move (319).

Two generations earlier, in his *Initia doctrinae physicae*, Melanchthon had still held it to be good and right 'to conform philosophy to the divine communications and in such great obscurity of the human spirit to ask divine authority for counsel wherever we can'.[55] Now this step, which was so generally illuminating and apparently unconditional, was stood on its head. Galileo required that the 'divine communications' should be conformed to the insights of philosophy. Here, however, he had in mind only such communications as related to phenomena within the limits of human possibilities of knowledge. What lay beyond those limits should still be subject to the authority of scripture. But who could lay down these limits? Galileo himself raises the question: 'And who will set limits to the human spirit? Who will claim to see and discover all that there is in the visible world and all there is to know? Perhaps those who in other matters concede (quite rightly) that what we know is only the smallest part of what we do not know?' (p.320). In fact, once the principle had been recognized, it was impossible to see where criticism would end.

Our glance back to Melanchthon shows where the watershed between Middle Ages and modernity runs on this question. Experience and proof are set over against the traditions, even the most sacred, by which the intellect had previously been shaped. And to the degree to which the former gained certainty and reliability, the latter lost credibility and authority.[56] Biblical criticism had to some degree become involved with this thinking.

The decisive insight was that the greater, indeed the quite compelling conclusiveness lay on the side of experience and not on the side of tradition. Galileo puts it like this:

'I would like to ask those wise and foresighted fathers to consider with all diligence the distinction between knowledge that can be demonstrated and knowledge which allows of opinions: if they consider with what force necessary conclusions compel their acceptance, they may become all the more aware that it is not in the power of those who acknowledge demonstrable sciences to change their opinion at will and put themselves now on this side and now on the other...' (326).

Here we have a clear formulation of the difference between scientific and theological statements as understood in the new age. In contrast to the statements of scripture, the regularities of nature do not depend on our interpretation. They come about independently of us, in accordance with eternal, unchangeable laws. Once we have recognized and demonstrated a law of this kind, knowledge and proof take on the same eternity and immutability as the law which they follow. They are removed from human whim and have the character of strict necessity. Therefore it is never possible to decide against their authority, even where they contradict the wording of scripture. For scripture – and this to some degree is the complementary argument – has no such compelling truth. Its statements need interpretation and are at the mercy of human whim.

So Galileo goes on to ask the fathers to remember, 'that it makes a great difference whether one is commanding a mathematician or a philosopher, or using a merchant or an attorney; for statements about natural phenomena and heavenly bodies which have compelling proofs cannot be changed with the same ease as opinions on what is permissible or not in a contract, a property transaction or money changing' (326). It reads rather like a commentary in anticipation on his own trial when Galileo recalls that his kind of truth can in no circumstances be suppressed, either by closing someone's mouth or by banning the books or views of Copernicus, or by a ban on astronomy generally (328.10ff.).

And he declares, boldly enough, that here even the power of the Pope has its limits: 'For in respect of this and other similar statements which are not directly *de fide*, there is no one who would doubt that while the Pope always has absolute power to accept or reject them, it is not in the power of any creature to make them true or false, i.e. other than they are by nature and *de facto*' (343).

In fact the course Galileo adopted was the only possible way of avoiding the difficulties. If on the one hand he did not want to attack the authority of the church,[57] and on the other could not attack the authority of reason, he had to deny scripture and tradition all competence in these questions and assign them entirely to the sphere of the metaphysical. However, experience and proof alone might reign within the sphere of physics. That despite all the efforts of the Copernicans this did not solve the problem, but simply formulated it correctly for the first time, became clear from subsequent events.[58]

4

It is clear that underlying this conflict was no longer just a dispute over the salvage of particular astronomical observations. What was involved here was a new principle of knowledge, which ran contrary to the old biblical-Aristotelian picture of the world. And at the same time this demonstrated the connection between new scientific knowledge and the position of the older theology: it was not the individual fact which provoked such disquiet so much as the spiritual claim based on the facts. The decisive step taken between Copernicus and Kepler and Galileo was that the latter disputed tradition in the name of reason, proceeding in a methodical way, and in so doing continually referred to facts.

That was the very moment at which the facts now also had to become important for church and theology. As individual opinions, no matter how revolutionary, they were only individual instances. Now, in the context of the new model of the world, it proved that along with the recognition of them went a universal claim. Anyone who wanted to dispute this claim had to dispute the facts. That was one of the reasons why Christian theology of all confessions refused for more than a century to recognize the new results.

Dijksterhuis has listed the most important characteristics of the new principle in connection with Kepler's work:

'1. The rejection of all arguments which are based only on tradition and authority.

2. Independence of scientific research from all philosophical and theological principles.

3. The ongoing application of mathematical thought in the positing and development of hypotheses.

4. Inexorable application of the results derived from this by means of an empiricism taken to the highest possible degree of accuracy.'[59]

While the independence mentioned under 2 – as Dijksterhuis rightly adds – initially did not mean a general independence, but only an independence related to particular scientific thought-processes, the basis of the principle and therefore of all its consequences lay here. One of these consequences was biblical criticism.

The reaction of the Roman church is well known. In March 1610, seventy-three years after it appeared, the work of Copernicus was suspended by the Congregation of the Index. This action had been preceded by an admonition to Galileo from Cardinal Bellarmine to desist from his views (but this was presumably not an absolute prohibition).[60]

The church's decision was based on the famous opinion of 23 February 1616, in which the statement 'The sun is the centre of the world and consequently does not move in space' was declared to be 'foolish and absurd in philosophy and formally heretical, in so far as this explicitly contradicts the statements of Holy Scripture in many places according to their real wording and according to the general interpretation and understanding of the Holy Fathers and learned theologians'.[61]

There is no doubt that the churches of the Reformation also largely concurred with this verdict. The trial in the course of which seventeen years later, in humiliating circumstances, Galileo was compelled publicly to renouce his belief in the Copernican theories which had been condemned, did not in fact add anything new, and belongs more in the unpleasant history of the practices of the Roman inquisition than here. The one point of interest is the date, which roughly coincides with the beginning of deliberate anti-Copernican polemic from the Christian churches throughout Europe.

It is conceivable that Galileo would have avoided trial had he followed Bellarmine's advice. In an answer to the open letter by Foscarini of 12 April 1615 Bellarmine had urgently recommended the Carmelite and Galileo to speak hypothetically in these matters, along the lines of Osiander: 'It seems to me that you and Galileo would be wise if you contented yourselves speaking not in absolute terms but *ex suppositione*, which is what I have always believed Copernicus to have done.'[62]

The modest beginnings of an attempt to follow this advice made by Galileo in his most famous work, the *Dialogue on the Two Main World-Systems*, seem so much of a concession in their context that they did not deceive anyone.[63] And that should not surprise anyone who has read the letter to Christina of Lorraine. For there could be no more open statement of the power with which the necessary conclusions compelled acceptance despite all authorities.

Galileo's name does not appear in the history of biblical criticism, but he was the first to formulate its basic principles. In a highly paradoxical way, it was in fact the trial of Galileo and its consequences that brought this truth to light.

FOUR

The Credibility of the Biblical Picture of the World: II. The Problem of World History

1

We can put an exact date to the classical period of astronomy, in the course of which the new physical picture of the world came into being. It begins in 1543 with Copernicus' *De revolutionibus orbium caelestium* and ends in 1687 with Newton's *Philosophia naturalis principa mathematica*.[1] There are no similarly precise dates for the no less momentous parallel development: the replacement of the biblical picture of history by a new picture of the real course of world history, based on experience and evidence. There is no Copernicus of historiography, who first expressed the idea of a logical-empirical universal history, and no Galileo who deliberately called it to attention. There is nothing brilliant or spectacular about this development, and that is perhaps the reason why it is always overshadowed by the great astronomical revolutions. That is certainly a mistake; for which insight in the end changed our understanding of reality more deeply is a completely open question.

Because there are no great names in seventeenth-century historiography, Voltaire is often mentioned as its founder, and his *Essai sur les moeurs et l'esprit des nations* is often cited as the first work of the modern historical consciousness.[2] But Voltaire stands at the end of a long development and not at its beginning; if we can return to our comparison once again, he was to some degree its Newton, not its Copernicus.[3]

Jacques Bénigne Bossuet's famous *Discours sur l'histoire universelle* of 1681 is no proof to the contrary. Even if the great Bishop of Meaux could here once again rehearse for the Dauphin of France the tradition of mediaeval Christian conceptions of history in all their glory and give the impression of their unassailable validity, there is no doubt that the foundations of this noble edifice had long become shaky.[4] For Bossuet already saw himself confronted, 'though he objected to them, with the new aspects of a world-historical contemplation of universal history, as they had gradually come into being from the middle of the sixteenth century in the disclosure of historical realities which hitherto had been unknown or had not been taken into consideration'.[5]

In fact that was the age of the great discoveries which, with the transformation of the cosmographical views of the Middle Ages, provided the most important basis for a revision of the old view of history, a transformation which was essentially completed around the middle of the seventeenth century. After the discovery of America, in the first half of this century it was the much-noted voyages of the Dutch with their circumnavigation of the greater part of the continent of Australia which finally established the broad outlines of the modern map of the world.[6]

Now we must free ourselves from the illusion that the abundance of such reports, which flooded into Europe throughout the sixteenth century, immediately had a direct effect on the geographical and historical view of the world. On the contrary, it remains astonishing how little the great discoveries managed to change the traditional ancient-Christian framework of world history.[7]

It seems that serious reflection on the significance of the discovery of the 'New World' started only at the beginning of the seventeenth century.[8]

One sign that at this time the newly-discovered parts of the earth were gradually penetrating people's consciousness and taking on a life of their own is the argument of Fausto Sozzini in his *Praelectiones theologicae*, in which he disputes the possibility of a natural theology on the basis of reports from the New World. 'Not only individual men but whole peoples are being discovered today who do not have the least conception or intimation of any deity. These live in the new Western hemisphere in the province of "Bresilia", as historians report and as a reliable man who spent time there has assured me on his sacred oath. But the new history of India attests that such people are also to be found elsewhere.'[9]

This argument led directly to the question how these 'nations lacking all religion'[10] could be reconciled with the historical and geographical conceptions of the Bible.

Isaac de la Peyrère raised this question for the first time in his *Pre-Adamites*, which appeared in 1655, and backed it up with a wealth of material.[11] There is no more impressive evidence than this remarkable book of what a profound problem the old view of history had already become by the middle of the seventeenth century. With it – almost a century before Voltaire – the development of the new universal-historical conception of world history begins.

2

The mediaeval view of history was closely bound up with biblical conceptions. Werner Kaegi has painted a large-scale picture of it for us: 'The age-old Christian view of history depicted the course of humankind through this world like an altarpiece in three biblical scenes. The central one portrays the birth of Christ or his death; of the two wings, the one on the left depicts Adam's expulsion from Paradise or another theme from the creation stories, and the one on the right the return of Christ and the last judgment. These are the great epochs: the history of creation, the life of the redeemer and the end of the world. Between these two main scenes the literary historical narrative portrays like an infinite predella the course of humankind down the centuries, beginning with Jewish history as reported in the Old Testament, occasionally reaching out into the histories of the great empires of Egypt and Mesopotamia, then shortly before the birth of Christ interpolating a section of Roman history, with the life of the saviour meeting up with the course of the history of the Roman empire, and ending up in a broad portrait of the particular present of the historian concerned, in which the description is alternately marked by two main accents: confidence and faith in the salvation foretold by the prophets, proclaimed by Christ and consummated in his return - and gloomy pessimism as a result of human corruption, the decline in public morals and the coming of judgment.'[12]

The agreement between the elements which go to form this historical picture and those of the old physical picture of the world is obvious. Both owe their origin to the encounter between Christianity and antiquity; for both, the biblical framework is normative and the Bible is taken for granted as an authority. Ancient traditions which had been in conflict with this authority had long been excluded. This view of the world was a unity and remained so until the eve of the seventeenth century.

There is hardly any area in which the significance of the Bible as the presupposition and consequence of this unity can be better demonstrated than in that of history. In what follows I shall attempt to do this through the Reformers.

If scripture was already no textbook of mathematics and physics, it was certainly a historical textbook. It was a textbook of incomparable status and unique quality. Melanchthon put this very well in the preface to the *Chronicon Carionis*.[13] The status of scripture as a source for history is based on the will of God, which through scripture teaches us above all about the church: 'Therefore God willed for history to be written for us through the fathers and prophets in the best order and with careful transmission of the dates.' But its quality lies in the fact that it is older, more complete and more accurate than any other sources: 'And it is a special glory of the church that nowhere else in the whole history of the human race is there an older enumeration of kingdoms and times. And no other people has dates in the past which have been reliably transmitted.'[14]

We also find this confidence in the unconditional reliability of scripture as a historical source in Luther. In the preface to his *Supputatio annorum* of 1541[15] he goes on at great length about certain differences between his chronology and others and supposes: 'We all complain about the other historians, and they complain among themselves that they lack any certain reckoning of the years. Therefore I have tried to do that in this work and have sought to produce this calculation primarily from Holy Scripture. For on this we can and should truly rely, and with constant faith.'

The main point of dispute is the exegesis of the seventy weeks in Dan.9.24ff. Here Luther must with a heavy heart criticize even Philo because in this question scripture is the ultimate authority. So he says at the end of the preface: 'This cause has moved me, while not despising the historians, to prefer Holy Scripture to them. So I use it in order not to be compelled to go contrary to scripture. For I believe that in Scripture God speaks, who is true, but that in other histories very subtle people use their best diligence and faithfulness (however, as human beings), or at least that those who copied them could have made mistakes.'[16]

Scripture, church and world history form a unity. That is evident from the fact that for Melanchthon, biblical and pagan historiography run into each other with barely a seam: 'And the younger ones[17] may reflect that Herodotus begins his history at the precise point where Jeremiah ends, namely with king Apries,[18] who killed Jeremiah. So there is a consecutive history of the world: the prophetic books, Herodotus, Thucydides, Xenophon, Diodore... Polybius, Livy and then the others after Livy.'[19]

This unity also makes it possible not only for scripture to disclose history but also for history to make scripture comprehensible, and indeed to serve as a proof of its truth. For example, we know from history that particular prophetic oracles were fulfilled. That compels us to concede that not only those prophecies, but the prophets' proclamation of God, is true. So among the grounds on which Melanchthon demonstrates the indispensability of historical knowledge is the following: 'Secondly, that to understand the prophetic books better one must know the history of all times.'[20]

The Bible also serves as a basis and starting point in the division of the enormous amount of material. Since Augustine developed the doctrine of the six or seven great ages of the world on a late-Jewish model in connection with the story of creation, and the Venerable Bede established it in the West,[21] this doctrine remained *the* scheme for universal history throughout the Middle Ages. The chronicle of the world which appeared in 1493, by the Nuremberg doctor and humanist Hartmann Schedel, is quite naturally divided in accordance with the six ages of the world.

Over against this the Reformation accounts of history[22] for the first time returned to an earlier set of ideas: the doctrine of six millennia of the world deriving from late Judaism. It occurs in Melanchthon as 'a word which is presented in the commentaries of the Jews' under the heading 'tradition of the house of Elijah: the world lasts for six thousand years, then comes the end. Two thousand years are empty. For two thousand years the law rules. The day of the Messiah lasts for two thousand years. And because of our sins which are numerous and great, the years will lack which will lack.'[23]

Luther put the prophecy as a preface to his *Supputatio* as 'A Saying of Elijah the prophet', and referred to Paulus Burgensis as a source.[24] In connection with Osiander's *Coniecturae de ultimis temporibus ac de fine mundi*,[25] underlying which is similarly the 'tradition of the house of Elijah', Hirsch investigated its origin and traced it back to Pico della Mirandola.[26] But we can happily leave the question of source open here. More important is the reason why the Reformers went back to this late Jewish doctrine against the whole of tradition.

If we follow Melanchthon here, there can be no doubt about the explanation: the saying of Elijah enjoyed biblical authority. 'In this way Elijah prophesied about the duration of the human race,' declares Melanchthon on the saying itself, and ends this section by saying that he wants to divide his account into three books *iuxta dictum Eliae*.[27]

But on the basis of a 'word of scripture' world history is divided not only in its temporal span but also in terms of content. Melanchthon introduces the picture of the monarchies from Dan.2 and the vision of the four world empires from Dan.7 into the scheme of thrice two thousand years. 'But the book of Daniel shows that God himself numbers four world empires.'[28] The function of this prophecy is to strengthen the pious: when we see that the order and sequence of the monarchies took place precisely as was predicted, we will not doubt that the last judgment will also come. The danger of this argument is obvious. For any justified criticism of the historical validity of the scheme of four monarchies would inevitably mean that theology was criticizing the authority of scripture and thus of God himself.

But this historical criticism had to come, given a division which after the kingdoms of the Chaldaeans, the Persians and Alexander the Great left for the whole of the rest of world history only the Roman empire, which God had entrusted to the Germans: 'But we should be grateful for the consideration that God has marked out the Germans for such honour that in accordance with his will they are heirs of the Roman empire and the chosen protectors of Europe.'[29] This was a conviction that France, for example, was in no way ready to share. But we shall have to discuss it later. Here the prime concern was to try to make clear the unity of historical understanding in this period, and within this unity to understand the central position of the Bible as its presupposition and consequence. The Bible was a presupposition, in that history as a whole and in detail was found in it, related to it, understood through it and divided in accordance with it; it was a consequence, in that all this was possible only within the relatively closed sphere of Western Christian culture.

The powerful revival of historical interest, which can be observed
in connection with humanism and the Reformation in the sixteenth
century generally, further strengthened this central position of the
Bible rather than weakening it – at least as far as the Reformers
were concerned.

Everywhere we find evidence of this newly-awakened interest,
but at the same time it always proves to have a connection with
theology and the church.

Alongside Melanchthon ('knowledge of history is particularly
necessary in the church'),[30] J.Aurifaber's introduction to his translation of Luther's *Supputatio* is a fine example of this: 'It is highly
necessary for all men to know thoroughly the ordering of the years
from the beginning of the world and the chiefest stories of divine
revelations and witness, the beginning of true religion and divine
churches and the ending of supreme rule...'[31]

The reason why this is necessary is so that history can enlighten
human beings about themselves and about God's plan for the world:
'For otherwise men would not know the beginning of the world
and divine revelations; people would live in cruel darkness and
uncertainty; they would not know about their origins and how this
noble creation and the human race in the image of God fell into
cruel destruction, into sin and death, nor what is righteousness and
what is sin, as God has graciously revealed...'[32]

Theodor Bibliander, Zwingli's learned successor in the Zurich
school of theologians,[33] also begins his chronology with an extensive
preface in praise of history. He wants history to be read and
understood as salvation history and writes of it: 'It is the light of
truth which is remote from any deception; a mirror and a teacher of
life, which brings the greatest things before the eyes: the true
happiness of men, the supreme good, the true worship of the one
God, the true art of living well and happily and finally the true and
holy church of God, outside which no one can find salvation.'[34]

These voices make clear the relevance of historical research and
historiography for the church and theology which, in the view of
many contemporaries, both possessed to an extraordinary degree.
So Sebastian Franck was not wrong when he also called his great
chronicle of the world a 'bible of history'. For history writing could
not be other than a continuation, extension and addition to the
biblical material. But in also becoming that it took on something
like biblical status and respect. It ordered the world within the

biblical framework in a biblical perspective, determined the status of the present in relation to the past and the future, and explained what otherwise would inevitably have remained incomprehensible: the significance of all the wars, terrors and atrocities from the beginning of time to the historian's day. And by taking up, explaining, ordering and evaluating all this, it really became what Bibliander said it was: a mirror and a mistress of life.

3

A historical picture of such power and coherence, on which so much of the reality of faith and experience depends, does not collapse overnight. In fact it took a century of work for even the critical questions to be formulated in context. Most of the work went on in secret. Only here and there in the period between 1550 and 1650 can we see some signs which indicate that this picture of history was now no longer being taken for granted. The unity of the historical universe as Melanchthon and his disciples saw it depended on the power of religious conviction. Anyone who was no longer quite so certain could see some things differently. The church and theology and the whole aspect of salvation history could fade into the background and be replaced by a stronger interest in things which were closer at hand: say in constitutions, in political complications and legal problems. Here there was still no question of criticism in principle; what was heralded here was just the slow re-structuring of historical and political consciousness.

We can see all this very well in Jean Bodin, the French advocate, historian and politician,[35] whose *Methodus ad facilem historiarum cognitionem* produced the first criticism of Melanchthon's picture of history. Its circulation throughout Europe guaranteed the work a special place in the history of the historical world-view.[36]

Bodin, too, begins with a 'Prologue on the Possibility, Delight and Utility of History', in which he celebrates history as the 'mistress of life' (1).[37] Here he in no way forgets its theological relevance, but it is clear that his interest lies elsewhere. In the reason he gives for his undertaking the theological perspective appears only under *Postremo*, 'finally': 'So I have been moved to the composition of this writing because we receive thorough instruction from history: not only in the skills which are needful to life but also in what we are to strive for and what avoid, what is shameful and what is honourable, what are the best laws, what is the best state, what is a happy life; finally because in the course of time cults, religions and prophecies are celebrated as God's exalted history...' (8). But not only is the sequence changed. The substance itself seems to be seen from a different perspective. Bodin finds 'God's exalted history' not in 'the word of God handed down through history' but in a multiplicity of 'cults, religions and prophecies', which already hint at the natural religion of the *Colloquium heptaplomeres*.[38]

The knowledge of state constitutions which Bodin mentions as the finest fruit of the study of history[39] not only indicates his predominant interest but also forms the presupposition for his criticism of Melanchthon.[40] It is directed above all at the scheme of four monarchies. Bodin thinks this an inveterate error which is so widespread that one can hardly hope to eradicate it. Numerous interpreters of the Bible – among others he mentions Melanchthon, Sleidanus and Funck - had confirmed this error. Once he had even thought on their authority that he should not doubt it. Then follow some highly characteristic and important statements: 'I was also moved by the prophecy of Daniel, to challenge the credibility of which would be a crime and to diminish the authority of which would be a sin.' So he is concerned formally to maintain the credibility and authority of the prophecy, but: 'Later I understood that the obscure and enigmatic words of Daniel could be twisted in different directions; and in the interpretation of prophecies I preferred to make use of the legal formula "not proven" rather than rashly to assent to something which I had not understood on the opinion of others' (346). Not unbelief, but an eye for political realities, is what forces him to this critical 'Not proven'.

How, for example, can the Germans claim that they are the fourth monarchy of the world, when they rule over barely a hundredth part of the world's surface? Does not the king of Spain have a much greater empire? 'Both as to the magnitude of the population and the extent of the territory involved; here I do not even mention the regions of America, over which he largely rules and which are three times greater than Europe' (347). Even the king of Portugal ('by force of arms he has seized almost the whole coast of Africa') rules over a greater territory, not to mention the Sultan of Turkey who, according to Bodin, 'possesses the richest parts of Asia, Africa, and Europe and largely rules the whole of the Mediterranean and all islands, with the exception of only a few' (348).

The consequence is clear: 'It is therefore nonsensical for the Germans to believe that they possess an empire – which according to Philip's understanding is the most powerful of all empires – and even more nonsensical if they believe that they possess the Roman empire. That all seems quite ludicrous to anyone who has a precise knowledge of the earth' (348).

Bodin goes on to support this statement by enumerating numerous great empires of history which cannot be reconciled with Daniel's oracle.

There is no doubt that Bodin has a very much clearer picture of the historical and political forces of his time than Melanchthon and his disciples. The Frenchman seems much more modern – not least in his sense of nationalism, which has evidently sharpened his gaze. 'For in no other part of the world are all sciences so flourishing as in Europe, and in no part of Europe has there ever been a more renowned science of law than there is at present in France (which even foreigners now concede).'[41] This evidently leads him to suppose that something similar is involved in the German interpretation of the Daniel oracle: 'So in my view what is written about the Germans has been written in praise of their name and empire; for it has absolutely nothing to do with the prophecy of Daniel' (347).

It is also an eye to the realities of the present (the 'precise knowledge of the earth') which makes Bodin criticize the theory of decline. In a brilliant plea he argues for human progress: 'For that age which they call golden could have seemed like iron in comparison with ours' (353). For what did that allegedly golden age look like according to reliable reports from antiquity? 'These were gold and silver ages in which people lived scattered like wild beasts over field and wood with only what they could obtain by force and injustice, until gradually they were brought from that wild and barbaric state to the human customs and the community based on law, such as we see it...' (356).

It is not so much the detailed results as the spirit of the whole which makes this view of history so different in character from that of Melanchthon.

That becomes clear once again in the discussion of the tricky question of chronology, to which Bodin devotes a whole chapter.[42] It begins by stating that chronology is the presupposition of all historical understanding: 'Anyone who believes that he can understand history without knowledge of dates deceives himself...' (362).

From this there follows the need to discover about the beginning of time. But did time and the world have a beginning? Are they not perhaps eternal? Bodin is very concerned to demonstrate what after twenty pages of argument he puts like this: 'As things are, it is clear that the times have their beginning and their end...' (383).

Now it would be natural to resort to the biblical accounts on this question, if on anything. And Bodin, too, stresses that the authority of the one figure of Moses is so great for him that he prefers him by far to all the statements of the philosophers. Nevertheless he is not prepared to make decisions on Moses' authority. 'This question has to be settled not so much by authority, which is worthless to those who want to be guided by the understanding, but rather by compelling arguments' (362).

Is it a coincidence that this formula unintentionally recalls Galileo's 'necessary demonstrations'? It is not authority but compelling proof, compelling argument, that is binding.

Bodin thinks that he has found such arguments for the beginning of the world and the period which has elapsed since then.

Of course there can only be speculations about the end of the world. It is therefore consistent for Bodin to refuse to discuss this in any way. The future is not a field for the historian. And the 'tradition of the house of Elijah' is no substitute for compelling aruguments, all the more so since it is only a rabbinic conjecture: 'This conjecture many have taken to be a divine prophecy, since they regarded Elijah as a prophet' (402). Bodin knows better. So he can end this section tersely: 'But to investigate more closely what can neither be grasped by the human spirit or understanding nor be proved by divine prophecies seems as inappropriate as it is godless' (402).

If we compare the method with that of the roughly contemporaneous works of Reformation historians, a restructuring of the historical-political consciousness seems unmistakable. The more marked consideration of political realities, the extension of perspective beyond the limits of the West, the demand for compelling arguments even where tradition has long decided – all this points to the beginning of an emancipation from a purely biblical-theological understanding of the world and the history of nations.

However, we must guard against seeing these beginnings as a critical revolution in themselves. This is only the departure from the Holy Land, and the way is long. While Bodin seems modern and critical in some questions, he seems unmodern and uncritical in others.[43] The Frenchman famed for his free gaze was at the same time the author of a work which was relied on again and again as a basis and justification for the trial of witches.[44] There is no doubt that he believed in demons and spirits.[45] And the *Universae theatrum naturae* which appeared in 1596, the year of his death, clearly shows no trace of critical method. But perhaps it is precisely the fact that Bodin has no critical method, indeed not even a recognizable concern for criticism, but is ahead of Melanchthon only in his concern for historical and political arguments, that confirms Kaegi's theory: '...that the epoch-making transformation of the historical world-view, the final breaking asunder of the traditional Christian framework, did not derive from a new method and a new cultural and scholarly approach but from the experience of some powerful external realities.'[46]

4

In short, evidence was mounting that neither the biblical geography (or what this was taken to be) nor the biblical chronology corresponded with reality. Or, to cite Kaegi once again: 'That altarpiece (the old picture of history) had lost validity for historical scholarship not because an impious attitude alien to religion and Christianity had seized people, but because new undeniable historical realilties were being forced home on them which the old picture was quite incapable of incorporating within its intellectual system.'[47]

The question of chronology played an important role in this connection. Previously, the age of the world had quite naturally been calculated from the information in the Bible, in accordance with the principle that e.g. Johann Heinrich Alsted stil put at the beginning of his *Thesaurus chronologiae*: 'Holy Scripture provides a complete chronology from the foundation of the world to its end.'[48]

According to this, Adam lived for 930 years, Seth for 912, Enoch for 815, etc. And as the list of the generations of the patriarchs gave each a relative date of birth, the time from Adam to the flood could be easily calculated: it amounted to exactly 1656 years. Then things became more difficult, and in the historical books there were not inconsiderable differences, depending on the basis of the calculations. Still, up to the beginning of the sixteenth century, the age of the world was relatively firm: from the creation of the world to the birth of Christ was calculated to be around 4000 years. This calculation, however, from the beginning contained one uncertainty: the Masoretic text and the Septuagint differed in the information they gave by more than 1500 years. But the Middle Ages evidently at first felt no need to balance out these contradictions. Augustine considers the question and can leave it open; so did the mediaeval chroniclers.

However, in the course of the sixteenth century, interest grew in a more precise dating, of course without initially doubting the principle. Luther is a good example of this. In the preface to his *Supputatio* he takes great pains to explain his divergence from Melanchthon's calculation (amounting to two years!), and then consoles himself with the thought: 'That it is a small matter if the whole calculation is otherwise certain and a doubt remains in only two or four years. For if in this way it will all work out until the end of the world apart from two or four years, faith and the church are in little danger. Indeed we may with good conscience disregard four years in such difficult matters over the course of the whole world.'[49]

However, people became less satisfied with this consolation in the course of time, when the differences in fact amounted to considerably more than two years. In 1561 Bibliander, who had already produced a list of the 'different calculations of time from the founding of the world to the birth of Jesus Christ', could already count 24 different results which varied[50] between 3944 years (J.Carion) and 6984 years (King Alfonso).[51] Alsted's list contains 22 possibilities, which similarly differ by almost 3000 years.[52] By 1691 this number had reached seventy;[53] and in 1728 in his *Chronologie de l'Histoire Sainte* A. de Vignolles happily referred to two hundred ways of dating.[54]

Now in this context the extra-biblical sources also became a problem, above all the chronology of the Egyptians. Alsted resorted to the expedient of beginning with the Seventeenth Dynasty and supposing that the first eight, which according to the biblical information had to be far older than the creation of the world, had been invented by the vainglorious Egyptians. The passage seems to me so characteristic of the confusion of the time that I quote it here: 'The kingdom of the Egyptians is divided into thirty-two dynasties up to the reign of Augustus. Of these, the first eight and a half are proleptic and fictitious, that is, they were introduced by the Egyptians, who boasted that they were older than the Greeks and had been there long before the creation of the world; the rest are historical, so that the 110th year of the ninth dynasty coincides with the first year of the world...'[55] Similar problems arose from the Chaldaean and then, after the end of the century, also from the Chinese chronologies.[56]

Indeed, the stronger the uncertainty about biblical chronology became, and the more extra-biblical details gained credibility – two developments which supplemented each other – the greater, of course, was the doubt about the credibility of biblical historiography generally.

A picture of history develops not only in time but also in space. Bibliander therefore rightly referred to geography even before chronology, saying that without its help history would be blind and mutilated: 'I see two things without which history, as it were robbed of both eyes, is blind, or is as mutilated as if its arms were cut off. One is geography, i.e. the description of countries and places where the remarkable events took place...; the other is chronography and chronology, which divides times by firm boundaries and gives the date of each event briefly and clearly.'[57] In fact geography was the second point from which a critical examination of the mediaeval picture of history began. An understanding of history which began from demonstrably false geographical presuppositions was in the long run untenable in an age which increasingly looked for 'compelling arguments'. And doubts about the ancient biblical cosmographies arose early, even if for a relatively long period they had no visible consequences.

Like the chronological conceptions of the Middle Ages, its geographical conceptions were in principle orientated on the Bible. According to this, the earth was a circular surface, bounded on all sides by the ocean, beyond which eternal darkness began (cf.Isa.40.22; Job.26.10).[58] In the middle of this round disc lay Palestine (Isa.28.12), and in the middle of Palestine was Jerusalem (Isa.55: 'That is Jerusalem, which I have set in the midst of the heathen with lands around'). 'So to this degree the Bible itself had already given cosmographers a plan of the world, and this basic scheme was also preserved throughout the Middle Ages.'[59] Accordingly, as a rule the mediaeval maps of the world were round (though this was not necessarily connected with the disc theory) and put Jerusalem at the centre of the earth, a position which gave cosmographers considerable difficulties from the thirteenth century on, as a result of discoveries in Asia.[60] The classical threefold division of the earth into Asia, Africa and Europe could also be derived from the Bible, notably from the narrative of the occupation of the world by the three sons of Noah (Gen.9 and 10). 'The mediaeval exegetes... thought that the division was carried out like this: Shem was the firstborn, from whose descendants the elect people came. He had been assigned the whole eastern part of Asia, Japhet the northern part of the western half, Europe; and Ham the southern part, Africa.'[61]

The mediaeval cosmographers constructed their maps of the world according to these basic principles. Up to the second half of the fifteen century they show irregularly divided but interconnected masses of land surrounded by water.[62]

One might suppose that the wealth of new geographical reports which flooded into Europe without a break from the end of the fifteenth century on would inevitably very soon have led to the abandonment of these conceptions. However, that was by no means the case. In the eventful history of discoveries the tenacity of the old views remains one of the most astounding facts. And that was doubtless not just because of the difficulty of putting the numerous individual reports in a rational order; it was the unity of the old picture of the world which was opposed to the recognition of the New World as a world with its own history and culture.

The traditional geographical sphere was indeed more than a scientific hypothesis which was now obsolete. It was the sphere which had been filled with Christian history, and therefore its uniqueness had been stressed above all others. It had made sense to think of this sphere as being geographically at the centre of the world, just as the world formed the centre of the cosmos. So it is quite understandable that the new discoveries initially had 'reality only for commerce and colonial politics': what went out from the West remained related to the West.[63]

How far the world in the sixteenth century was still understood as the sphere of Christian history and in geographical terms was interpreted accordingly can be seen, say, from the *Epitome trium terrae partium* of the humanist and physician Joachim Vadian, who became known as the reformer of St Gallen.[64] This work is particularly interesting in that it shows Vadian to be competent in the sphere of geography. He had already interpreted one of the most famous geographical authors of antiquity, Pomponius Mela, in summer 1514, when he was a thirty-year-old professor at the University of Vienna.[65] Four years later his extensive book of scholia on this author appeared, and was immediately reprinted in Basel and Paris: 'a monstrous collection of geographical science and geographical knowledge'.[66] The geographical picture of the world that Vadian outlines is surprisingly modern for his time. Against the errors of ancient and Christian authors, he argues that the earth is a sphere and has antipodes; he rightly sees the New World as a new continent and is one of the first to call it America: for him its discovery marks major progress towards correct geographical ideas.[67] But almost more important are Vadian's theoretical discussions as they are collected in a polemical document directed against his friend and former colleague Johannes Camers.[68] Camers had professed the view that it was impermissible to pursue enquiries beyond the old authorities and especially the Bible. By contrast, Vadian had already stated in 1518: 'In the tradition of the location of the earth, the more recent reports are always to be believed more than any old ones.'[69] Now, in refuting Camers' criticism, he gives detailed reasons for his attitude. The truth is always of prime importance. 'No true knowledge – as long as it does not contradict Holy Scripture, which is a reservation Vadian makes at just one point - may be restricted by the authority of an author: What deception would it have been to prefer authority to truth in the tradition of a report!'[70] In Vadian's view, in questions of a geographical kind, observation and natural laws are the deciding factor: 'the calculating, exact sciences, mathematics and astronomy, drive the literary authorities and even theological arguments from the field'.[71]

Among Vadian's contemporaries, one will not find very many who so clearly and resolutely put forward the principle of the future, that standpoint which we found a century later in Kepler and Galileo as the presupposition of their biblical criticism.

The fact that this standpoint could already be formulated so early does not make the influence of the Reformation on the free development of science, which is so often taken for granted, any more probable. At the same time, however, we are also forced to a more cautious approach to the concept of humanism, the ambivalent character of which becomes evident here. For doubtless in this question Camers, and not Vadian, represented the genuinely humanist line.

So in 1534 this modern and critical geographer put forward a kind of biblical geography which came into being in connection with an interpretation of the Acts of the Apostles and was then expanded into a general description of the earth.[72] And it is precisely here that we can see most clearly the power of the old geographical picture of the world and its origin, Holy Scripture. When Vadian speaks 'about the division of the inhabited earth and of the Ocean and our sea', then for this Swiss 'our' sea is still the Mediterranean. And although he has long taken note of the existence of America as a separate continent, he divides the earth in accordance with the old scheme: 'What lands stretch from the straits of Cadiz (i.e. the straits of Gibraltar) to those rivers [namely the Nile and the Tanais, which is the Don] is called on the one side Africa and on the other Europe: to the Nile, Africa and to the Tanais, Europe; what lies beyond them Pomponius regards as Asia.'[73] Europe, Asia and Africa are grouped around the Mediterranean; the whole of the inhabited earth looks to the scene of Holy Scripture. Everything else fades into the background by contrast: 'That other tremendous sea which with its embrace encompasses the places already mentioned and washes round the complex as it were like an island, in the real sense called Ocean...'[74]

A long, highly characteristic, chapter is concerned with the geographical situation of Paradise. Vadian is critical enough not to adopt any of the current hypotheses here. As he demonstrates, they do not stand up in face of the facts. On the other hand, the authority of scripture is so great, and what it says on this point is so clear, that there can be no doubt in principle about the existence of paradise. Vadian's way out is significant. Paradise was a separate continent which in the meantime has been submerged: 'So Paradise was neither a place divided or set apart from the continent of other lands, nor elevated to an unusual height, but was itself a continent of lands.'[75]

It is clear that this theory of Vadian's is not developed in accordance with his principles, but is forced on him by the authority of scripture.

Scriptural authority underlies the whole mediaeval picture of the world. It delayed the real discovery of the New World, though it could not prevent it in the long run.

For it becomes clear even in someone like Vadian that it could only be a question of time before the critical principles, along with new facts, would direct their thrust against the Bible.

5

That became manifest for the first time in 1655 in a work which nowadays is almost forgotten: Isaac de la Peyrère's *Pre-Adamites*. At the time it caused a considerable stir, and rightly so; for here was a summary and critical evaluation of the problems, questions and doubts which had accumulated over a century and a half. It proved that this was enough to make the biblical accounts seem highly questionable at many points.

The author, born in 1594 the son of Reformed parents in Bordeaux, entered the service of the Condé family at an early stage and later became the Prince's librarian. It seems that he was in touch with many of the critical spirits of his time. But we do not have many details.[76]

The work which made him famous appeared in Holland, as a precaution without details of printer and author. Nevertheless it was very soon attributed to La Peyrère. His later fate is remotely reminiscent of that of Galileo: during a stay in the Spanish Netherlands, perhaps at the instigation of the Inquisition, he was put in prison and was probably released only on condition that he would abjure his Reformed faith and the theory of the Pre-Adamites.[77] At all events we find him soon afterwards in Rome, where he went over to Catholicism and made the required abjuration. There is a good deal of evidence to indicate that his contemporaries did not take this abjuration very seriously.[78] After 1659 he lived on a pension from the Condés in the seminary of Notre Dame des Vertus near Paris, where he died in 1676, evidently maintaining his convictions to the end.[79]

The book containing La Peyrère's thesis, which was very soon known and discussed throughout Europe, is in two parts. The first: 'The Pre-Adamites, or a Discussion (*Exercitatio*) on Verses 12, 13 and 14 of the Fourth Chapter of Blessed Paul to the Romans, by which First Men are Said to have Existed before Adam', provides the exegetical argument and justification. The second part, which is very much more important for us, the 'Theological System, on the Hypothesis of the Pre-Adamites, Part I',[80] is much more important for us; it also provides the material on the basis of which La Peyrère saw himself compelled to criticize the previous understanding of Holy Scripture. And in it we rediscover almost everything that we have already encountered here and there in isolation.

The first surprising thing is the clarity with which La Peyrère sees the problem.[81] 'It is a natural suspicion,' the preface to the 'System' begins, 'that the time of the establishment of the earth cannot be derived from that beginning which is usually associated with Adam.' And then the author goes on to enumerate the reasons which justify mistrust of the information in the Bible: 'Ancient Chaldaean calculations, the earliest documents from Egypt, Ethiopia and Scythia, newly discovered lands of the earth including those unknown lands to which Dutchmen[82] have recently sailed and whose inhabitants probably did not descend from Adam' (61).[83]

So it is the new results of chronology and geography which cannot be reconciled with the biblical picture of universal history. La Peyrère goes on to describe how doubts occurred to him even as a boy when he heard the creation stories, but how he only ventured to make room for this doubt when from Romans 5 the possibility of Pre-Adamites had become clearer to him.

For a man like La Peyrère, at any rate, the authority of scripture is no longer enough to oppose to the new facts. But on the other hand it is still far too great simply to be able to be by-passed, as it could be by Voltaire a century later.

And so La Peyrère has no other expedient than to seek a balance in some way, an explanation of the manifest contradictions which will reconcile scripture with the new picture of the world and restore the damaged unity of thought.

That is precisely what he describes at the end of the *Exercitatio* as his task and purpose: 'to reconcile Genesis and the gospel with the astronomy of the men of old, the history and philosophy of the most ancient of peoples. So that if the astronomers of the Chaldaeans were to come, or the Egyptians with their primaeval dynasties, if Aristotle himself were to come, and with him the chronologers and philosophers of the Chinese, or if an at present unknown but perceptive people were to be discovered in the south or in the north who had an ancient culture and tradition extending over tens of thousands of years, each from his position could readily accept the creation stories and happily become Christian' (58).[84]

On these presuppositions La Peyrère's thesis is quite consistent. In a sentence: Adam was not the first man, but merely the tribal ancestor of Israel.

In order to prove this thesis he makes use of the two ways which are possible here.

From the passage in Romans which he mentions (and from some passages in Genesis) he attempts to provide positive proof that the Bible itself begins from the existence of pre-Adamites. This proof, which culminates in a distinction between a heathen humanity outside or before the law and an Adamitic humanity under the law, is abstruse, and is of interest in our context only because it shows how important it still is to demonstrate that a theory is in accordance with scripture.

In the nature of things he succeeds far better with his negative proof, which is aimed at demonstrating the contradictions within the traditional understanding. Here his book becomes a collection of critical arguments with which the French freethinkers and English deists were able to stock their critical armouries for a long time.

The negative proof is based on two lines of argument. One – which one might call Socinian – operates with logic and experience, makes the numerous statements of scripture seem quite incredible, and constantly throw up inconsistencies in the accounts. The other – historical and empirical – makes use of the results of the exact sciences, in order to shake the possibility and reliability of the previous understanding of the biblical narratives.

La Peyrère finds a wealth of 'Socinian' questions, for example in the story of Cain and Abel in Gen.4 ('System' III.4, 160ff.). Abel was a shepherd. He looked after his sheep – why and to guard against whom other than thieves? Where did Cain get his murder weapon from? He smote Abel in open country – presumably as opposed to a city? Of whom was Cain afraid when he said to God after the murder: 'So it will come about that whoever finds me will slay me?' 'He was afraid,' says La Peyrère, 'of his judges, and the laws which threatened him with the death penalty.' It is clear at what the answers to these and many other similar questions are aimed; they are meant to support La Peyrère's theory of the heathen population before Adam. He is convinced that there is simply no other explanation. It alone can bring Genesis into harmony with itself.

The proofs which La Peyrère adduces to make it clear that at many points the biblical history is to be understood 'in more special' and not 'in more general' terms serves the same purpose: 'There is quite often sin in reading the sacred documents when something is understood in general terms which should have been understood specifically' ('System' IV.3, 208). That is true, for example, of the darkness at the death of Jesus, which only covered Palestine; of the star of the wise men, which appeared only to them (certainly the other men and not just the wise men would have seen that [star] in the heaven); of the shadow that went backwards on Hezekiah's sundial (II Kings 20), where only the shadow went back on the dial and not the sun in the heavens ('System' IV.3, 4,5). In these passages historical and empirical arguments predominate. Thus, for example, the sun may have continued to move on Gibeon and only its rays remained behind in the atmosphere. 'So we must understand this miracle to mean that as the sun itself sank, and the natural and heavenly order of things did not cease in the meantime, the rays of the sun would have remained in the atmosphere without the sun itself and without a great miracle.' To prove this possibility La Peyrère cites an experience of his own, when in a valley in the Pyrenees he saw a quite similar phenomenon: 'I saw... on the opposite mountain sunshine without sun for several hours...' (215). It is simply the laws of the refraction of light which make this possible.

Also characteristic is a conversation between an eminent mathematician and an insignificant theologian which La Peyrère cites in this context on Josh.10.14 ('And there was no day like this neither before nor afterwards'). The mathematician explains that there are days which are very much longer than that of Joshua, namely six months: 'In accordance with the tendency of the sphere of the earth under the conditions of the polar circle.' Thereupon the theologian angrily supposes that such a godless assertion must be punished with the stake, that here Holy Scripture is being made a liar, and that the ruler who banished mathematicians from all Christian countries was correct. 'Not so strongly, little priest, retorted the mathematician to the theologian. Your piety turns your senses. For the word of God is true and mathematical calculations are also true.' La Peyrère's solution is that the scripture was true for Gibeon. But one may not extend the miracle to other spheres and regions.

Again along the lines of his idea, the critical fertility of which seems inexhaustible, La Peyrère examines the extra-biblical historical sources and nowhere in them finds a reference to the descent of the heathen world of nations from Adam ('System' III.5, 165ff.). An investigation into the accounts by Diodore, Manetho and Herodotus of the age of the Egyptian dynasties and an examination of the astronomical tablets of the Chaldaeans leads to the result that these figures cannot in any way −a priori− be rejected as lies ('System' III, 6 and 7, 171ff.). Rather, there is everywhere also an amazing agreement with the prehistory of newly discovered peoples: 'In those thousands of years which are reckoned to the beginning of things, there is evidently a miraculous correspondence between those people who have been most recently discovered and the people of the Chaldaeans, Egyptians, Scythians, Phoenicians, Gauls, etc., who have been surveyed and known for a long time...' ('System' III.7, 180). Again and again it is the new discoveries which fascinate La Peyrère and which he thinks could not remain without consequences for the understanding of scripture. He wishes that Augustine and Lactantius, the greatest opponents of the idea of the Antipodes, were alive and could see and hear what had now been found out and reported about Americans and Australians: they would doubtless be ashamed of themselves ('System' IV.17, 245).

I cannot develop further and use here the wealth of La Peyrère's critical insights. But it is important to recall one more of his discoveries, because Richard Simon made it famous in the history of Pentateuchal criticism. Quite incidentally, La Peyrère is one of the first to develop the idea of a literary history of the Pentateuch, pointing to something like a fragmentary hypothesis. In connection with indications of earlier sources in the historical books, he writes: 'But I do not know through what sufficiently reliable author it has been guaranteed that the Pentatech was written by Moses himself. It is generally asserted, but not proved by all. These reasons move me to regard those five books not as the originals of Moses but as texts which have been extracted and written out by another' ('System' IV.1, 198).[85]

The work evidently sold like hot cakes. McKee reports four editions which appeared in 1655, two English translations in 1656 and a Dutch translation in 1661.[86] However, a far more reliable indication of the great success of the book is the extent of the polemic which it provoked. La Peyrère had had a foretaste of what the author of the *Pre-Adamites* might expect after its publication from Hugo Grotius, who had given a confidential report on the manuscript of the *Exercitatio* ('System' IV.14, 247). Grotius replied: 'If this is believed I see a great danger for piety' (ibid., 249). In fact a storm of indignation arose immediately the book appeared. In 1656 it was publicly burnt in Paris by the hangman. Again, as early in the question of Copernicus, the three great confessions were at one here. Roman, Lutheran and Reformed theologians competed in their refutation of the 'pre-Adamite fable'; here Micraelius, the Rector of Stettin, probably expressed the general conviction when he opened his counterblast with the words: 'I declare that no more pernicious heresy has ever been circulated in the church than this doctrine.'[87]

The orthodox critics, who hurled themselves above all on the exegetical section, of course had little difficulty in demonstrating that most of what was said here was wrong. However, evidently there continued to be no comprehension throughout orthodox criticism of the problem which had given rise to the offence and which was in fact only heightened by an exegetical refutation of the pre-Adamite thesis.[88]

This inability to see the question at stake behind the answers – an inability which all Christian confessions had in common – lay like a cloud of doom over the beginnings of biblical criticism.

La Peyrère never grew weary of stressing that this purpose was not to 'destruct' but to 'reconcile': Genesis with itself, the biblical accounts with all possible and conceivable documents, sources and testimonies, old and new, and the Bible generally with the results of all investigations, inventions and discoveries that had already taken place or were to be expected. All critical approaches were initially dominated by this situation and saw themselves as positive solutions. That was as true for the Socinians as it was for Kepler and Galileo.

La Peyrère could think of nothing better than the pre-Adamite theory. And because he was convinced that this was the only way of continuing to preserve the authority of the Bible, he applied great perspicacity to the arguments for this theory. The criticism he applies is in their service.

But at the same time it becomes evident that here criticism is in process of making itself independent. Anyone who disputed La Peyrère's theory without replacing it with a new and better one was cutting the last tie which still held criticism back.

In the end, precisely that was the result of orthodox polemic.[89]

FIVE

Theology, Philosophy and the Problem of Double Truth

1

It is worth investigating, for a moment, the real purpose of La Peyrère's remarkable book. In the eighth chapter of the *Exercitatio*, as we have seen, he explains the significance of his new hypothesis. After explaining that it is not in contradiction with scripture, but on the contrary can be derived from it, he continues: 'Consider further that through this position, which assumes that the first men were created before Adam, the history of Genesis appears much clearer. It is reconciled with itself. It is also in a surprising way reconciled with all profane documents, ancient and more modern, for example, of the Chaldaeans, Egyptians, Scythians and Chinese. The earliest creation which is depicted in the first chapter of Genesis is reconciled with the Mexicans, whom Columbus reached not so long before. It is reconciled with those people in the north and south who have not yet been discovered. All of these, like those of the first and oldest creation which is reported in the first chapter of Genesis, were probably created along with the earth itself in all lands and were not descendants of Adam.'[1] And then follows a sentence which makes clear in a flash what all these individual questions are in fact about: 'Through this position faith is again reconciled with natural reason...' That, then, is in the background; the threat of an irreconcilable contradiction between faith and reason.[2]

La Peyrère's theory is an attempt once again, albeit with desperate means, to restore the unity of scripture and world-view which has already almost been lost, the unity which the Middle Ages had experienced and which the Reformers still took for granted as their starting point. The French Calvinist – with far more acumen than most of his theological contemporaries – saw the deep rifts which ran through the old foundation. And in order to avoid falling into them, like a balloonist who sees himself foundering, he was prepared to throw out anything that could be dispensed with as ballast: the priority of the primal history, the authorship of Moses, the universality of miracles – all this seemed to him to be dispensable if only the principle, the unity of the world-view, could be saved.

Reconciling faith with natural reason: that was the task. There were different possible solutions, but none which avoided the claims of reason. For – and here was the nub of the problem – reason was no longer prepared to submit to the authority of scripture and tradition. And it had good, indeed irrefutable, arguments for this on its side. As things were, anyone who could not or would not offer the sacrifice of reason demanded by orthodoxy had only two possibilities: mediation or accepting a twofold truth. Mediation was inconceivable without a critical interpretation or restriction of scripture. But that still seemed better than the second way, which was intolerable for both faith and reason, because it destroyed the unity of thought and action and necessarily had to lead to scepticism.

The extent to which the beginnings of criticism are in fact bound up with this problem has become particularly clear from our sources.

When the Socinians challenged the doctrine of the Trinity, their purpose was the same as that of La Peyrère with his Pre-Adamites: to reconcile faith with true reason. How had Stegman Sr put it in the context of a list of the most important principles of true reason? 'These and similar principles which are not unknown to anyone of sound mind form the foundation of our knowledge, even in respect of the authority of Holy Scripture and its true sense.'[3] There was only one truth, only one 'foundation of our knowledge'. This truth and its principles applied everywhere, even in the sphere of scripture and its interpretation. There might be things which were above reason, but there was nothing that was contrary to reason, for that would have meant the acceptance of a double truth, which was contradicted by the universality of reason and the universality of faith. The challenge to the early church doctrine of the Trinity and christology was necessary for the sake of unity of thought. Only at this price, it seemed, could it be rescued.

It is characteristic that Osiander could still leave the problem hanging. The conflict was in fact only just beginning to take shape.

That he saw it is clearly demonstrated by that somewhat enigmatic statement which postulates an astronomical and a philosophical truth and denies final certainty to both: 'Let no one expect anything certain by way of hypotheses from astronomy, as it cannot offer anything of the kind, lest if he takes as the truth what is devised for another purpose, he depart from this discipline more foolish than when he came to it.'[4] Moreover Osiander's theory of hypotheses – especially in the form in which it was later presented and applied – was naturally also an attempt to solve the task of reconciling faith with natural reason.

If Kepler almost bitterly rejected *this* solution, it was not because he did not see the problem, but because for him the truth was indivisible. 'But holier to me is the truth' – so runs the decisive sentence with which he challenges the binding character of theological authorities for all philosophical questions – 'which I demonstrate from philosophy, that the earth is round and is inhabited at the antipodes, that it is quite insignificant and small and finally that it is borne through the stars – with all due respect to the doctors of the church.'[5] Is it a coincidence that La Peyrère referred to the same principle? 'For although I am dearest to myself, the truth is a greater friend to me.'[6]

For the sake of the worth and holiness of truth, Kepler too was compelled to look for a way out. He finds it in that theory which remained the classical solution of our problem up to the end of the eighteenth century: scripture speaks with human beings 'in human fashion'; it accommodates itself to the spirit and comprehension of its readers and hearers. Its aim is not the communication of physical or mathematical facts but the revelation of God's greatness and glory. In principle this opens up the way to criticism, but it should be remembered that Kepler still had no conception of what the extent of this criticism would be.

Kepler is convinced that truth demonstrated by mathematics will hold up against all authorities. Galileo was also of this opinion when he allowed only the experience of the senses and compelling proofs to hold in all scientific questions. He draws the radical consequence and calls for an exegesis of scripture in these questions in accord with the results of the exact sciences. He indeed concedes the possibility that some things may be above reason, but it seems inconceivable to him that anything should be contrary to reason. In the letter to Christina of Lorraine the law of modern biblical criticism becomes clear for the first time. When Galileo speaks of the 'force' with which the 'necessary conclusions compel acceptance', and sets against them the insights 'which allow of opinions', we can feel something of the power which criticism wields against all authorities.

This letter, too, was written with the purpose of reconciling faith with sound reason. I have already indicated that this in no way solved the problem but really only posed it correctly.[7]

In fact at first a 'solution' of this question was unthinkable. It was ruled out simply by the dimensions of the problem. For that old unity of world-view and faith, backed up by the authority of scripture, associated with the power of tradition and given life by the trust and hope of many generations, could not be 'refuted' overnight even by the most compelling evidence. It had too much life, too much history, too much destiny, to be ready without further ado to fit in with precise arguments. On the other hand, however, the advocates of the new world picture knew that they were in accord with the eternal laws of reason, which it was not in their power to alter. They found confirmation in the wealth of facts which could not be explained in any other way. And they lived by the solemnity of truth which compelled them to continue along new untrodden ways.

It says much for the power of tradition that the advocates of the new world-view all without exception sought to prove that their results did not infringe the authority of scripture. And it says much for the power of the new ideas that their defenders ventured to put them forward in the face of any danger. Nevertheless they could not prevent their results causing deep disquiet on all sides. For as things were around the middle of the seventeenth cenutry, the unity of thought in fact seemed seriously threatened.

2

The problem of double truth was not new to the West. And a situation which had already raised it had a certain similarity to that of the time with which we are concerned.[8]

On 7 March 1277 the Bishop of Paris, Stephan Tempier, condemned certain heresies which had been published by the faculty of arts in the university. This action had been prompted by a letter from Pope John XXI in which he expressed his disquiet about the news from Paris.[9]

In a letter which the bishop prefaced to 219 statements that were expressly condemned, he also went into certain practices with which representatives of the faculty of arts sought to conceal their true opinions. They presented heathen errors as truth, but so as not to come under the suspicion of agreeing to these sentences, explained that they were 'true according to philosophy but not according to the Catholic faith, as though there were two opposed truths, and a truth in the statements of the heathen who are condemned stood over against the truth of Holy Scripture.'[10] A look at the statements which were condemned makes it clear what the issue was. They contained essentially Aristotelian material, as presented by Averroes.

As is well known, in the second half of the thirteenth century a trend had developed at the University of Paris, alongside traditional scholastic philosophy with a Neoplatonic Augustinian stamp and the ecclesiastical Aristotelianism of Albert and Thomas, which in the wake of Averroes advocated a radical Aristotelianism.[11] Its main representatives were Siger of Brabant,[12] Boetius of Dacian and Bernier de Nivelles. Following the commentaries of the great Arab, this trend developed his philosophy regardless of church doctrine. 'For the first time since the earliest Christian period, the Christian thinkers of the thirteenth century found themselves confronted with a purely "natural" scientific system and a heathen world view' – a situation which not only led to 'the decisive crisis of growth in the Middle Ages',[13] but also to that assumption of double truth which was now contested by Bishop Tempier.

The question whether this theory already appears in Averroes – who was no less in conflict with the teaching of the Qur'an than his Christian disciples were in conflict with Holy Scripture – is answered in different ways and can be left open here.[14]

It is certain that the advocates of Averroism in Paris put forward this doctrine. That emerges not only from the bishop's letter but also from some of the propositions which it quotes. Thus e.g. the view is condemned: 'That the natural philosopher must deny the unique creation of the world because he bases himself on natural reasons and considerations. The believer, on the other hand, can deny the eternity of the world because he relies on supernatural reasons.'[15] Aristotle's doctrine of the eternity of the world was one of the points which was in decided conflict with church teaching. Anyone who advocated it as a Christian theologian had no other expedient than to assume a twofold truth, namely philosophical and theological. And in fact the distinction between natural and supernatural causes in this connection goes in precisely this direction. In a quite similar way Proposition 184 asserts: 'That a creation is not conceivable, although the opposite must be maintained in faith.'[16] Aristotle's doctrine of the soul also proves irreconcilable with Christian dogma, so Proposition 113 states: 'That the soul separated from the body is unchangeable according to philosophy, though according to faith it undergoes changes.'[17]

Generally speaking, there emerges from the 219 statements condemned a remarkably complete picture of a world understood and interpreted exclusively in rational and philosophical terms: from the denial of the Trinity, which recalls the Socinian arguments,[18] through critical observations on the foundations of theology,[19] to the exclusion of revelation as an epistemological principle.[20]

The parallel to the development which was beginning in the first half of the seventeenth century is obvious. And it is only natural that as a result particular questions and problems repeat themselves.

However, the assessment of the theory of double truth is both difficult and disputed. The two extreme positions are represented by Colpe, who thinks that 'the revealed Christian statements of faith were described as truth only for opportunistic reasons'[21], and Van Steenberghen, who suggests that Siger von Brabant 'no more taught a double truth than did Averroes' and ' – in contrast to the rationalist Averroes – remained true to faith all his life'.[22] I shall leave the question open here because in this context there is no need to do more than describe the problem.

There is a series of sure indications that despite the condemnation of 1277[23] and the Thomistic mediation in the West this problem remained alive. A.Maier reports an oath which the Faculty of Arts of the University of Paris required of its newly admitted masters in the fourteenth century: 'that in questions in which philosophical and theological views diverged, they would defend the orthodox view and refute the opposed view' – doubtless an effect of the controversy in the 1270s.[24]

However, certain developments in Italy are more important. Here Averroism had found a home in the fourteenth century after the doors of the University of Paris had been closed to it.[25] In the arts faculties of Bologna, Padua and Pavia, Averroistic schools came into being in which the principle of double truth evidently increasingly became the means 'of at least formally harmonizing the new philosophical views and Christian convictions'.[26]

In the first half of the fourteenth century Averroistic theories were being openly discussed in Bologna, including the notorious principle of the unity of the intellect, the complete determination of all events or the question whether God knows nothing outside himself.[27] Here we continually come up against the assumption of a double truth as a last way out of the contradiction between philosophical evidence and theological authority: 'on the one hand there seem compelling reasons for the doctrines which are condemned and on the other people cannot and will not depart from faith'.[28] But if things here are still in flux, towards the end of the century the situation had clearly become more acute.

A notary's instrument from the year 1396 reports a revocation offered by a Magister Blasius of Parma, Professor in the Faculty of Arts of the University of Paris, before the Bishop and in the presence of some colleagues. Anneliese Maier, who has investigated the affair,[29] has reconstructed from manuscript sources the doctrine which is presumably being revoked here. According to her Blasius advocated an extreme determinism and materialism which also took up again a series of Averroistic theses condemned in Paris. What is most interesting in this connection is the clear formulation of the principle of double truth in Blasius. At the end of an epistemological excursus in the context of a discussion *de anima intellectiva* there are the following two corollaries: 'Corollary 1: It is inconceivable that this is known by you if you believe that...; Corollary 2: If term *a* is known by you, then *a* lies outside all faith, opinion, etc. And I wanted so to say to this end, that you should not bring together opposed opinions about the separation of the soul from the body and its perpetuity... Consequently, where you purpose to support faith, the nature of which is to believe, divest yourself of the philosophical approach, the nature of which is to have evident proof; here, on the contrary, you must give up faith in Christ.'[30]

The principle can in fact hardly be put more sharply. Here Blasius is asserting the absolute impossibility of reconciling faith and knowledge. Faith includes belief and opinion, and the philosophical approach contains evident knowledge which excludes faith in Christ. That recalls, even down to the wording, Galileo's distinction between doctrines which are a matter of opinion and doctrines which can be demonstrated.[31] But whereas Galileo – at least at one point – derives from this the demand that theological statements should be corrected in accordance with the results of the exact sciences, Blasius keeps to two mutually contradictory principles: 'But that the soul can be separated from the body, this can only be believed on the basis of hope and the authority of that which says it (i.e. the church). And these reasons are enough for faith.' By contrast, according to the schools of philosophers, it follows that: 'It is more probable that the individual soul, be it created or not, must end, than that it lasts eternally, and this conclusion was arrived at from the principle of the question.'[32]

After the whole discussion, which of the two positions Blasius regards as the truth, 'according to faith' or 'according to the schools of philosophy', can hardly be in doubt. For him, evident knowledge is binding. Here the doctrine of double truth really seems to be merely 'a convenient cover' under which it is possible to go on philosophizing undisturbed. At any rate, Anneliese Maier is convinced of this.[33] If she is right, however, the problem has thus ceased to be a problem. For where the position 'according to faith' can be advocated only out of opportunism, there can really be no longer any talk of a double truth. In that case, in fact only one truth – philosophical truth – is recognized as truth, whereas all validity is denied to faith. So one can talk meaningfully of a double truth only where the claim of faith in the form of tradition, authority of scripture, or whatever is taken as seriously as the claim of reason in the form of 'evident knowledge', without the contradiction being balanced out in a system. It is obvious that such a question could not be left unresolved for long, but called for a decision. The fact that Siger of Brabant can be claimed for both positions seems to indicate that he had not yet made this decision. That might also still be true of the Averroist school in Bologna in the first half of the fourteenth century[34] and for Johannes Buridan.[35] But the direction in which the problem is developing is clear. It is getting towards the point where the question is seen: from double truth to single truth – philosophical-rational truth. That is already evident in Blasius of Parma. It is even clearer in Petrus Pomponatius, one of the leaders in Italian renaissance philosophy at the end of the fifteenth century.[36] This older contemporary of Luther, from 1488 professor in the faculty of arts of the University of Padua, and later, after it was dissolved in 1509, in Ferrara and Bologna, is regarded as the most famous advocate of 'double truth'. But here the position 'according to faith' is even more clearly the result of practical considerations – we can hardly talk any longer of a serious conflict.[37]

Moreover Leo X's bull of 19 December 1513, which was directed against Pomponius's tractate *De immortalitate animae*, condemns less the doctrine of double truth than the old Averroistic principles ('especially of the nature of the rational soul, namely that it is clearly immortal, or one and the same in all men'), and their philosophical champions ('as some, who philosophize ignorantly, seriously claim to be true at least in philosophy'). Church doctrine cannot acknowledge a real contradiction between reason and faith: 'And because the truth does not conflict with the truth in the slightest, we declare any assertion that is contrary to the truth illuminated by faith to be utterly false.'[38] This definition did not introduce anything new, but merely summed up the development hitherto. In a formula, it represented the solution of the problem which had fallen to the Middle Ages, 'that of building up and preserving the unity of the "Christian" world'.[39] It was a unity full of tensions that had come into being here, but it remained a unity because it was basically subordinated to the authority of the church, which in principle excluded conflict without suppressing reason.[40]

This unity seems to have been seriously endangered only once in the Middle Ages: with the Aristotelian invasion. Here Christian theology for the first time saw itself confronted with an utterly rational and closed system of knowledge, the consequences of which for a world-view became clear above all in physics and metaphysics. Coupled with the enormous number of new elements in learning of Arabic and Jewish[41] origin, the great pagan exercised enormous fascination, and for a tense century that unity in fact seemed to have been shaken. The repeated bans on Aristotle in the University of Paris (1210 and frequently thereafter) and the condemnations of 1270 and 1277 are telling evidence of this danger. But at the end of the thirteenth century the synthesis had been achieved: it was not Siger of Brabant but Thomas and Bonaventura who determined further developments. Church doctrine had won, and unity had not only been preserved but had emerged from the controversy extended and strengthened. Averroism and the Renaissance could not seriously endanger it.

The process was repeated 400 years later. Once again the Christian church was faced with the task of integrating an enormous wealth of new material and new insights. But what could be achieved in the thirteenth century could not be achieved in the seventeenth. Now the philosopher of the future was no longer Aristotle but Descartes, and the new unity was dominated by reason and not by authority. It is, if one cares to put it that way, a late victory of Averroism, and in this sense (but only in this sense) one can speak of an 'unbroken tradition' which runs from the Averroism of Paris and Padua 'through Pomponazzi, Bodinus and Bruno to Spinoza and the Enlightenment'.[42] The question arises why the seventeenth century could not repeat the synthesis of the thirteenth. Clearly our sources can show us only one aspect of this question. But according to it the answer seems clear: because the new picture of the world based on proof and experience had incomparably greater evidential power than Aristotelian physics and metaphysics. Even where late-scholastic natural philosophy began an independent investigation going beyond Aristotle, in principle the result remained within the sphere of probability. For scholastic science was and remained a science without exact measurements. It is a constant source of amazement that the scholastic philosophers evidently did not arrive at the idea of examining individual phenomena precisely – despite the quantitative ideal that they wanted to realize, 'and the far-reaching dominance of mathematical method on the one hand – and the correct insights into the essence and value of induction, experiment and individual experience on the other'. 'That is the decisive gap in the late scholastic system of natural philosophy, at which the great turning point comes with Benedetti and Galileo.'[43]

In fact, where Aristotle stood over against Holy Scripture it was just a matter of one conviction against another. One was a conviction based on the authority of a divine revelation and the other a conviction which claimed evidence for itself derived from inductive philosophy. Neither of the two positions could be proved in the strict sense, nor could they be refuted.[44] It remained a question of decision which one took – and it was obvious that in the Christian world this decision was finally made in favour of the authority of revelation.[45]

However, the situation inevitably changed the moment that mathematical proof took the place of philosophical evidence on an inductive basis. It is no coincidence that Galileo continually pointed out that he was not just expressing a conviction but was standing under a law which had nothing to do with his preferences. It was compelling proof that gave philosophical proof priority over

theological truth and thus destroyed the old unity of faith and
knowledge which had been ensured by subordination to church
authority.

3

The presupposition that all philosophical knowledge is only probable
still applied for Luther. On the basis of this presupposition it was
beyond question for him personally that in cases of doubt the truth
lies on the side of theology and not of philosophy. In principle
scripture and faith have priority over rational conclusions. Without
this presupposition that in principle philosophical statements are
only probable, which is part of his world-view, many of his statements
on the relationship between philosophy and theology seem hard to
understand.

In fact for a number of reasons the problem may hardly have
bothered him. Luther had a deep antipathy to philosophy as being
a possible truth, which from the beginning prevented him from
seriously taking a philosophical position.[46] Indeed – we must go on
to add – what position should he and could he have adopted?
Aristotle, accepted for 300 years and continually commented on
anew, of course no longer had much fascination. The natural
philosophy of Scholasticism nowhere broke through to arrive at
mathematical evidence; the Renaissance and Humanism, at least
from Luther's perspective, and as far as they came within his field
of vision, remained within the frameworks of the old philosophical
and theological view of the world. There was no philosophical
alternative to theology – such as Aristotle had possibly represented
in the thirteenth century – and to this degree it is also objectively
understandable that Luther's whole interest in this question was not
in 'an antithesis between philosophy and theology in general' but in
'an antithesis between good and bad theology, between true theology
and pseudo-theology'; and it is the significance for this purpose of
the distinction between theology and philosophy that interests him'.[47]

Luther was never fully challenged in the rational field. And it is
certainly no coincidence that Luther research 'has hitherto been
relatively little concerned with the problem of reason in Luther's
theology'.[48] The questions which were to oppress theology increasingly from the seventeenth century on were quite remote from him.
His direct comments on the relationship between philosophy and

theology are often based on presuppositions which had fundamentally changed a century later. That does not mean that his theology would not have offered possibilities of maintaining its evangelical approach even on these changed presuppositions. But to develop these possibliites in so dangerous a situation was evidently beyond the powers of his orthodox followers.

I shall examine this point in detail by means of a disputation in which Luther directly tackles the problem we have discussed. It is the *Disputatio de sententia: Verbum caro factum est (Joh.1.14)* of 11 January 1539.[49]

Luther's theme is the relationship between philosophy and theology, and his polemical starting point is the principle that what is true in philosophy must also be true in theology. He attributes this principle to the Sorbonne, the 'mother of errors': '(4). The Sorbonne, the mother of errors, has made the very bad definition that one and the same truth holds in philosophy and theology.' So far it has not been possible to demonstrate that this thesis is a definition made by the Sorbonne.[50] But it is clear that it is connected with the repudiation of the Averroistic errors of 1277 and is equivalent to the assertion of the bull of 1513: 'And because the truth does not contradict the truth in the slightest, we declare that any assertion which is contrary to the truth of illuminated faith is utterly false.'

If the Sorbonne thesis cited by Luther in fact belongs in this context – and anything else is hardly conceivable – then it is directed against all attempts to oppose a distinct philosophically-based truth to church doctrine. The assertion that there is one truth for both philosophy and theology is meant to safeguard the priority of theology.

Surprisingly, Luther understands the thesis in quite the opposite sense. In his conviction it serves to subject the truths of faith to the judgment of reason: '(6) For with this abhorrent statement it (the Sorbonne) has taught that the articles of faith are to be brought under the judgment of human reason' – an attempt that is utterly meaningless. (7) That was tantamount to including heaven and earth in its centre or in a grain of millet.' This understanding shows that the Averroistic possibility of an autonomous scientific philosophy evidently lay completely beyond Luther's horizons. So there cannot in fact be an 'either-or of philosophy or theology generally', but only an 'either-or of good and bad theology'.

However 'Averroistic' the whole disputation may seem to be in places, it is far removed from defending a 'double truth'.[51] What Luther is attempting to do is merely to provide a basis for the distinctive character of theological statements and thus for the distinctive character of theology generally.

'(1) Though the principle must also be maintained that all truth corresponds with all truth, nevertheless the same thing is not true in different spheres.' That is Luther's own thesis, which he puts forward against the Sorbonne thesis. Here he is solely and exclusively concerned with theology, which in no circumstances may be made philosophically comprehensible; for in that case the articles of faith would be made subject to the judgment of human reason.

Luther attempts to demonstrate this distinctive position of theology by pointing out numerous contradictions. '(2) In theology it is true that the word has become flesh, but in philosophy that is quite impossible and absurd. (3) The proclamation "God is man" is far more contradictory than the assertion "Man is an ass".' Luther does not weary of enumerating such contradictions between the theological and the philosophical aspect of a matter, e.g.: (18) The Father has the whole of the divine being. The Son is divine being. Therefore the Son is the Father. (19) The premises are correct, nevertheless the conclusion is false, and the truth corresponds entirely with the truth here but not there. Or, (22) What has become flesh is creature. God's Son has become flesh, therefore God's Son has become a creature. That is correct in philosophy. (23) Even if this conclusion could be defended by the artifices of sophistry, it cannot be tolerated in the church. (24) Far less can we tolerate the conclusion: All flesh is creature. The Word was made flesh. Consequently it is a creature... The conclusion he draws from these contradictions is, however: (27) So in the articles of faith we must turn to a different dialectic and philosophy, namely the Word of God and faith.

The decisive point is that in all this Luther is not primarily concerned with contradiction, but to establish the commensurability of philosophy and theology. They are 'different professions' (1), and anyone who mixes them up (as Scholastic philosophy has done), is fundamentally corrupting theology. The following group of arguments shows that the real concern is incomparability, of which these contradictions are only a sign.

(29) Even in other disciplines we are compelled to state that the

truth is in no way the same in all matters. (30) It is false and an error in weighing to suppose that weights can be measured by points and mathematical lines. (31) It is false and an error in measurement to measure volume by feet or ells. (32) It is false and an error in linear measurement to calculate length in ounces or pounds, etc., etc. The consequence is: (38) If one thus goes through individual arts or, better, activities, one will never find that truth is the same throughout.

Heim thought that 'the similes which Luther uses here from measurement' did not lead further because between these spheres it could never be the case 'that the same statement is true in one sphere and seems a logical contradiction in the other'.[52]

This criticism is characteristic of the misunderstanding to which the whole disputation continued to be exposed and still is.[53] It is not concerned to demonstrate a contradiction in principle between philosophy and theology as in the case of the Averroists – the series of arguments would in fact have been so unsuitable that this fact must already have struck its author – but with the demonstration of incommensurability. The argument seeks to convey that to apply philosophical categories in the sphere of theology is as nonsensical as to apply lines and points to weights or linear measures to volume. So at the end of this group of theses we find: '(39) How much less can the same thing be true in philosophy and theology, the difference between which is infinitely greater than that between different arts and activities!' And that is the only way in which we can understand that remarkable sentence which to some degree sums up the whole series of theses, and demands nothing less than learning to speak with new tongues. '(40) Thus we would have acted more correctly had we left dialectic or philosophy in its sphere and learned to speak with new tongues in the realm of faith outside that philosophical sphere.'[54]

Once again, Luther is not concerned here with a double truth, the presupposition of which is that philosphical and theological arguments must be thought of as lying on the same ontological level. Luther contests that there is such a common level when he speaks of the virtue and majesty of matter, which cannot be enclosed within the narrow limits of reason or rational conclusions (20). The 'truth of faith' is as different from the 'truth of dialectic or theology' as is heaven from earth. But strictly speaking that excludes any contradiction between the two truths. At least in one thesis – perhaps the most characteristic of the whole disputation – he even says that explicitly: '(21) Just as this matter is not indeed in opposition to, but outside, inside, above, below, this side, the other side of all dialectical (i.e. philosophical) truth.' With this 'outside, inside, above, below, this side, the other side, of all dialectical truth', he is expressing that incompatibility in principle[55] which in fact rules out the possibility of any fundamental contradiction in terms of Averroistic positions 'according to faith' and 'according to philosophical schools'.[56]

If it was the purpose of the disputation to stress the 'outside, inside, above, below, this side, the other side, of the substance of faith' – and as we have seen, that is quite probable[57] – it did not exclude the possibility of another understanding. A formulation like that of the second thesis, '(2) In theology it is true that the word was made flesh, but in philosophy that is simply impossible and absurd', can doubtless also be understood as a contradiction in principle. And occasionally this contradiction is even formulated directly: for example, when in connection with correct philosophical premises and false theological conclusions we read: '(17)...from the truth follows falsity against philosophy'. Here there seems to be an assumption of precisely what thesis 21 excludes: the possibility of a direct conflict between reason and faith on the same ontological level. What is also meant here is the essential difference which is only a sign of that false conclusion. But these formulations can doubtless also be understood in terms of a general opposition, where naturally in any case of doubt, primacy would be accorded to the 'truth of faith'.

If in this context we recall that for Luther all philosophical knowledge was regarded, and could be regarded, as being in principle only probable, the dangerous consequences of this understanding or misunderstanding become clear. The necessary result would be that theology rejected all the results of philosophical work in the sphere of truth that it possessed which contradicted or seemed to contradict this truth.

The question is so difficult because Luther himself clearly took precisely that for granted – and on his presuppositions, rightly. For in his perspective there were indeed logical contradictions between philosophy and theology, but no convincing counterpositions against statements of scripture for which compelling proof could be given.

A statement like 'for the authority of scripture is greater than any capacity of the human spirit for comprehension',[58] which was doubtless Luther's lifelong deep conviction, in fact allows both possibilites of understanding. It can mean the 'outside, inside, above, below, this side, the other side, of the substance of faith' over against all 'human capacity for intellect': but it can equally mean an absolute opposition to any possibility of conflict between the authority of scripture and human intellect. On the basis of the presuppositions already described, Luther was never compelled to make this distinction precise. For the only science which in his time provided not only probable, but evident results, mathematics, did not directly contradict theological statements directly, but only through particular conclusions. Still, it is interesting that Luther regards mathematics as the greatest enemy of theology and is particular insistent that it remain in its sphere and place. I quote the passage here because it once again makes clear the connection between incommensurability and objectivity. This is Luther's response to the thesis that philosophy is necessary for distinguishing unity from trinity.[59]

'In every respect mathematics is the greatest foe of theology, because there is no part of philosophy so in conflict with theology. For example, the mathematician says that one cannot equal two and three cannot equal one, as is taught in the article on the Trinity. That also goes for the sacrament of the altar. The mathematician does not believe that the bread is the body of Christ and the wine the blood. So we say that mathematics must remain in its sphere and place. Discussions about unity and its numerical value get us nowhere, because mathematics cannot concede that a trinity is a unity. Nevertheless it is true that unity and trinity in God are quite different. Although it is not true in nature, it can be and is true in God.'[60] If the 'quite different in God', which is none other than the 'outside, inside', etc. of thesis 21, were consistently maintained here, the introductory statement which refers to a clear opposition could not be put in this way. Why should the mathematician in particular be the one not to believe in transsubstantiation? It cannot contradict his science *qua* science any more than any other person's art or activity, because the break is not between knowledge and faith but between belief and unbelief. However, evidently Luther sees not just a difference but also a contrast here. The designation of mathematics as 'the greatest foe' similarly goes in this direction. Still, Luther does not plead like that 'insignificant theologian' in La

Peyrère[61] for a ban on mathematics, but merely wants to point out its limitations.

That did not produce any serious conflicts for mathematics, for the contradictions between mathematical and theological statements did not arise directly but through conclusions which could be said to be unacceptable without entailing the need to dispute mathematical results.[62] This demand only became problematical when it was transferred to other sciences, e.g. astronomy, cosmography or chronology. Here, as we have seen, Luther was in no way restrained, although (or precisely because) these questions were quite marginal for him. He thought the ideas of Copernicus, like the divergences in chronology, to be an unjustified interference of philosophy in theology: reason being led astray by the flattery of worldly wisdom.[63]

'But the position is that he who would be wise should not allow himself to be pleased by the estimation of others. He must make up his own mind, as does he who seeks to overthrow the whole of astrology. Nevertheless, I believe Holy Scripture...'[64] 'I hold to Holy Scripture alone, therefore I must even reject Philo – which I am very reluctant to do...'[65] There is no doubt that here Luther sees the 'substance of faith' as being not 'outside, inside', etc., but contrary to philosophical truth, and decided accordingly – as became clear a century later. Even Osiander's hypotheses theory can be explained as an attempt to apply the 'each in its sphere and place' to astronomy as well, with the difference that here, in contrast to mathematics, this demand interfered in the substance of the science.

In view of the problems connected with this (though these became visible only later), we must ask whether this involvement was fortuitous or necessary. Or more exactly: was the freedom from contradiction within the world picture which was taken for granted possibly the presupposition for Luther's ideas about the incommensurability of philosophy and theology? Only in this way could he develop his bold theory against the background of a fixed world in which the authority of scripture was nowhere seriously threatened. One may be inclined to answer this question in the affirmative if one remembers the way in which it is connected with the scriptural principle.

As Heim has rightly brought out, incommensurability meant that here the substance of faith had 'no expressible relationship to logical thought'.[66] At the same time it meant that theology depended on scripture and its authority solely and exclusively. That in turn presupposed the clarity of the statements of scripture, if the door was not to be opened to enthusiasm. It was the only guarantee against those who for their part appealed to a 'new tongue'.

Holl has shown[67] how in contrast to late mediaeval exegesis, which looked for a deeper sense in the texts that in fact 'had no intrinsic connection with the literal sense',[68] for Luther with his 'conviction of the clarity of the Bible'[69], 'the literal or, as Luther prefers to say, the grammatical sense... basically occupies the decisive place'.[70] This return to the literal sense did not have a 'historical-critical' basis but was exclusively theological, arising out of the need to preserve clear statements. Here exegesis in principle remained in the sphere of scripture and did not have to seek other than theological criteria. That is the significance of the famous formula 'scripture its own interpreter'.[71] The incommensurability of the substance of faith thus called for clarity in scripture and this in turn required the literal sense. However – and this is the necessary consequence – the literal sense had to extend to the whole of scripture unless hopeless uncertainty was to be the consequence. So the position of the 'outside, inside, etc.' seemed necessarily bound up with that of the 'contrary to' – at any rate where the critical function of 'spiritual understanding',[72] i.e. orientation on Christ as the Lord of scripture, had been lost.

We do not have to decide here whether the further development of the idea of incommensurability could have freed Christian theology from the critical situation in which it increasingly found itself as a result of the philosophy of the seventeenth century. What is certain is that at the same time this would have presupposed a resumption of the Lutheran concept of faith, and as things were, this was hardly conceivable.

The fact is that orthodoxy resolutely took the other course. We cannot claim that basically it would not also have been inclined to do so. And the insight that compelled a change in its theology which could still have applied in the sixteenth century could no longer apply in the seventeenth: the nineteenth century was in fact the first century really to bring out this insight.

4

For orthodoxy I shall limit myself to some general comments, especially as here our question has been sufficently clarified by a series of admirable investigations.[73] There is no question whatsoever that no problem of double truth existed either for Lutheran or for Reformed orthodoxy.[74] H.E.Weber even goes so far as to say that the mere question of the relationship between reason and revelation in Lutheran orthodoxy was possible only at a time 'for which this dogmatics and its philosophy as such belongs to history'. 'For the consciousness of the time whose work we are considering, it is a question only of the natural application of the given scientific means of description.'[75]

So firm is the absolute authority of the Bible that it would be quite crazy to doubt it.[76] It extends not only to the substance of faith but also to the natural sciences. Theology is an unrestricted mistress and philosophy is a mere servant. The scripture principle sees to it that this conviction does not remain mere theory but is in fact practised. Any contradiction between philosophy and theology is ruled out *a priori*; otherwise one would arrive at the absurd principle of double truth. 'From this firm standpoint theology can calmly accept the work of philosophy as far as it is usable; it may be certain that the *ministerium* will not turn back into a *magisterium* in the hands of another. The old conflict between reason and faith which resounds in Luther's polemic against Aristotle the scholastic seems to have been overcome.'[77]

Althaus' investigation of Reformed dogmatics comes to the same conclusion. The Reformed high schools continue to be governed by Melanchthon's university reform, and a particular relationship between philosophy and theology is already expressed in the structure of the faculties.[78] It represents the unconditional rule of theology, which can reject anything that is contrary to its truth. Althaus illustrates this among other things with a fine quotation from Amandus Polanus's *Syntagma theologiae christianae*, which states with reference to theology: 'It also has to judge on other things by virtue of its greater and more infallible truth;... for whatever is found in other sciences as being in conflict with theological truth is condemned as utterly false.'[79]

One example of the universal validity of the authority of scripture is the concept of theosophy which Keckermann introduces. Because theology as a practical discipline is concerned only with the question of blessedness, and the knowledge of God does not end in its soteriological reference but also extends to philosophical knowledge, Keckermann seeks to find a higher concept which to some degree overshadows philosophy and theology, namely theosophy. It 'treats God as the first and most simple essence, the supreme principle of all other sciences'. Here Keckermann is in no way thinking of a natural theology but is explicitly stating 'that even theosophy can ultimately derive its doctrine of God only from scripture'.[80]

At the centre of works on the orthodox doctrine of principles there is now above all the question of the intrinsic connection between philosophy and theology, which, as we know, could be given very different forms within the general principle. The details can be seen, for example, in the treatment of so-called 'mixed questions', those problems in which theological and philosophical questions were mixed. Here today the general distinction between a Reformed type with a more strongly rational stamp and a Lutheran type more inclined to a positivism of scripture may be regarded as the accepted view.[81] H.E.Weber has made clear the increasing rationalization of Lutheranism also.[82] But this inner process of rationalization leaves the principle unassailed. And in our context the most important issue is this principle and its consequences for the problem of the relationship between the authority of scripture and philosophical evidence.

Two things are worth noting here.

First is the question of the use of real philosophy. This is its organic use 'as a real explanation of biblical material with the help of the philosophical disciplines'.[83] In the case of Johannes Gerhard's *Loci*, Troeltsch has shown how this organic use 'quite quietly and under the title "biblical terms" imputes to dogmatics the world-view and anthropology of Aristotelianism as the basis on which the divine comedy of the redemption of the world which it unfolds is played out'.[84] Althaus has drawn attention to the same process within Reformed theology, especially in Polanus.[85] The consequences of this theological insistence on the Aristotelian world-view will concern us later. How this use of real philosophy is intrinsically connected with the scriptural principle, understood formally, has already become clear: unless the idea of incommensurability is strictly maintained, Luther's theological totality must almost of necessity lead to a biblical-theological universal science which in some circumstances could not but look Aristotelian.

That is in a sense the internal aspect of our problem. Ernst Troeltsch described the external aspect very well: 'The question whether a philosophical view of the world and of life could not develop on the basis of them [the real disciplines] and offer dangerous competition to the biblical foundation, and the question whether the contradiction to it which emerged at certain points could be the symptom of a more general difference, did not bother an age which believed in the scriptures. For there was no overall philosophical view, and in the case of such an individual conflict the only important thing was to demonstrate the emergence of such an appearance as ignorance of the true doctrine of principles or atheistic arrogance.'[86]

In J.Baur's study of Quenstedt's theology, this closedness of orthodoxy to the really urgent problems of its time becomes impressively clear. Quenstedt's *Systema theologicum*, 'one of the most important systems of high orthodoxy',[87] which appeared for the first time in 1685, follows Melanchthon and J.Gerhard in the application of our principle as naturally as if half a century or indeed a whole century – and what a century! – had not passed.

The fact that in the meantime a new 'overall philosophical view' had emerged is not felt to be a problem. Certainly Descartes comes within Quenstedt's horizon, 'but the not very thorough controversy to which in particular the Reformed Cartesians applied themselves remains on the periphery... We can see no serious engagement with this modern philosophizing which would correspond to, say, Musaeus' work on the questions raised by deism. It is no more than a brief, sweeping No.'[88]

Baur speaks in a section entitled 'Reflections and Criticism'[89] of the watchfulness of orthodoxy, which opposes 'the autonomy of an independent view of the world wherever orthodoxy sees a contradiction to the truth break out'. 'In the tradition of this watchfulness any limitations on a statement of scripture recognized as a truth of revelation are not allowed.'

However, the fine words should not disguise the fact that in the second half of the century orthodoxy increasingly resembled the troops of Leonidas who were defending a pass which had long since been traversed. For the unwearying watchfulness of orthodoxy began from the false presupposition that the philosophical situation had not changed since the beginning of the century and that as a result theology still had to establish, secure and defend these same positions.

Baur, of course, could count this among 'what is taken for granted by thought', which 'could not include even this strenuous watchfulness in the sphere under examination'. But could these presuppositions still really be taken for granted in 1685, after the Socinian criticism, after Kepler and Galileo, after Bodin and La Peyrère, and finally and above all after Descartes? Or might the more correct historical question be: what moved Lutheran orthodoxy in Germany still to maintain as self-evident what had long lost that character throughout Western Europe?

In the face of this blindness can it really be said that orthodoxy resolutely carried on 'in the context of an understanding of the world in terms of fate and history that which no generation of the church and no theologian can choose for themselves: concepts and statements arising in the encounter with revelation'? Did it not rather neglect this, and this above all?

For there can be no doubt that the position of radical criticism which the eighteenth century developed is largely also an answer to the exasperating lack of understanding by orthodoxy of the new 'modern' problems which are associated with that term.

SIX

Cartesianism: Orthodox Opposition, Mediation and Radical Criticism

1

So far we have made a detailed investigation of the questions which arose with the origin of the modern world-view and the beginning of the emancipation of reason from the Bible and its traditional exegesis. The picture that presented itself to us here was the same everywhere. There were individuals who saw the problem, and they always saw only a particular aspect. The Socinians, for example, show no interest in the Copernican question; by contrast Kepler and Galileo were not at all interested in dogmatic criticism. La Peyrère was merely troubled with the problem of chronology; everything else in his work is incidental to this. In this connection one might also think of the example of Newton, who in outlining a pattern of universal history still unsuspectingly trusts the biblical information, though in connection with astronomy it had long since ceased to have any binding quality for him.[1]

This picture of individuals who see one particular question fundamentally changes around the middle of the century. This is the moment when the spirit of modernity first takes philosophical form in Descartes.

In 1637 Descartes' first published work appeared in Leiden, the *Discourse on the Method of Properly Conducting One's Reason and of Seeking the Truth in the Sciences*. In 1641 there followed the *Meditations on the First Philosophy in which the Existence of God and the Real Distinctions between the Soul and the Body of Man are Demonstrated*, and in 1644 the *Principles of Philosophy*.[2] With them began a triumphal course which is unprecedented in the history of philosophy.[3] 'In fact towards the end of the century Descartes is king. He is not an absolute ruler, because there never is such a thing in the realm of the spirit, and because even in the most abstract formulations which are most remote from reality there is still a remnant of national and racial peculiarities which cannot be removed... But to the degree to which thought moves on the universal level, Descartes prevails.'[4]

The significance of Cartesian philosophy lies in its principle and not in its results. A generation later Fontenelle had already seen that very clearly when he commented: 'It was he (Descartes), it seems to me, who introduced that new method of thinking, and it is to be rated much more highly than his real philosophy, a large part of which has proved false or uncertain on the basis of the very rules which he taught us.'[5] It is this 'new method of thinking' that is important. It – and not individual results and conclusions – changed the cultural map of Europe. In our context three aspects of this new method are particularly important.

1. For Descartes, the thinking subject takes the place of the object to be thought of as the given starting point for philosophizing. That is the significance of that famous formula from the *Discourse*: 'And observing that this truth "I think, therefore I am," was so certain and so evident that all the most extravagant suppositions of the sceptics were not capable of shaking it, I judged that I could accept it without scruple as the first principle of the philosophy I was seeking.'[6] Thus however one sees things, the reflecting I is brought to the centre of the universe. Gerhard Krüger at one point sought to clarify the significance of this principle by means of the difference between Augustine and Descartes. In his view this difference 'does not consist in the fact that Augustine did not yet know the problems of consciousness and its foundation, and on the other hand that Descartes spoke only of a fictitious God: rather, both see man before God. But in Augustine this seeing itself receives its criterion from God, and in Descartes from the human spirit. For the one, God is the original "truth itself"; for the other, God is the I of his self-awareness.'[7] Now the decisive question is what possible basis there is for a philosophy: is it 'in something outside itself... or only in philosophizing itself understood as laying its own foundation'? 'Descartes is the first to lay this foundation in this, our sense.'[8]

2. The break with tradition is consistent with this principle. Among the four main rules which Descartes proposes in the *Discourse*, the

first is 'never to accept anything as true that I did not know to be evidently so: that is to say, carefully to avoid precipitancy and prejudice, and to include in my judgments nothing more than what presented itself so clearly and so distinctly to my mind that I might have no occasion to place it in doubt'.[9] That means that reason has nothing but itself on which it can rely. No tradition may stand as the truth for it, no authority give it the certainty which it achieves solely through its own judgment. This is not only a new way of knowing, but also a new concept of the 'true'. What is true is primarily no longer what is guaranteed but what is evident; no longer what is handed down but what is demonstrated and proven. The passion of Descartes and his time for mathematics is no coincidence: it seemed to correspond most completely to this concept of truth.

Here we also find a connection with our previous reflections. For this is the same concept of truth which already heralded itself in Vadian and which compelled Kepler, Galileo and La Peyrère to engage in critical disputation with the old authorities, as Kepler's formulation made clear: 'Therefore Lactantius is holy, Augustine is holy... the Holy Office of today is holy... But holier to me is the truth' – namely the truth demonstrated by philosophy and proved conclusively.

The decisive progress represented by Descartes' system is the methodological grounding and generalization of this conviction through the principle of universal doubt. It is beyond question his most important and most successful discovery that sure knowledge can be gained only through doubt – doubt in everything, even the existence of God. 'The significance of doubt,' Krüger puts it, 'is the serious break with tradition, i.e. finding firm ground in a situation where there is absolutely no spiritual ground.'[10] As is well known, Descartes was always very cautious over the consistent application of his principle – not least because he was frightened by the result of the Galileo trial[11] – wherever there was the risk of a clash with the Christian authorities. Thus for example his remarks on the truth of the Copernican system were very restrained, and in the *Principles* he resorted specifically to the hypothesis theory: 'In order not to appear arrogant here, if I claim to have found the authentic truth in the investigation of such great matters, I would prefer to leave this undecided and offer all that now follows only as a hypothesis. Even if it were false, though, it would seem to me to be worth all my trouble, in so far as all its results accord with experience...'[12]

On this question his successors were rightly much more consistent, and on the basis of Cartesian principles asserted the reality of the Copernican system – not without continually being referred by their opponents to the hypothetical formulations of the master. In fact Cartesian philosophy first helped the new world-view to break through generally, because it made a specific problem in mathematics and astronomy a basic philosophical decision which in the long run simply could no longer be avoided.

3. Descartes decided the question of double truth which lurked as a danger behind all the controversies for modern times in favour of the universal rule of reason.[13] With this decision philosophy replaced theology as the guarantee of the unity of thought. Contradictions between reason and revelation, previously in principle transcended by the higher authority of scripture or church, are now brought before the judgment seat of reason and solved. This development, too, had previously been in the making, not least in the inability of theology to overcome the confessional divisions theologically: if the Socinians here already appealed to reason as a transcendent, generally binding authority, this course was consistently taken further in Cartesianism.

However, here Descartes himself is again very much more cautious than his successors. Several times he expressly excludes the mysteries of faith from the verdict of reason, as for example in the *Principles*: 'So if God were to reveal to us something of himself or other things which transcends the natural powers of our understanding, as is the case in the mysteries of the Incarnation and the Trinity, although we cannot see them clearly, we cannot refuse to believe them, and we shall not be surprised that much transcends the power of our comprehension partly in its own unfathomable nature and partly in the things created by him.'[14] The question whether this and similar remarks are opportunistic or really reflect Descartes' convictions is disputed. It is certain that they clash with the consistency of his system and that he never attempted to balance out this contradiction or to lay down particular limits for reason in principle. On the contrary, his system is based on the unshakable conviction of the universality and ubiquity of reason, in the activity of which 'there can be nothing so distant that one does not reach it eventually, or so hidden that one cannot discover it'.[15]

The course of our investigation may have made clear why this new philosophical approach was largely felt as salvation and was accepted with such great enthusiasm. In view of the crisis in which the traditional authorities had been placed by modern developments, it must have seemed a liberation, the solution of all those problems on which people had worked in vain for centuries. A sign of this effect is the unbridled optimism with which the Cartesians set to work.

And so now in fact the picture fundamentally changes. It is no longer individuals in whom the new spirit is embodied but a whole generation of young philosophers, physicists, mathematicians, physicians and theologians. Nor is the concern any longer only with individual problems but with the basic question of what authority will be given priority in the future.

In Germany, however, little can be detected of this change. Here the church and theology still long enjoyed halcyon days. But in Western Europe, and particularly in Holland, orthodoxy found itself forced on the defensive almost overnight. In what follows we shall be dealing with the way in which it coped with this new situation. Here we shall not be so much concerned with the historical course of the controversy; rather, I shall attempt to make a cross-section through the discussion and provide an account of the most important positions within Dutch theology.[16]

2

In the year 1677, Peter van Mastricht, pupil and successor of Voët in Utrecht and an unbending representative of the old Dutch orthodoxy,[17] complained about the extension of Cartesianism. He thought that it should be borne in mind, 'How those [viz. Cartesian novelties] have in a short time, within thirty or forty years since the appearance of that philosophy, crept from person to person, from city to city, from province to province, from university to university, so that almost no part not only of Belgium, which is so keen on innovations, but of all Christian Europe, has been spared that poisonous brand...'[18] This vivid description completely matches the impression of Balthasar Bekker,[19] but as a follower of Descartes he welcomes this development in triumph: 'For thirty years ago one found hardly anyone among our native theologians who had not completely rejected that philosophy of Descartes. Today, however, the majority of them accept it, or at least permit it.'[20]

These voices do not just demonstrate how quickly and intensively

Cartesian ideas were received in Holland.[21] They also indicate something of the changed situation which had arisen as a result. This situation was characterized on the one hand by a resistance against the old forces with an increasingly strong polemical accent, and on the other by an almost boundless confidence in the capacities and possibilities of reason. The front line, which ran right across all the sciences, no longer merely divided two philosophical parties, the Cartesians and the Aristotelians; at the same time it separated ancient from modern, conservative from progressive.[22] Orthodoxy, which challenged the new philosophy, automatically aligned itself with the opponents of science and progress, a stigma from which it was never again able completely to free itself.

Perhaps the self-confidence of reason, this almost boundless confidence in its capacities and possibilities, is the characteristic mark of the young Cartesians. It is a new spirit which pushes itself forward here, a spirit which is almost uncannily sure of itself. We encounter this new spirit in many forms in the literature of the period.

We find it, for example, in the form of the confession of Daniel Lipstorp,[23] who describes his 'conversion' to Descartes in his *Specimina Philosophiae Cartesianae* which appeared in 1633.[24] In it he reports how from the beginning he could find nothing in the *Philosophia Peripatetica* 'in which the spirit longing for truth could have found rest'; how in Galileo, Gassendi and others he encountered only a 'diversity of principles' and finally made the acquaintance of Cartesian philosophy in Holland. 'It in fact pleased me so much that from that moment on I accepted it before any other...' It is above all the clarity and certainty of mathematical proof which fascinates Lipstorp: 'For mathematics itself is the true and best philosophy, and of all the sciences it teaches us most beautifully and and most happily to philosophize and to argue.' The narrative ends with an enthusiastic acknowledgment of the new philosophy and its possibilities: 'And I can really say that since the time that I began to revere it, I have made such great progress in the study of wisdom and such a great light has dawned on me as I could scarcely have hoped for in all my life, when I was still occupied in ordinary philosophy.'[25]

The consciousness of the infallibility of their method which is expressed to a greater or lesser degree by all the Cartesians is a characteristic of the new spirit. Johannes Tepelius,[26] as a Tübingen

Magister the author of a history of Cartesianism (albeit quite a modest one), cites as a deterrent some remarks by Tobias Andreae,[27] which in fact convincingly express this consciousness. Descartes, Andreae says, investigated the way of wisdom exactly and infallibly: 'He disclosed the nature of things themselves... so happily that neither he himself nor any of those who followed in his footsteps could even now be accused of any error, let alone be convicted of one, in things which they discovered in this way, as long as there are people with sound understanding and true, upright, honest philosophers in the world.'[28]

We also encounter the new spirit in numerous eulogies of the power and greatness of human understanding, formulated in a way which Hegel himself could not have excelled. Thus for example in the inaugural speech of Hermann Alexander Roëll,[29] which he delivered on becoming professor of theology in the University of Franeker: 'The power of understanding is quite amazing and even divine. It can move miraculously and without wings, without the aid and support of others, fly not only over the immeasurable expanses of the earth and the sea but also round the world in a moment and reach up to the clouds of heaven; it can also understand the remotest of things...; it can see through human customs and even improve nature by art; it can discern justice and injustice, the limits of good and evil...; it can not only recall things long past but, as it were, transcending its limits, also know in advance of future things; finally, in a word, not without an enormous wonder which one must recognize, it becomes everything, changes itself into all forms and, becoming greater than itself, in some way embraces and encompasses the whole universe and all the powers of the world, if the expression be allowed, within its own bosom.'[30] The dawn of a new age seems to be being announced here. It is also expressed in the hopes which a new generation associated with the rule of reason. Ludwig Meyer, the Amsterdam physician and friend of Spinoza,[31] expressed these hopes in 1666 at the end of his *Philosophia scripturae*. This most radical among the younger Cartesians sees the dawn of a hope 'that in our days the philosophical field' will be expanded in all directions by the followers of 'our greatest innovator and pioneer, Renatus Des Cartes, who has born the torch before the academic world and preceded us with his example'. 'Theories emerge about God and the rational soul, about the supreme happiness of men and women, and about other questions connected with the gaining of eternal life, theories which will complete the explanation of the scriptures of the Old and New Testaments. They will prepare the way by which the church of Christ, hitherto divided and torn apart by incessant dispute, will come together in love... May they then for the future flourish, grow and blossom here on earth as one and of one opinion, draw to them hosts who are still alien, and finally triumph blissfully in heaven.'[32]

If we take these voices together, we get a good picture of what I have called the 'new spirit', which more than any individual results inevitably had to disturb orthodoxy, as indeed it did. The unbridled optimism with which the Cartesians set out to solve the riddle of the world, their rocklike confidence in the reliability of their methods and the certainty of their results, and the boundless hopes bound up with this – all this could appear to the representatives of the old Reformed doctrine only as hybris, as a claim to power over God's creation born of the evil spirit himself.

And so, if we look through the orthodox replies, we continually find as one of the main charges that the Cartesians have exchanged the roles of God and man, of creator and creature. Cyriacus Lentulus,[33] who was one of the first to see the approaching danger, put the epithet 'proud' in first place among the fourteen transgressions which he attributed to the 'Spiritus Cartesianus'.[34] And he had a right feeling for the spirit at work here when he wrote: 'The learned theologians say on the basis of Holy Scripture that the earth and what lives on it is subject to human beings. Descartes promises the possession and lordship of heaven, fire, air, water, the earth and all nature.'[35] 'The former offer this benefit that they have received to God, the latter to themselves and those who follow their philosophy...'[36] In theological terms the new spirit is often evaluated as a kind of super-Pelagianism. The Leiden pastor Jacobus du Bois thought that 'in intellectual matters and free judgment Descartes seems to surpass even Pelagius',[37] and Nicolaus Arnoldus, Professor of Theology at Franeker,[38] agrees with him. The assertion (Arnoldus is attacking L.Meyer's *Exercitatio paradoxa*) that the impossibility of error is a condition of exegesis, is pure Pelagianism. 'In fact that amounts to making the human understanding God... do you not see the godless person? That is to deny the fall of the first man and the subsequent blindness of human knowledge... to deny the state of sin, the necessity of rebirth.'[39]

In fact, orthodoxy can and must set against the optimism of the

Cartesians, their trust in the certainty and infallibility of methodically trained reason, the human 'state of misery'. And it does not tire of doing that, time and time again: 'And so one can consider reason in two respects, either in the idea, or as it once was in the state of innocence, namely perfect in every respect, as it is not in human beings – at least after the fall: or in nature, as it is now found in human beings: blind in things human and divine; one-eyed in natural things, and fatally wounded; and in all things imperfect.'[40]

The fundamental repudiation of doubt as the way to knowledge which constantly recurs in the orthodox polemical writings also belongs in this context. While the Cartesians take enormous trouble to neutralize this principle theologically to some extent as being merely a question of method, the anti-Cartesian theologians saw things more clearly here.

There is no question that the Reformed orthodoxy of the Netherlands understood that the controversy with Cartesianism was one over fundamental issues. Nor can one say that they took the matter too lightly. Mastricht, for example, sees very clearly that the new philosophy has produced a particularly difficult situation: 'It is also equally indubitable that between those two realms, of Christian theology and utterly pagan philosophy, there will be constant disputes and the severest controversies.'[41] However, Voët's successor already doubts the possibility of a victory, nor is he the only one. Arnoldus, too, knows that the position of orthodoxy is seriously threatened, and is afraid of a schism – which in fact happened, though not as might have been expected: 'I see nothing if I do not see this: a schism will arise between the disciples of the Cartesians and those who reject Descartes which will be more dangerous than the Arminian schism. The fear is that within a few years, wherever Cartesians have gained a majority in the Classes (i.e. the provincial governments), the whole system of Reformed theology will be so destroyed that the orthodox professors find themselves exiles in another land.'[42]

Orthodoxy rightly saw the decisive point of the whole controversy – namely the new definition of the relationship between philosophy and theology. It knew what it was doing when it resolutely opposed the rational optimism of the Cartesians. Nor did it have any illusions about the significance of the problem or the seriousness of the situation. That makes all the more pressing the question why it finally proved incapable of continuing to put forward its position credibly in the new situation.

The answer to this question takes us back to the heart of our problem, to the understanding of scripture. For it was here that the decisions were made, in the argument over the authority of scripture. And it is tragical to see how the orthodox finally came to grief on scripture – precisely at the point where they felt most secure and most unassailable.

The connection can be seen everywhere. 'Whatever reason brings out of its stinking heaps must be subordinate to the word of God and be measured by it as its touchstone but not opposed to it. One may not produce any axioms or devise any hypotheses by which one does not bring out the meaning from scripture but reads it in.'[43] Here Arnoldus is in fact merely drawing conclusions from his presuppositions: on the one hand the divine perfection of scripture and on the other the human imperfection of reason. Where the two conflict, the verdict cannot be in doubt. No matter what, it must turn out in favour of the 'written word of God'. There is no third possibility. For Arnoldus sees this question only as a specific instance of the relationship between philosophy and theology generally. Just as theology must in principle meet the Cartesians' claim to perfection and optimism about progress by referring to the human 'state of misery', so it must act accordingly in each individual instance.

Now the Copernican principle is one such individual case. Arnoldus cannot see anything in it other than one more case of 'making reason God'. 'The creator of the universe says "The sun rises." The Holy Spirit, the teacher of all philosophers, says, "The sun sets." But the pig that wants to teach Minerva grunts: "The sun neither rises nor sets, but rising and setting are attributed to the sun by the Holy Spirit on the basis of a false human view."'[44]

The pre-Adamites theory is also one individual case. Arnoldus polemizes against its author in the same peeved tone as against the Copernicans: 'Noah's flood is polluted, he discredits Moses as an inventive fantasist, he does away with the biblical canon after the fashion of Lucian, he basely debases many scriptures, he belittles and scorns the divine miracles, and whatever sins against the Holy Spirit can be invented, that man has suggested.'[45]

In Peter van Mastricht the connection between principle and consequence takes the form: 'We solemnly declare that philosophy is subordinate to theology and at its service.'[46] That is the principle.

But in practice it means that the 'utterances of reason about natural matters' are to be subordinated to the 'dictates of scripture on the same matters', and that in all cases the decision lies with the latter whether the 'utterances of reason' are to be accepted or rejected.[47]

Examples of this connection can be multiplied almost at will. They make it clear that in defending the old world-view against the Cartesians orthodoxy believed that it was defending a principle that it must have felt it quite impossible to surrender.

And there is no doubt that here too orthodoxy had a right insight. For in fact Socinians, Copernicans and the followers of La Peyrère had found in Cartesianism their common philosophical basis and justification. Accordingly scriptural criticism, previously to some degree practised only in casuistic fashion, was here elevated to a principle. Now from the middle of the century the author of this principle seemed increasingly to be the new spirit: for orthodoxy a spirit of hybris, the primal sin of man since Adam's fall.[48] That sin was attacking scripture here. Could, indeed should, one acknowledge its results if one saw this? Was one being an accomplice of sin?

'What the saints inspired and instructed by God have written, they have at the same time believed and taught... I would rather err according to scripture, not only with the people but also with the prophets, than with the innovators feel that there is prejudice in the Bible. I do not want to die with those philosophers but with the prophets.'[49]

To prefer to err with scripture than be right with the innovators: that is the pathos of orthodoxy.

We may not doubt the seriousness and honesty of this position.[50] But we must also see that it is governed more by fear than by freedom: fear of losing the foundation and the certainty of faith; fear of giving in to a spirit which was bold enough to raise questions where orthodoxy did not seem to allow any; fear, finally – and that is perhaps the deepest reason for our discontent about this position – of any change whatsoever.

Here, in the repudiation of Cartesianism, there begins that alliance between fundamentalism and conservatism which is so characteristic of the church history of the modern period.

'And so for the sake of the peace and harmony of souls, in the schools the boundaries that the fathers set may not be trangressed. Anyone who attempts that is rightly accused of a breach of the peace.'[51] Here is that same fatal argument with which Melanchthon already warned against Copernicanism. Now it runs like a scarlet thread through all the anti-Cartesian literature. From the opinion of the University of Utrecht, which above all warns against leading the young astray,[52] to Jacobus Koelman, the faithful disciple of Voët,[53] who in 1692 still appeals to the Classis of Walcheren to take proceedings against these 'dangerous and damaging novelties',[54] anti-Cartesian literature is tuned almost without exception to this tone. The stigma of hostility in principle to progress which theology and the church were thus given has lasted – as I have already said – down to the present.

3

Among the three conceivable positions over scripture which were possible in the face of the new philosophy, namely that reason should be subordinate to, set alongside, or set above the Bible, orthodoxy resolutely adopted the first. It did that not least because it saw that if reason and revelation were set side by side with equal rights, unity of thought would collapse and there was the danger of a double truth.

Mastricht saw things like this: 'So whereas on the one hand scripture insists on knowledge of the Trinity, on the other side this is denied by philosophy. Who will give way if one is not subordinated to the other? Where will there be an end to the disputation?'[55] This is the consequence of the course that the generation after the Reformation adopted on this question. On the same ontological level, the elevation of philosophy from handmaid to partner inevitably led to a double concept of truth and faith, to a divine philosophical and a divine scriptural faith.[56] Leydekker sees the same problem in terms of interpretation. Anyone who puts philosophy and theology side by side 'like two daughters of the same father', will arrive at a twofold norm of exegesis.[57] 'The innovators want a double norm in matters of faith and the exegesis of scripture: scripture itself and, as among the Socinians and Remonstrants, human reason (which hitherto has never had the role of a criterion or norm among the orthodox in theological questions)...'[58] In fact this was a weak point in the argument of that group of theologians which sought a mediating position between orthodoxy and radical criticism. We might call it the Cartesian centre party. On the one hand full of respect for the authority of scripture, on the other hand fascinated

by the method and results of Descartes, they saw as the only course
the strict separation of philosophy from theology. Here philosophy
was to be assigned the sphere of 'natural things' while scripture had
to decide on 'supernatural things'.

The remarks of Balthasar Bekker in his *Admonitio de philosophia
Cartesiana* are characteristic of the standpoint of the Cartesian
centre party. For a moment we shall follow the argument, because
with clarity and brevity it makes this position very clear.

Bekker begins by asserting: 'And it is certain that philosophy
considers all that is accessible to reason, while theology teaches
that which transcends the power of comprehension of the human
spirit...'[59] Here the change of verb is illuminating: philosophy
'considers' but theology 'teaches'. This is connected with the different principles with which both are associated, and which are
described in the following way: 'So as the principle of philosophy is
reason, and that of theology revelation, the philosopher recognizes
in his way something as true when with the help of reason it can be
proved beyond objection that a matter is so; the theologian believes
that everything is true, whether or not reason may grasp it, which
the holy claims of God, that can neither deceive nor be deceived,
regard as a binding matter of faith' (10f.).[60] Here beyond question
there are two different concepts of truth: the philosophical, which
needs compelling proof and is understood; and the theological,
which depends only on the authority of scripture and has to be
believed. Each of these two truths, with its own principle and its
own method, extends over the one particular ontological sphere and
may in no circumstances be transferred to the other. 'So one may
not listen to any theologian who attempts to read out of Holy
Scripture that the essence of the soul is rational or animal, or that
the earth stands still and the sun revolves around it... But on the
other hand one may not tolerate a philosopher contemplating the
deeply hidden mysteries of the worshipful Trinity or the incarnate
Christ in the light of reason' (17f.).

The decisive presupposition of this position is the demonstration
that reason and revelation are free from contradiction. This demonstration is so important because, once the possibility of a contradiction is allowed even theoretically, the whole thought-process will
unavoidably end up in a double truth.

The argument in this question is the same throughout the centre
party: 'And God is the creator both of reason and of revelation, just

as he is also the source of all good' (18). Since God is the creator equally of reason and revelation, of scripture and nature, he must necessarily have created both free of contradiction. This statement is quite axiomatic for the Cartesians.[61]

The consequence of this axiom, which Bekker also draws, is obvious: 'What manifestly contradicts philosophy cannot be believed in theology, nor can one know in philosophy something that scripture disputes' (18). But here comes the problem. For what scripture says or does not say is manifestly a matter of interpretation, whereas philosophy provides objective results. We can therefore hardly follow Bekker when on the basis of these principles he regards as vain the attempt to derive transsubstantiation and ubiquity from scripture, as they would manifestly contradict the principles of reason, whereas on the other hand Trinity and Incarnation may not be disputed, as these are clearly presented by scripture (18f.). One need only think of the Socinian arguments against the scriptural nature of the doctrine of the Trinity to see on what a weak basis these considerations rest.

Basically the two principles of separation and freedom from contradiction clashed because the latter called for what the former disputed, namely the necessary accord between scripture and reason. Nevertheless, given the presuppositions, this way was the only possibility of combining the orthodox approach with the new philosophy.

And beyond question that was the task of the time. For the Cartesians had at any rate understood one thing: the progress of philosophical knowledge was unstoppable. It was given with the principle of modern philosophy. And therefore a separation between philosophy and theology was necessary if the church were not to become increasingly incredible: 'And as all philosophy must recognize experience as its mistress, so it is manifest that often innovations become necessary where one day it teaches something about which among the ancients deep silence reigned; so that even Aristotle could learn today from Descartes about magnetic force; or Ptolemy from our seafarers about the inhabitants with which the two halves of the earth are populated; or Lactantius and Augustine from Bishop Virgil of Salzburg,[62] who recognized the existence of antipodes' (43).

Here Bekker avoids biblical examples, but it is clear that this also applies to scriptural conceptions: so far as they deal with natural matters, they too stand under the law of progress.

A limitation of the philosophical demand as required by orthodoxy[63] is unthinkable because its very nature is freedom: 'Now freedom is to some degree the basic possession of philosophy' (109) and '... one will seek in vain to subject the scholarly republic of philosophers, whose real law is freedom, to alien laws' (111).

So the Cartesian centre party begins from four presuppositions:[64] 1. The unqualified authority of scripture in all theological questions where it makes clear and unequivocal statements on them. 2. The certainty and reliability of philosophical knowledge in the sphere of natural matters and its right to examine all things freely and critically in this sphere. 3. The separation in principle between philosophy and theology as two ways of knowledge based on different principles and working with different materials. 4. The freedom of philosophical and theological statements from contradiction.

In this way scriptural criticism was for the first time given a basic principle. For if on the one hand philosophical knowledge was regarded as certain, and on the other the possibility of contradiction was excluded, criticism of scripture was required in principle, where clear dogmatic statements did not impose limits on it.

To quote Bekker once again: 'I unreservedly deny that Cartesius contradicts clear passages of scripture in the Copernican question. And those who dare to assert this make either ill use of their discernment in their reading of scripture or no use of it at all' (94). It is a misuse of scripture to seek to oppose it to reason: 'What if by a statement of sound reason it is established that the earth in fact moves? Or should we believe that God challenges in scripture what he proclaims in nature?' No grounds can be derived from scripture either for or against the movement of the earth: 'I do not say that the earth moves. I say that I cannot learn from Holy Scripture that it nevertheless rests unmovingly at the centre' (95).

It is above all Christoph Wittich and Balthasar Bekker in whom the critical effect of the new presuppositions becomes clear. Here Wittich is without doubt more significant theologically,[65] whereas with his *The Bewitched World* Bekker above all had a broad influence.

It is Wittich who gives the whole discussion of the authority of scripture which now breaks out in all its acuteness the decisive slogan which is cited countless times in assent or polemic: 'Scripture often speaks of natural things according to the view of the people (its opponents tended to put in an 'erroneously' at this point), and not in accordance with the exact truth.'[66]

Here is the classical formulation of the accommodation theory which until the discovery of the historical character of the biblical writings, i.e. up to the end of the eighteenth century, would in fact remain the only possibility of giving the contradictions a satisfactory theological and philosophical explanation.[67]

Now of course Wittich is by no means the inventor of this theory. We have seen how Kepler and Galileo already attempted to solve the emerging difficulties with its help and in almost the same words. And Wittich is well aware of his predecessors when he talks of 'a form of speech used frequently by the Copernicans' which he is employing here.[68] But Wittich is the first *theologian* to make use of this argument and to elevate it to the status of a principle in the context of a hermeneutical system. At the same time this substantive and historical context shows the degree to which things had in fact changed under the influence of Cartesianism. Kepler's and Galileo's opponents saw themselves confronted with an individual view. In the accommodation theory Wittich's opponents were warding off the general attack on the authority of scripture.

'O how dangerous and suspicious a thing it is into which the Cartesians want to seduce us', exclaims Arnoldus,[69] and du Bois specifies the fears of orthodoxy like this: '... if we are allowed in matters of physics and astronomy to represent at will words which are in themselves easily understandable and appropriate as tropes or phrases accommodated to our terminology, why not in theological matters and in the things of faith? For there are many who are of the view that in matters of faith Holy Scripture speaks according to appearances and the opinion of the common people, like the Marcionites and the Manichaeans, who deny the reality of the birth and passion of Christ, etc., etc., by representing the holy testimonies as being according to the appearance and opinion of the common people.'[70]

Does that not mean, as Maresius thinks, making scripture 'a wax nose'[71] and representing God as a liar and deceiver?[72] Does that not lead directly towards Rome, where what holds is not the word but the exegesis of the church?[73] In short, is not here the authority of scripture, and thus all certainty and all security, utterly destroyed?... 'If scripture in natural and moral matters does not speak according to the truth of the matter, but according to the erroneous view of the people, then the basis for infallible belief will become deceptive. God will endanger his own authority and that of his word or scripture, and prepare the way for doubt even in matters of faith: whether they have been handed down according to the truth of the matter or only according to the view of the common people...'[74]

Wittich defends himself against these charges with a reference to the 'scope' of scripture, i.e. its spiritual aim. This scope consists only in the tradition of the truths of faith, and not in the communication of a picture of the world.[75]

As we have seen with Kepler and Galileo, this thought, too, was in no way new. Nevertheless Bizer rightly sees the development of this concept as the real theological contribution of this significant Cartesian.[76]

Like all Descartes' theological followers, Wittich starts from the principle of the separation of philosophy and theology. This principle can, of course, have different aspects in view: it can above all aim at the liberation of philosophy from all theological limitations; on the other hand, it can also seek to secure the independence of theology from all ties to a world view. And if one constantly finds both aspects also among the Cartesians, some different accents are unmistakable. For instance, Bekker and Velthuysen seem more concerned about freedom for philosophical research, whereas Wittich wants above all to restore theology to itself. In the preface to his *Theologica pacifica* he expressly acknowledges this task: 'They (the Cartesians) do not introduce a new language into the schools, but they want to drive out that which was once introduced into theology by people to whom Aristotle was more important than Paul, along with the early Reformers, and in its place reintroduce the genuine language of Canaan and the words of the Holy Spirit...'[77]

That is the 'scope' of scripture. While one may not mix up philosophy with theology, one may not confuse theology with philosophy either. 'This is done by those who make us a Mosaic or a Christian physics and want to develop the intrinsic connection and the nature of things from scripture. They cite many passages of scripture in which individual bodies are mentioned, which are adduced as examples of divine providence and potency. To serve this aim, a common notion is enough, such as can be understood by anyone. The Holy Spirit subordinates this simple notion to its far finer aim. Those who assume a reliable knowledge of natural things and true knowledge in such accounts therefore only deceive themselves, because they either do not raise human beings above the ordinary or general conception, or confirm and implant prejudices. For those authors have mixed in some other things from the scholastic or usual philosophy in which they grew up...'[78]

Here it emerges that Wittich has a clear conception of the time-conditioned nature of the biblical picture of the world. However, it has a completely rational and philosophical basis, namely in the good Cartesian concept of 'prejudice', which is overcome and corrected by the progress of science. The question why the Holy Spirit accommodated himself to those prejudices and did not correct them is solved by the concept of the 'scope': his task – and thus the task of scripture generally – was and is solely 'to lead us to salvation'. That here he made use of the conceptions and prejudices of his time is, in Wittich's view, only too understandable.[79] So we must guard against wanting to see an early form of historical interpretation already in Wittich's hermeneutical reflections. The accommodation theory derives utterly from rational thought and virtually excludes a historical understanding. So its rule ends with the beginnings of historicism, as is convincingly demonstrated by C.Hartlich and W.Sachs' investigation into the origin of the concept of myth in modern biblical scholarship.[80] In the detailed interpretation of the disputed biblical passages, Wittich follows the example of Kepler, to whom he explicitly refers. So for example he explains the *locus classicus* of the ancient world-view, Josh.10.12f., just like the great astronomer. Joshua here was simply asking for an extension of the day in the terms that anyone would have used at the time: 'He wanted the sun to stand still for him so that he could achieve his aim; in other words, he wanted the sun to remain above the horizon longer. Now this could have happened just as well if the apparent course of the sun had been stopped by the halting of the earth as if the sun itself stood still.'[81] The main question of the possibility of such a miracle is not raised by Wittich: it took place, but it cannot be the basis, confirmation or refutation of any theory in astronomy or physics. In his interpretations of the psalms, too, there is nothing which essentially goes beyond Kepler. We already know that, and there is no need to dwell further on it.

Generally speaking, Wittich's significance lies less in his actual criticism than in his insight that the old hermeneutical position of orthodoxy had become untenable. By introducing the concepts of accommodation and scope against the background of Cartesian philosophy, he attempted to show theology a way out of the difficult situation from systematic considerations. He did not see this as a criticism of scripture but as an endorsement of its authority, which in the future would no longer be exposed to any suspicions.[82]

And yet it was precisely this approach which was to provide the systematic presuppositions for the criticism of the content of the Bible. Wittich establishes a philosophical foundation for the accommodation theory in the concept of *praejudicia*, those time-conditioned prejudices which it is the most important task of philosophy to correct and put right. At all events, that is Descartes' conviction, and not just his: a whole generation derived its philosophical life from doing away with the old prejudices and as a result introducing a realm of reason, peace and progress. 'The world "prejudice" is the most appropriate expression for the great desire of the Enlightenment, for its concern for free, open examination: "prejudice" is the clear polemical correlate to the all too ambiguous word "freedom".'[83]

Wittich still limited the concept to particular scientific questions connected with the Copernican world-view. Only here does he see prejudices at work among the biblical writers which must be understood hermeneutically as an 'improper mode of speaking' in scripture. But already among his contemporaries there are some who are not at all content with this. Could not the biblical reports be caught up in prejudices in other areas too? What about their notions of spirits, angels and the devil? Descartes had required that in principle anything that was not evidently proved had to be doubted. Were spirits, angels or the devil evidently proved? But if they were not provable, could they possibly owe their existence not to God but merely to human prejudices? Moreover the nearest and most extreme step had already been taken: in the end was not the whole of religion just one giant prejudice, at least in its traditional form?

It was Wittich's contemporary and fellow combatant Balthasar Bekker who for the first time raised the question of the biblical world of spirits and subjected it to a comprehensive critical examination in connection with the new philosophy. His *The Bewitched World* not only made a decisive contribution to depriving the witchhunting of the time of its theological and ideological foundations, but also belongs in the first rank of those works with which modern biblical criticism begins. That this earned it the grim enmity of the orthodox of all camps was unavoidable in the circumstances.[84] The structure of the work shows Bekker's purpose and method clearly.[85]

The first book seeks to demonstrate that there are prejudices - which are demonstrable by psychology and history – which make us find a world of spirits in scripture. Bekker sees the same superstitious conceptions widespread throughout the old pagan world. They are characteristic of paganism, as is also shown by a reference to the New World which has now been discovered (I.10). Now superstition was inherited from the pagans by the Jews, and from the Jews by Christians, as Bekker demonstrates by an abundance of quotations from the Fathers (I.15). Small children are already brought up in these prejudices, impressions of which the author of *The Bewitched World* knows 'that they implant the deepest fears and the clearest forms which afterwards are very difficult to uproot again' (I.24.6).

'We come to the exegesis and explanation of scripture with so many prejudices; we have never doubted things and therefore never investigated what the truth of them is.' So Bekker requires 'scripture to be so explained as though no one had ever explained it' (I.24.21), i.e. with a free, unprejudiced examination and exegesis under the prompting of sound reason.

Bekker undertakes this examination in the second book, a complete compendium of all related concepts and passages in the Old and New Testaments. Here he works just like Wittich, above all with the concepts of scope and accommodation.

So we read in connection with the investigation of the biblical doctrine of angels that scripture never makes comments about their nature and being: 'And why should it do that, since the Bible is not for angels but for men, to whom the way of blessedness is shown in it. It teaches us to seek this alone in Christ, who became neither angel nor spirit but man for our sake...' (II.8.1). 'Therefore scripture only reports that of them which concerns men from God' (ibid.). It is vain to develop an angelology from the Bible, 'in which it is taught what angels and spirits really are in themselves, for what they are made by God and what they do' (II.8.2), because this does not correspond with the aim of scripture.

The connection between scope and accommodation becomes clear from the following passage: it is not the task of scripture 'to teach us natural things as they are in themselves but to contemplate them to God's glory and man's blessedness... From which it follows, as specially comes about here, that God, who does not explain nature himself nor alter language, speaks of himself in human fashion...' (II.10.15). It does not occur to Bekker to deny the existence of angels (II.15.11). What he is disputing is merely traditional angelology, which seems to him compatible with neither the rule of God, the purpose of scripture nor the demands of reason.

Those are the terms in which he summarizes his view about Jacob's struggle in Gen.32; on the exodus of Israel from Egypt in Ex.14.19; on the stone which was moved from Jesus' tomb in Matt.28.2; and on the freeing of the apostles from prison in Acts 5.19 – all passages in which the Bible reports the direct intervention of an angel: 'It all amounts to one thing. God himself did it: the angels are nothing but a sign of the divine majesty...' (II.11.9).

Bekker deals in a very similar way with the devil, but of course in a different setting. The good things that have happened have been done only by God, even if in the language of the time they were attributed or still are attributed to angels. Conversely: the evil that is done and is attributed to the devil is solely the work of human evil. 'What then do I conclude? That so many writings are not there to teach us what the devil in fact does but to teach us what the corruption of humankind itself causes, and that is attributed to the devil as the one who first did evil' (II.18.12).

However, we may not overlook the fact that there are already powerfully rationalizing tones in Bekker. Thus for example he asks of the temptation story how the devil could have brought Jesus to Jerusalem without many thousands of people seeing him, unless it was by night ('but it does not say that', II.21.7); how one could see all the kingdoms of the world in a moment, as the earth was certainly already round in those days (II.21.8), etc. None of this is with a critical intent, but to demonstrate 'that this story about Christ and the devil must not be understood literally' (II.1.8). Rather, the fight with the devil must be explained in the same way as 'that which he later fought in the garden, consisting merely in the alternation of dangerous thoughts...' (II.21.17).

At the end of this book Bekker points once again to the un-Christian convenience which seeks to attribute everything to the devil, instead of man looking into his own conscience: 'there he will see the true beginning, the source of his torment and plagues' (II.36.18). It is not fear of the devil, but only fear of God that will free him from this: 'If I sometimes deviate from the interpreters and translators, I still keep to scripture. If I give little glory to creatures, I give all the more to God; if I belittle the devil's deceit and power, I magnify the wisdom and power of the saviour... And if I do this, I demonstrate that I do not want to make people fear the devil, but fear God' (II.3.22).

If there is no devil, then there cannot be those who traffic with him. The third book of *The Bewitched World* draws this conclusion. Again Bekker goes through the relevant passages of scripture. He finds 48 of them: 38 in the Old Testament and 10 in the New, where 'in our German Bible there is mention of wizards, witches or magic under this name or of soothsaying or the devil's arts' (complete list in III.4.2). Bekker's interpretation, which makes use of philological, philosophical and theological arguments, seeks to demonstrate that here in fact we have either apostasy (II.17.5) or secret crimes, the perpetrators of which are 'to be deemed highwaymen and murderers' (III.17.8).

Summing up, Bekker says: 'The alliance of wizards and witches with the devil is only an invention which is not in the slightest contained in God's word. Indeed it goes contrary to God's word and covenant, and is quite impossible, the most utter nonsense that was ever invented by the pagan poets...' (II.19.1).

Finally, in the fourth book the bold author subjects a series of contemporary reports to a critical examination which shows them to be either unproven or capable of rational explanation. Here above all he resorts to his own experiences and gives a convincing picture of the people who invented such things and the treacherous guile of those who exploit this superstition. Finally, he requires that in all witch trials the church should act not against the accused but against the accuser (IV.34.10), an idea which already appears at the end of the third book as the fruit of his considerations: 'The judge and the lawyer will no longer burden their consciences with the shedding of so much innocent blood of those who are put to death for imputed and invented witchcraft...' (III.23.11).

We have to compare Bekker's work with Voët's two-part 1638 disputation, *De natura et operationibus daemonum*,[86] to see the enormous progress which his work represents from a theological point of view. In fact we can see *The Bewitched World* as the first attempt at a comprehensive 'demythologizing' of the world of biblical conceptions. There is nothing comparable to it on the continent during these decades. It is hardly a coincidence that in many respects Bekker's results seem surprisingly modern. For his presuppositions are in principle the same as those of modern exegesis: the recognition of the modern world-view on the one side and the scope or kerygma as the distinctive feature of scripture on the other. However, in the meantime a highly differentiated historical understanding has replaced the fateful theory of accommodation. But this transition changed the general understanding of scripture far less than the move from orthodoxy to the exegesis of the Cartesians.

Furthermore Bekker's work is an impressive demonstration of the way in which the roots of modern biblical criticism in no way lie in a scepticism of some kind or another. It is more concerned to provide a basis and guarantee for the authority and freedom of scripture even in a changed world. That is as true for Bekker as it is for Wittich and the whole Cartesian centre party. What distinguished these Cartesians from orthodoxy were not theological doctrines – in doctrine they felt that they were quite orthodox – but their eye for modern problems and the impossibility of avoiding them. By raising these problems and adopting a new way of understanding scripture, they made Protestant theology possible beyond orthodoxy. We can say that, even if to begin with not many followed them on this course.

4

The Cartesian centre party did not have any great historical influence on theology. That was less because of their opponents than because of their friends, real or supposed. In fact nothing harmed these Cartesians more than the fact that they spoke at the same time as and in the name of the philosopher who called for and practised the unconditional subjection of theology to the universal rule of reason.

Among the three conceivable positions in the relationship between reason and scripture, namely subordinating reason to scripture, setting the two side by side, or putting reason above scripture, this group represented the third. What began here was the way to a religion of reason, a consistent thinking through to the end of the Cartesian approach without reference to dogma, tradition and history.

For the centre party this position meant the need to wage a constant war on two fronts. On the right they had to defend themselves against the charge of philosophical heterodoxy, and on the left distinguish themselves from the radical Cartesians. The latter in particular they did with great passion and acuteness,[87] but without always managing to be completely convincing. For beyond doubt their approach had a tendency towards progressive rationalizing. Thus above all for those who had not yet understood the problem – and among them we have to include all orthodoxy – the radical position could appear to be an anticipation of the consequences of the moderate approach. The centre party never completely succeeded in freeing themselves from this suspicion.

The most important – though by no means the most significant - voice in radical theological Cartesianism was that of the anonymous author of that *Exercitatio paradoxica* which already announced its programme in its title: 'Philosophy the interpreter of Holy Scripture'.[88]

With this work we find ourselves in that group of questions which the first chapter of this book sought to sketch out: the problem of a sure norm of faith, raised by confessional divisions and kept alive by the incessant bloody controversies to which it led. What was more natural than that the 'new spirit' should also deal with this question and attempt to solve it with the principles of Cartesianism? Did not this system promise that sure knowledge which the confessions had evidently so hopelessly lost? Should not trained reason be in a position, by removing the countless prejudices, to be able to penetrate to the matter itself, to some degree to the basic Christian substance which now seemed so utterly displaced?

These were the thoughts which led Ludwig Meyer to write his work, and which he develops in the prologue.

It is not the quest for vain praise but 'furthering the truth, the benefit of one's neighbour and the reunion of divided and dissenting Christianity' which is the aim of his book (xvi). There must be a way whch leads out of the sea of doubt and uncertainy, where everyone disputes and no one wins (xix). In this situation he comes upon the method of Descartes, that 'most noble and incomparable man', who renewed philosophy from the ground up by seriously renouncing all prejudices and recognizing and accepting nothing that was not clear and easy to understand. 'I have long and often considered most zealously whether, like him, in philosophy, I was allowed immediately to reject as false whatever could be doubted, until I finally arrived at something certain and firm in theology, too, on which one's foot could rest in confidence' (xix).

The decision to make a free and open examination of scripture which Meyer arrived at also seems to him to be in line with the Reformed fathers, whom he cites in abundance.

It is clear what is happening here, namely precisely what the centre party wanted to avoid in all circumstances: the resolution of genuinely theological problems with the help of philosophical categories. Philosophy is not limited to 'natural matters', but decides on the aim of scripture. But that means that this aim can only be 'rational': the way to a religion of reason is open.

We need not follow Meyer's hermeneutical reflections in detail here, especially as E.Bizer has already described them.[89] It is his approach and its result that is most important for us.

Meyer's starting point and first principle is the statement that 'the books of the Old and New Testaments are the infallible word of God' (xxii and I.1). Anyone who disputes this statement puts himself outside theology; to him the saying of Aristotle applies: 'one cannot dispute with those who challenge the principle' (xxii). Unity also prevails among all Christians over this. Dissent only begins with the question of exegesis. That poses the problem, which is that of finding a norm or rule which is certain, clear and obvious, or, to quote Meyer, 'A norm and a criterion, certain and indisputable, by which the truth of any interpretation can be tested, investigated and decided as by a touchstone' (I.1).

Neither the church nor scripture's interpretation of itself can provide an infallible norm in this sense, but – so Meyer argues – only philosophy: '…this is the task of true philosophy, and it is the certain and indisputable norm both in the interpretation of the holy book and in the testing of these interpretations' (V.1).

However, not any philosophy can do this, but only that which begins from that true and indubitably certain concept of things which reason works out and brings to light – 'free from any covering of prejudices, supported by the natural light and acuteness of understanding … on the basis of principles which are unshakable and intrinsically clear, logical conclusions and clear proofs, which are known clearly and openly' (V.2).

This reason is of divine origin, and God, as creator and preserver of all true philosophy and wisdom, has in no way created it blind (V.3, 4, 5).[90] Therefore a contradiction between reason and

revelation is unthinkable (V.6). Both the truth disclosed by reason
and revealed truth have the same force (V.7; cf. VIII.1).

The following chapters serve to refute the various objections.
What is interesting here is the comment that theologians have always
made use of a philosophy: Justin, the Areopagite and Origen used
Platonic philosophy, and the Middle Ages and – though not so
resolutely – the Reformers used Aristotelian philosophy: 'Until
finally in this century the light of Cartesian philosophy shone on
theologians' (VI.2). He discusses at length scriptural passages which
seem to run contrary to his theory (VII.3-5). He disputes the
Roman principle of an interpretation governed by the church, by
demonstrating a number of contradictions (IX.1), and the Protestant
principle that scripture is its own interpreter by referring to the
problem of illumination by the Spirit. The argument with Reformation hermeneutic takes up a good deal of space (X-XV), but it
produces little that is new; one can find most of it in Valerianus
Magni.

The Amsterdam physician has occasionally been accused of being
'completely dependent on the Socinian method of interpretation'[91]
and of 'not having produced a single new thought'.[92] In fact a degree
of kinship to Socinian arguments is unmistakable.[93] And yet the
Exercitatio paradoxa differs from all the Socinian writings in a highly
distinctive way.

Meyer himself sees this distinction at three points: 1. He asserts the
certainty and infallibility of both understanding and interpretation,
about which they (the Socinians and Arminians) had said nothing;
2. he disputes the clarity of scripture 'in matters necessary to
salvation' which both these groups affirm; 3. he makes philosophy
the only norm in the exegesis of obscure passages of scripture, where
they use reason, circumstances and parallels as expedients (XVI.8).

In fact in these three points the decisive step that Meyer took
beyond the Socinians and the Arminians becomes clear. It was the
step from rational praxis, which always had a contingent aspect, to
a rational system, which in principle excludes anything that is
contingent or uncertain. True philosophy takes the place of sound
reason. A dialogue between reason and scripture such as was still
attempted by the Socinians was thus ruled out. Since Meyer disputed
the transparency and sufficiency of scripture, and in the same breath
censured tradition and history, philosophy alone remained as the
norma normans and the *norma normata* of all theology. As Bizer

rightly says, this is the solution of all the enigmas and difficulties of the theology of the time – 'but the price was that theology should surrender itself'.[94]

Nowhere does the *Exercitatio paradoxa* lead significantly beyond the sphere of hermeneutical theory. The few examples which Meyer cites[95] are so conventional that they hardly indicate the real consequences of his position.

These consequences become very much clearer in a book which, also anonymous, appeared in Saumur in 1670 and which in some respects seems like a more practical sister to the *Exercitatio paradoxa*: *La Réunion du Christianisme ou la manière de rejoindre tous les Chrestiens sous une seule Confession de Foy*.[96] The author was Isaac d'Huisseau, and when he wrote it he was a pastor in Saumur.[97]

The title of the work indicates that d'Huisseau has the same aim as Ludwig Meyer: the reunion of divided and dissident Christianity. And like the Amsterdam physician, he sees the way to this in the application of Descartes' method.

'For some time a way has been proposed in philosophy of thinking clearly and finding a sure way to truth. It is held that to do this one must be unconditionally free from all preconceived opinions and all spiritual prejudice. That one must first accept only the simplest notions and propositions which cannot be disputed by anyone who makes even the slightest use of his reason. Can we not also imitate this process in religion?' (117).[98]

However, d'Huisseau's argument is not hermeneutical but dogmatic. Does not Christianity rest on a few quite simple and generally acknowledged facts and concepts? Is not everything that stands between the confessions merely a question of historical, theological and psychological prejudice? At any rate, this is the way in which the pastor from Saumur sees things.[99] And he thinks that simply the removal of these prejudices and a return to the old simple truths is enough to secure the reunion of all Christians.

In this connection d'Huisseau formulates a creed which, he is convinced, contains all these simple truths that are common too all Christians, namely, 'that there is a God, who created heaven and earth; that he requires of us perfect holiness; that we have violated his ordinances, as a result of which we have become unworthy of his grace, and that he nevertheless invites us to repentance and salvation. That consequently he sent the one whom he himself calls his Son; that his Son died for our sins; that he rose for our justification; that he ascended into heaven where he intercedes for us; and that we achieve eternal salvation when we are wholly permeated by these truths and are zealous in seeking piety towards God and love of our neighbour' (161).

This creed has to be compared with the creed of the early church if we are to see the decisive changes which have been made here. First of all, it is striking that the third article is reduced to the concept of 'eternal salvation'. There are no statements about the Holy Spirit, the church, and the resurrection of the dead. What remains is a general conception of immortality. The achievement of this immortality as an aim is associated with two conditions: the acceptance of the basic Christian truths and the practice of honourable piety towards God and practical love of one's neighbour.

But that means that the whole of christology – despite the orthodox-sounding formulae 'died for our sins', 'rose for our justification' basically becomes homeless. It is no coincidence that this creed is silent about the second coming of Christ. In this it betrays the fact that it understands sin morally, and not theologically. For the second coming and the judgment correspond dogmatically to original sin, and neither of these can be formulated as a simple truth which is universally understandable and acceptable.

In fact here everything has become very simple, very clear and very rational. Although d'Huisseau retains many traditional formulations, he in fact regards the whole dogmatic tradition as one great prejudice which hinders access to the basic concepts of the gospel. And these basic concepts are virtue and immortality. 'The main purpose of the gospel... is to lead people through the knowledge of its mysteries to the study of virtue and to bring them to the enjoyment of happiness and glory by the practice of this virtue' (23). It is this that is the will of God, what scripture teaches and what man has to do. D'Huisseau is still at the very beginning of the road, but it is already clear where it will lead: to a religion of reason, morality and humanity.

When the author of *The Reunion of Christianity* keeps requiring his readers 'to distinguish exactly between the doctrines which Holy Scripture offers to believers for them to believe, and what concerns only the external nature of the church and its ceremonies' (130f.), then in connection with the concepts of virtue and happiness, that can lead only to a comprehensive critique of scripture, to a radical exclusion of all dark, unclear passages which go against this aim.

It is the foundation for that critical programme to which the Enlightenment then applied all its strength and all its acumen – up to Reimarus, Semler and Lessing.

The hopes for the future which d'Huisseau attaches to his plan are as uninterruptedly optimistic as the plan itself. He sees one great Christian kingdom coming into being on earth (199), inhabited by people for whom good actions are more important than being right in theological discussions (203), who live truly Christian lives and act for the well-being of society (204f.). Disciples and apostles will celebrate a feast of joy in heaven if all this is finally achieved, and on earth peace, joy and unity will prevail (205).

Ludwig Meyer and Isaac d'Huisseau reflect only individual aspects of the spirit of radical criticism: Meyer in the form of a new hermeneutical theory, and d'Huisseau as a practical way to the reunion of Christianity. From these works it is only a step to Spinoza – but what a step!

In fact the *Tractatus Theologico-Politicus*, which appeared in 1670, is already something like a summary of the whole development. Not only does it completely incorporate the previous results of criticism in all spheres, but in addition, for the first time it puts them in the context of the modern criticism of religion. The extraordinary critical force of the *Tractatus* is the way in which it enlarges and combines these two principles; it is that which has ensured it its significance to the present day.[100]

There can be no doubt about the primacy of reason in principle in Spinoza's thought. Spinoza himself expressed this very clearly in an answer to Willem van Blyenbergh.[101] The latter had declared in a letter to Spinoza on 16 January 1665:[102] 'Though it has happened that after long examination my natural knowledge seems to contradict the word of God... this Word of God commands so much respect from me[103] that the conceptions which I regard as clear are becoming far more suspect to me, instead of my setting them over against the truths which have been prescribed for me in that book.' That is precisely the formulation of the basic question with which we are concerned here, namely whether reason is to be put above, alongside or below the authority of scripture. Spinoza – bolder in his letters than his writings intended for publication – replies on 28 January: if Blyenbergh is convinced that through scripture God 'speaks more clearly and effectively than through the light of natural understanding', then he has good reason to submit reason to those statements which he attributes to Holy Scripture. 'As far as I am concerned, I grant openly and frankly that I do not understand Holy Scripture, though I have devoted a number of years to it, and as it does not escape me that after arriving at a basic truth I cannot succumb to a thought which puts this in doubt, I console myself with what understanding offers me and do not fear that I am deceiving myself here, nor that Holy Scripture contradicts it, although I cannot fathom that Scripture. For the truth is not in conflict with the truth...'[104]

Thus Spinoza has in principle adopted the same position as his friend Ludwig Meyer, and we can understand why the *Exercitatio paradoxa* was at first universally attributed to the great philosopher.[105] We may assume that from the beginning Spinoza's thought here was quite consistent. At any rate, already in the *Cogitata metaphysica* he not only disputes the possibility that God could do miracles against the laws of nature, but also decisively rejects any action of God 'above nature': 'For most of the wiser theologians grant that God does not act against nature but beyond it, i.e., as I interpret things, that God also has many laws of action which he has not communicated to the human spirit. If they were communicated to the human spirit, they would be as natural as the rest.'[106] So there are no miracles, but only phenomena which seem miraculous to us because we do not know the natural laws underlying them.

Thus it cannot be surprising that for Spinoza, the traditional theology and its understanding of scripture falls under the heading of prejudices. He explicitly mentions the removal of prejudices as the first task of the *Tractatus Theologico-politicus* in a letter to Heinrich Oldenburg: 'I am writing a treatise about my opinion of scripture. I am moved to this undertaking by 1. The prejudices of theologians; for I know that they are the greatest hindrance in the way of people being able to pay attention to philosophy. I am thus concerned to demonstrate this and to banish it from the consciousness of the wise...'[107]

Those are the presuppositions from which Spinoza begins in the *Tractatus*. Even when in the course of it he constantly points out that 'between faith or theology on the one side and philosophy on the other there is no connection, nor affinity', because the foundation and aim of the two are quite different;[108] that is, only on these conditions.

'Philosophy has no end in view save truth: faith... looks for nothing but obedience and piety. Again, philosophy is based on axioms which must be sought from nature alone: faith is based on history and language, and must be sought for only in scripture and revelation...' Here theology seems to be accorded freedom to express its own subject matter. But the consequence which Spinoza draws is precisely the opposite: 'Faith, therefore, allows the greatest latitude in philosophic speculation' – in so far as philosophy does not teach opinions which are a summons to hatred, dispute and anger.[109]

The separation between philosophy and theology which Spinoza calls for is possible and conceivable for him only within the limits of universal reason: 'For what altar will shelter a man who has outraged reason?'[110] And so in truth what Spinoza teaches and achieves is only an apparent separation; for revelation, scripture and theology have – albeit in another way – to serve the same goal as reason, namely the furtherance of human virtue and happiness. The use and necessity of scripture and revelation lie in the fact that they proclaim this aim in the most understandable way: 'All are able to obey, whereas there are but very few, compared with the aggregate of humanity, who can acquire the habit of virtue under the unaided guidance of reason. Thus if we had not the testimony of scripture, we should doubt of the salvation of nearly all men.'[111]

In these presuppositions, which belong in the wider context of his philosophical system, lie the roots of the biblical criticism which Spinoza practises in the *Tractatus* with unusual acuteness. For only if the Bible was also deprived of the last semblance of a supernatural truth, i.e. one which is not evident to reason but only to authority, was the coherence of the system really secured.

So Spinoza criticizes Old Testament prophecy by stripping it of its supernatural character and deriving it from 'a more vivid imagination'.[112] The accommodation theory, which is used in sovereign fashion, takes up a good deal of space – as for example in the famous passages Josh.10.12f.; II Kings 20.11.[113] It also helps towards an understanding of the flood: 'According to the understanding of Noah it was revealed to him that God was about to destroy the whole human race, for Noah thought that beyond the limits of Palestine the whole world was not inhabited.'[114] Here, as in other passages, the influence of La Peyrère is evident; Spinoza had his *Pre-Adamites* and evidently used it a good deal.[115] In Chapter 6 of the *Tractatus* the miracles are subjected to critical examination, with the result that: 'We cannot gain knowledge of the existence and providence of God by means of miracles, but we can far better infer them from the fixed and immutable order of nature.' A real miracle, i.e. a transcending of or break in the natural order, 'not only can give us no knowledge of God, but, contrariwise, takes away that which we naturally have, and makes us doubt of God and everything else.'[116]

If here Spinoza – as we have seen – always takes familiar paths, he enters markedly new ground with his requirement of a 'history of scripture'. However, we must be cautious in seeing historical interest already at work here. On the contrary the foundation for this demand is thoroughly Cartesian. Spinoza states that 'the method of interpreting Scripture does not widely differ from the method of interpreting nature – in fact, it is almost the same. For as the interpretation of nature consists in the examination of the history of nature, and therefrom deducing definitions of natural phenomena on certain fixed axioms, so scriptural interpretation proceeds by the examination of scripture, and inferring the intention of its authors as a legitimate conclusion from its fundamental principles. By working in this manner everyone will always advance without danger of error... and will be able with equal security to discuss what surpasses our understanding and what is known by the natural light of reason.'[117]

We can see that this is the very notion that moved Meyer and d'Huisseau, namely the transference of the Cartesian method to the exegesis of scripture and theology, with the difference that Spinoza makes this transfer much more sensibly. The critical results which the application of this principle produces in the *Tractatus* are accordingly far more reliable and appropriate to the subject than anything which had previously appeared in this direction. We need not report them in detail here, as this has already been done frequently,[118] and in this context we are less concerned with the results than with the motives and presuppositions of the criticism.

And here it is decisive that with Ludwig Meyer, Isaac d'Huisseau and Spinoza, for the first time criticism is at the service of a system: the system of reason. If up to the middle of the century scriptural criticism had a completely positive tendency, now it began to be increasingly destructive. Socinians, Copernicans, the first critical chronologists and geographers were, like the Cartesian centre party, agreed that their criticism was necessary for the authority and credibility of scripture. Precisely because they saw a fatal danger to the authority of the Word of God in the contradiction between reason and revelation on the one hand and scripture and reason on the other, they gave themselves the task of reconciliation. But with growing self-confidence in reason, this aim receded. The new Spirit is so certain of itself that it no longer needs revelation. Authoritative though the rule of scripture had been, the rule of reason no longer tolerated any other authority. Now with this change the tasks and goals of criticism also changed. The increasing concern was systematically to shake the authority and credibility of the Bible, to unmask its history as obscure fiction and its theological statements as long obsolete prejudices which dissolved into insubstantial schemes in the light of reason.

For a century the radical position seemed to be the position of the future. From the time of Voltaire, the Europe of the Enlightenment was agreed on it until the earthquakes of the French Revolution. The aura of destruction and godlessness which has been attached to biblical criticism to the present day, derives from this time.

Only with the rise of historicism are new possibilities of understanding disclosed, and does a mediating position again emerge. Its basic principles were then taken up and developed further in nineteenth-century biblical criticism.

CONCLUSION

In the great controversy over the understanding and significance of the Bible which began with the rise of modern thought in the West, the most important positions were staked out around 1680. The Enlightenment may have changed the historical balance, but it did not introduce anything essentially new. Orthodoxy died out slowly, and with it the last group which held resolutely to the universal claim of scripture. By contrast, rational criticism was extended and made more radical. In between there were mediating positions of all degrees and shades from theological rationalism to supranaturalism, but none of them could escape the claims of reason. The less credible the historical statements of scripture appear in detail, the more theology takes refuge in 'eternal truths' which it believes that it finds there and which also exist before the forum of reason. The Bible becomes a handbook of morality whose doctrines are acceptable to any reasonable person.

This age of rational criticism is the first stage in the history of the development of historical-critical theology, in which its critical-rational component was formed. Initially as an antithesis to this utterly unhistorical criticism, the young Herder formulated his insight that human beings and their world are in principle historical. The price that the new possibility of the historical understanding of the Bible, which Herder thus opened up and practised with unusual historical sensitivity in his exegetical writings, had to pay was the abandonment of rationalist criticism. For Herder, the historical phenomenon as such is so singular that it rules out any criticism by analogy.[1]

The first to achieve a synthesis between rational criticism and historical understanding was Ferdinand Christian Baur, who thus becomes the founder of historical-critical theology in the modern sense.[2] The significance for modern intellectual history of the whole development, the beginnings of which I have attempted to describe here, can hardly be overestimated. The rise of criticism shattered natural trust in the literal truth of the Bible and thus robbed its authority of essential support. From now on, if its statements were held to be valid at all, they were held to be valid only in the religious sphere. But with the end of its universal rule there ended the rule of the mediaeval church, even if that only became clear centuries later.

Protestant theology will have to be careful to learn to see not only the loss but rather the gain in all this, and to teach what poverty and freedom have meant for the church at all times.

NOTES

Introduction: Historical-critical Theology as a Problem for Church History

1. R.Bultmann, 'New Testament and Mythology' (1941), in *New Testament and Mythology and other basic writings*, ed. Schubert M.Ogden, Philadelphia and London 1985, 1ff.: 11.

2. H.Liebing, 'Historisch-kritische Theologie. Zum 100. Todestag Ferdinand Christian Baurs am 2. Dezember 1960', *ZTK* 57, 1960, 303.

3. G.Hornig, *Die Anfänge der historisch-kritischen Theologie. J.S.Semlers Schriftverständnis und seine Stellung zu Luther*, FSTR 8, 1961. Similarly E.Hirsch, *Geschichte der neuern evangelischen Theologie im Zusammenhang mit den allgemeinen Bewegungen des europäischen Denkens* III, 1952, 59.

4. H.-J.Kraus, *Geschichte der Historisch-Kritischen Erforschung des Alten Testaments von der Reformation bis zur Gegenwart*, 1956, 64. Similarly P.Hazard, *La Crise de la Conscience Européenne (1680-1715)*, two vols, Paris 1935.

5. G.Bohrmann, *Spinozas Stellung zur Religion. Eine Untersuchung auf der Grundlage des theologisch-politischen Traktats*, 1914, 24. Similarly M.Grunwald, *Spinoza in Deutschland*, 1897, 12, and L.Strauss, *Die Religionskritik Spinozas als Grundlage seiner Bibelwissenschaft. Untersuchungen zu Spinozas Theologisch-Politischem Traktat*, Veröffentlichungen der Akademie für die Wissenschaft des Judentums, Philosophische Sektion II, 1930, 1.

6. G.Ebeling, 'The Significance of the Critical Historical Method for Church and Theology in Protestantism', in *Word and Faith*, London and Philadelphia 1963, 17ff.

7. Ibid., 42f.

8. F.C.Baur, *An Herrn Dr Karl Hase, Beantwortung des Sendschreibens der Tübinger Schule*, 1855, 22. Cf. also K.Scholder, 'F.Chr.Baur als Kritiker', *EvTh* 21, 1961, 448, 441ff., and W.Geiger, *Spekulation und Kritik. Die Geschichtstheologie F.Chr.Baurs*, 1964, 166ff.

9. Ebeling, 'Significance' (n.6), 42f. Similarly in 'Hermeneutik', *RGG*[3] III, 253: 'In terms of hermeneutics, the cultural change towards modernity sparks off a revolution which governs the whole future development, or itself represents a radical change in the conditions of understanding.'

10. See below, 169 n.73 and the literature in *RGG*[3] IV, 179f.

11. W.Krauss, 'Entwicklungstendenzen der Akademien im Zeitalter der Aufklärung', in *Studien zur deutschen und französischen Aufklärung*, 1963, 47.

12. On this see also M.Wundt, *Die deutsche Schulmetaphysik des 17.Jahrhunderts*, Heidelberger Abhandlungen zur Philosophie und ihre Geschichte 29, 1939, 18; he speaks of a 'resolute and almost unanimous repudiation of the modern mechanistic view of the world and thus of Western European philosophy by German thinkers'. Wundt's attempt to give a positive interpretation of this closedness 'under the notion of Volkstum' (I) has led to an excellent account of German scholastic metaphysics, but otherwise has not helped further.

13. K.Holl, 'Die Bedeutung der grossen Kriege für das religiöse und kirchlichen Leben innerhalb des deutschen Protestantismus', in *Gesammelte Aufsätze zur Kirchengeschichte* III, 1928, 317.
14. W.Elert, *Morphologie des Luthertums* I-II, 1931-32, here quoted from the revised edition of 1958.
15. Ibid., I., 364.
16. Ebeling, 'Significance' (n.6), 43.
17. Thus Hirsch, *Geschichte* (n.3), I, 135.

1. The Norm of Faith in Controversies between Catholics and Protestants

1. Quoted from K.Zeumer, *Quellensammlung zur Geschichte der Deutschen Reichsverfassung im Mittelalter und Neuzeit* ²1913, no.197, 395ff.
2. The corresponding article in the Münster Peace Treaty has almost the same wording. Cf. Zeumer, *Quellensammlung* (n.1), no.198, 434ff.
3. Surprisingly this aspect seems entirely to have escaped K.Heim, *Das Gewissheitsproblem in der systematischen Theologie bis zu Schleiermacher*, 1911, a fine account of the history of the problem of certainty; perhaps this is because he limits himself to the development of doctrine.
4. R.Descartes, *Meditations*, in *Discourse on Method and the Meditations*, trans.F.E.Sutcliffe, Harmondsworth 1968.
5. M.Pfaff, *Introductio in historiam theologiae literariam*, Liber II, Tübingen 1726, 290ff. Characteristically the titles appear under *Theologia dogmatica*; only a very few appear under *Theologia polemica*, III, 125f.
6. V.Magni, *De acatholicorum credendi regula iudicium*, Prague 1628. Here quoted from the reprint in the substantially enlarged *Valeriani Magni Iudicium de acatholicorum et catholicorum regula credendi*, Vienna 1641, in which the original writing is supplemented with six answers to various opponents [UB Tüb].
7. E.d'Alençon, *DTC* 9.2, 1927, cols. 1553ff.
8. J.Caramuel, *Theologia moralis fundamentalis* II, Rome ²1656, 14, quoted from *DTC* 9.2, col.1559.
9. *DTC* 9.2, col.1555.
10. For this and the preceding religious conversation see now H.Schüssler, *Georg Calixt. Theologie und Kirchenpolitik*, 1961, 118ff.
11. 'The Landgraf was convinced that real certainty about revelation could be found only in the infallible church...', ibid., 119.
12. G.W.Frank, *Geschichte der protestantischen Theologie*, Part 2, Leipzig 1865, 57.
13. For this see the contribution by H.G.Bloth, 'Der Kapuziner V.Magni und sein Kampf gegen den Jesuitenorden', in *Materialdienst des konfessionskundlichen Instituts* 7.5, 1956, 81-6, though this is not very illuminating. Unfortunately I could not examine the material cited on p.81.
14. *DTC* (n.7), col.1553. Moreover in his controversy with the Jesuits Pascal took up the case of Fr Valerian as an example of the slanderous methods of the order and thought: 'This Father has found your (the Jesuits') secret of keeping his mouth shut; that's what must be done whenever you accuse people without proof. One has only to reply to each one of you, like the Fr Capucin, "You lie shamelessly"' (15e lettre écrite par l'auteur des lettres au Provincial, *Oeuvres complètes*, Paris 1954, 845).

15. Bloth, 'Kapuziner' (n.13), 81.

16. I have not been able to discover the exact bibliographical title of the work. J.C.Zeumer (*Vitae professorum theologiae...in academia Jenensi*, ed. Christoph Weissenborn, Jena 1711, 117ff.) knows only of a *Iudicium de acatholicorum credendi regula*, Jena 1610 (sic!). Presumably the title was *Iudicium de acatholicorum credendi regula castigatum et confutatum*, Jena 1631 (S.Jöcher, *Allgemeines Gelehrten Lexicon* III, 1711, col.57).

17. J.Martini, *Vindiciae ecclesiae Lutheranae dei gratia ab absurdis superstitionis pontificiae sententiam eius de regula credendi*, Wittenberg 1631. For Martini and the 'Mirror of Reason' see E. Schlee, *Der Streit des Daniel Hofmann über das Verhältnis der Philosophie zur Theologie*, Marburg 1862, 49f. d'Alençon, *DTC* (n.9), col. 1559, wrongly locates Martini in Dresden.

18. J.Botsaccius, *Antivalerianus, sive religio romano-papistica probatur non esse vera, quia regulae credendi falsae innititur, contra Valeriani Magni iudicium*, Leipzig 1631.

19. For Stegman and his work see below, 22ff.

20. C.Bergius, *Praxis catholica divini canonis contra quasvis haereses et schismata, seu de fide catholica et christianorum quorumvis circa illud consensu vel dissensu. Dissertationes novem*, 1639. For C.Bergius, see *RE* II, 614, 12ff.

21. Here in the unpaginated foreword there is a list of his opponents which is partly more reliable than the information in d'Alençon, *DTC* (n.9), col.1559.

22. *Iudicium de iudicio Valeriani Magni super catholicorum et acatholicorum credendi regula, sive absurditatum echo*, Amsterdam 1644. *Iudicium Ulrici de Neufeldii de fidei catholicae regula catholica eiusque catholico usu. Ad Valerianum Magnum omnesque catholicos*, 1645. Valerianus' answer appeared in 1646; the two writings of F.A.Comenius under his name, but another title, again in 1658.

23. J.C.Dannhauer, *Gorgias Leontinus sophista in Valeriano Magno...redivivus, sive analysis iudicii de acatholicorum et catholicorum regula credendi producti a Valeriano Magno*, Strassburg 1652. For Dannhauer cf. *RE* II, 460ff.

24. Helmstedt 1654. See *RE* II, 269.

25. Straubing 1654.

26. *H.Conringii responsio ad Valerianum Magnum, pro sua concussione fundamentorum fidei pontificiae (sic!)*, Helmstedt 1654.

27. *Valeriani Magni capuccini Methodus* ἀμέθοδος *et ignis fatuus, sive I.Examen theologicum novae methodi ab ipso nuper profusae ad retrahendos protestantes sub iugam pontificis. II, Brevis refutatio libelli alterius quem postea subtitulo Lucis in tenebris lucentis emisit*, Groningen 1654. This title refers to two of Magni's works: *Methodus revocandi acatholicos ad ecclesiam catholicam*, Regensburg 1653, and *Lux in tenebris lucens quam tenebrae non comprehendunt*, Straubing 1654.

28. *RE* XII, 299.

29. *DTC* (n.9), cols 1561-3; Schüssler, 'Georg Calixt' (n.10); H.Liebing, *RGG*³ II, cols 601f.

30. For Magni's not insignificant philosophical works I must refer here to *DTC* (n.9), cols. 1556ff.

31. In what follows the page references in the text refer to the Vienna 1641 edition of the *Iudicium* (n.6).

32. The certainty and infallibility of scripture are generally grounded in divine authorship.This is in fact undisputed: 'When there is a question about the

authority of scripture, there cannot nor should not be any other response than that that divine authority of scripture is from God alone... And thus far the Papists are ready to agree with us.' But J.Gerhard, from whose *Loci theologici* this passage comes (1610-1625, here quoted from the second edition of 1657), immediately shows where the problem begins. 'But if it is further asked whence the divine authority of that scripture comes to us, there we divide in a difference of opinions' (quoted from C.H.Ratschow, *Lutherische Dogmatik zwischen Reformation und Aufklärung* I, 1964, 109).

33. It is clear that by taking up a thought from Gal.1.8 Magni is attempting to meet the Protestant scriptural principle as far as possible. That is also true of thesis 4. In fact Magni uses these theses against the traditionalists of the Roman church, especially the Jesuits, whose position E.Hutter (*Loci* [1619], Wittenberg 1661, *pro quaestio* VII, *propositio* II) reproduces as follows: 'Those things which are put forward under the heading and pretext of tradition, the same are to be believed by faith, as are those things which have manifest testimony in the scriptures. For after so many councils there is to be no more disputation on traditions but they are simply to be believed without any testing, because they are in truth apostolic, although they are manifestly in conflict with scripture' (Ratschow, *Lutherische Dogmatik* [n.32], 109).

34. Magni is thinking here of the so-called *Decretum Gelasianum* (cf. Denziger-Schönmetzer, *Enchiridion Symbolorum Definitionum seu Declarationum*, [3]1962, nos.350ff., esp., no.354; B.Altaner, *Patrologie*, [2]1950, 413f.; *RE* VI, 475, 15ff.). His dating is disputed. A Roman synod cannot be shown to have been held in 494.

35. Evidently Magni already succumbed to the misapprehension that the *testimonium Spiritus Sancti internum* is a movement in human beings, a *motus in mente Biblistarum*. In fact, however, by this term orthodoxy understands 'that within scripture by which it proves itself effective, and not anything within human beings' (Ratschow, *Lutherische Dogmatik* [n.32], 106).

36. There are some examples in Frank, *Geschichte* (n.12), II, 53ff.

37. *Loc.* I, *cap.* III, § 33 (Ratschow, *Lutherische Dogmatik* [n.32], 109f.).

38. The quotation appears in Magni's reply, ibid., 144. Similarly also J.Major: 'So the blemish of obscurity is not in the divinely inspired scriptures but in the minds of men, who walk in the vanity of their senses, having an intellect obscured with darkness, alienated from the life of God by the ignorance that is in them, for the blindness of their hearts, as Paul says in Ephesians 4.18,or because of the clouds remaining in their minds, or through blindness which the same apostle in II Corinthians 4.4 attributes not to so much to the malice and hostilities of the unfaithful as to the fraud and power of the devil' (ibid., 67).

39. For this see Quenstedt (*Theologia didacticopolemica*, 1685, Wittenberg [3]1696, *pars* I, *cap.* IV, *sectio* II, *quaestio* VII): 'The question is ...VI. not about obscurities of the scriptures in respect of the unregenerate... but in respect of faithful adults illuminated by the Holy Spirit. VII. Not about the transparency of scripture absolutely and taken by itself but about the transparency of scripture considered relatively, viz., in respect of our intellect. VIII. Not about this transparency apart from prayers, pious study, reading and meditation on scripture and in the first place the illumination of the Holy Spirit, and other aids in knowledge, but including these' (Ratschow, *Lutherische Dogmatik* [n.32], 125). The listing of the illumination of the Holy Spirit under the means of understanding is of course fatal and recalls Magni's formulations.

40. Ratschow, *Lutherische Dogmatik* (n.32), 72.

41. On this see also the answer to Botsack, ibid., 204, 217f.

42. M.Hafenreffer, *Loci theologici* (1600), Tübingen ³1606, *lib* I, *loc*.IV, *pars* 3.I-IV (Ratschow, *Lutherische Dogmatik* [n.32], 117).

43. *Gisberti Voetii selectarum disputationum theologicarum pars prima*, Utrecht 1648, p.1.

44. See above, 13f.

45. Eleutheropolis (i.e. Amsterdam) 1633. The work is extremely rare. C.Louise Thijssen-Schoute, *Nederlands Cartesianisme*, Verhandelingen d Kon.-Ned.Akad. van Wetenschapen, Afd.Letterkunde, NR LX, Amsterdam 1954, 395f., found the only known copy in the Koninklijke Bibliothek in the Hague. Here I quote from a microfilm of this copy, kindly provided by the library. I could not discover a London 1650 edition (*DTC* 9.2 [n.9], col.1560).

46. We owe our knowledge of the author of the *Brevis disquisitio* to C.Sandius, who in his *Bibliotheca antitrinitariorum* (Freistadt [Amsterdam] 1684, 133) gives J.Stegman (Thijssen-Schoute, *Cartesianisme* [n.45], 396). The 'three Stegman brothers' mentioned in *DTC* must be a mistake. We know of only father and son. Cf. O.Fock, *Der Socinianismus nach seiner Stellung in der Gesamtentwicklung der christlichen Geistes, nach seinem historischen Verlauf und nach seinem Lehrbegriff*, 1 Abt., Kiel 1847, 200f. This work, which is still indispensable because of its wealth of material, suffers above all from the lack of any historical differentiation between earlier and later Socinianism.

47. Fock, *Socinianismus* (n.46); cf. also E.M.Wilbur, *A History of Unitarianism, Socinianism and its Antecedents*, Cambridge, Mass. 1947, 505f.

48. Lessing's famous parable of the ring is the classical form of the answer which the eighteenth century attempted to give to this question.

2. *The Relationship between Reason, Scripture and Dogma among the Socinians*

1. E.M.Wilbur, *A History of Unitarianism, Socinianism and its Antecedents*, Cambridge, Mass. 1947, 525f.n.4. For further literature on Socinianism see below in the text; apart from the general works which he lists, E.M.Wilbur, *A Bibliography of the Pioneers of the Socinian-Unitarian Movement in Italy, Switzerland, Germany, Holland*, Sussidi eruditi 1, 1950, covers only the sixteenth century and breaks off with Servetus.

2. A.Calov, *Socinianismus profligatus*, Wittenberg 1652. J.G.Walch, *Einleitung in die Religionsstreitigkeiten… ausser der Evangelisch-Lutherischen Kirche* I, 1728, 579, thinks of this writing: 'Scholars have long noted that of all the works of Calov, those against Socinianism hold the prize.' Summarized in *Scripta anti-Sociniana in unum corpus redacta*, Ulm 1684ff. Cf. Wilbur, *History* (n.1), 525f., and M.Pfaff, *Introductio in historiam theologiae literariam*, Tübingen 1726, III, 325f., where the individual titles of this work are cited.

3. S.Maresius, *Hydra Socinianismi expugnata*, Groningen 1651-1662. We owe to this work knowledge of two otherwise lost Socinian tractates by J.Crellius (*De Deo et eius attributis*) and J.Volkelius (*De vera religione*), which Maresius prints complete and glosses.

4. J.A.Scherzer, *Collegium anti-Socinianum*, 1672, Leipzig ²1684: more than 1300 pages!

5. J.Stegman, *Photinianismus, hoc est, succincta refutatio errorum Photinianorum 56 disputationibus comprehensa*, Frankfurt 1653.

6. L.Diestel, 'Die socinianische Anschauung vom Alten Testamente in ihrer geschichtlichen und theologischen Bedeutung', *JdTh* 7, 1862, 711.

7. Pfaff, *Introductio* (n.2), III, 339f.

8. According to S.Kot, *Le mouvement antitrinitaire au XVIe et au XVIIe siècle, Bibliothèque d'Humanisme et Renaissance IV*, 1937, 16-58, 109-156, in its heyday in Poland, including foreigners the Socinian movement did not comprise more than a thousand families.

9. F.C.Baur, *Die christliche Lehre von der Dreieinigkeit und Menschwerdung Gottes in ihrer geschichtlichen Entwicklung*, Part 3, Tübingen 1843, 108. Cf.also G.Schramm, *Antitrinitarier in Polen, 1556-1658. Ein Literaturbericht*, Bibliothèque d'Humanisme et Renaissance XXI, 1959, 473: 'If the theses of the sixteenth-century anti-trinitarians also have points of contact with the Arian doctrines of the fourth century, this is not a mere historicizing reprise, but a position determined completely by contemporary forces.' Cf. also Wilbur, *History* (n.1), 416.

10. According to the report by Schramm, *Antitrinitarier* (n.9), 476.

11. Ibid., 478.

12. Wilbur, *History* (n.1), 523. The controversies with Servetus of course belong in the prehistory of modern antitrinitarianism but not necessarily in the prehistory of Socinianism. As Wilbur writes: 'Various attempts have been made to account for Socinianism as an outgrowth of earlier systems or thinkers, or as dependent upon them; but none of them is convincing. There are, indeed, resemblances to the thought of Servetus; but Socinus emphatically denied that he had drawn his views from that source' (416).

13. For the history and purpose of this dedication, which was felt by the Wittenbergers to be quite especial infamy, cf. H.-W.Gensichen, *Die Wittenberger anti-sozinianische Polemik. Ein Beitrag zur Auseinandersetzung von Reformation und Humanismus*, Göttingen theological dissertation, type-script, 1942, 38.

14. O.Fock, *Der Socinianismus nach seiner Stellung in der Gesamtentwicklung der christlichen Geistes, nach seinem historischen Verlauf und nach seinem Lehrbegriff*, 1 Abt., Kiel 1847, 183ff., and Wilbur, *History* (n.1), 408ff.

15. Of course a related factor here is that the printing of Socinian writings only began around 1600 (Wilbur, *History* [n.1], 524). They then left the Rakow press in quick succession and were circulated throughout Europe (Schramm, *Antitrinitarier* [n.9], 508). On the other hand Socinian ideas were already so well known anyway that about the turn of the century a Socinian circle could come into being at the University of Altdorf around the physician E.Soner, from which J.Crell and M.Ruarus emerged. Soner died in 1612 (Fock, *Socinianismus* [n.14], 234f.). C.Vorstius could also get to know Socinian writings at the University of Heidelberg as early as 1593 (Alexander Schweizer, 'Conradus Vorstius. Vermittlung der reformierten Centraldogmen mit den socinianischen Einwendungen', in *Theologische Jahrbücher*, ed. Baur and Zeller, XV, 1856, 437).

16. After the works by Wilbur and others (on this cf. the very instructive bibliographical account by Schramm, *Antitrinitarier*, n.9), we must put Poland's own contribution very much higher than has usually been done so far. Schramm thinks that the Polish scholars are quite right 'to evaluate anti-trinitarianism as a Polish contribution to European culture' (474).

17. In addition to the works by Baur, Fock and Wilbur already mentioned I

would cite here above all W.Dilthey, 'Weltanschauung und Analyse des Menschen seit Renaissance und Reformation', *Gesammelte Schriften* II, ²1960, esp.129ff.; A.von Harnack, *Lehrbuch der Dogmengeschichte* III, ⁵1932, 765ff.; H.E.Weber, *Reformation, Orthodoxie und Rationalismus*, 2, BFCT 2/51, 1951, 184ff. Socinianism is not discussed by E.Hirsch, *Geschichte der neuern evangelischen Theologie*, 1952.

18. Baur, *Dreieinigkeit* (n.9), 162.

19. Ibid., 183.

20. Ibid., 161.

21. Ibid., 162.

22. Harnack, *Lehrbuch* (n.17), 767.

23. Ibid.

24. Weber, *Reformation* (n.17), 192. That is also true in some respects of Ritschl's brilliant account (*A Critical History of the Christian Doctrine of Justification and Reconciliation*, I, Edinburgh 1872, 298ff.).

25. Harnack, *Lehrbuch* (n.17), 806.

26. Ibid., 798.

27. Ibid., 808.

28. Ibid., 807.

29. Perhaps also a more careful historical differentiation would have removed some problems here. One can hardly identify Socinian doctrine with F.Sozzini, find its content in the 1609 Rakow Catechism and cite this in the edition edited by Crell and Schlichting, with considerable changes, which appeared in Amsterdam around 1665 after the expulsion of the Poles.

30. Harnack, *Lehrbuch* (n.17), 786.

31. 'If this account of faith is censured for being defective, legalistic, Pelagian and Scotist, it is only because the real connecting thread through the Holy Scriptures is also all these things' (Dilthey, 'Weltanschauung' [n.17], 140).

32. Ibid., 137.

33. Ibid., 136.

34. Ibid., 137.

35. Weber, *Reformation* (n.17), 185.

36. Ibid., 188, 192ff., 197.

37. Ibid., 190 n.1.

38. Ibid., 184.

39. Ibid., 198.

40. On this see also K.A.Hase, *Kirchengeschichte, Lehrbuch für akademische Vorlesungen*, ¹⁰1877, 455: 'Socinianism... was never the heartbeat but the unrest in the Protestant church at the time of its increasingly rigid orthodoxy.'

41. *Catechesis ecclesiarum Polonicarum, unum deum patrem, illiusque filium unigenitum Jesum Christum, una cum spiritu sancto; ex sacra scriptura confitentium. Primum anno MDCIX in lucem emissa... atque per viros in his coetibus inclytos, Joh.Crellium Francum, hinc Ionam Schlichtingium a Bukowiec, ut et Martinum Ruarum, ac tandem Andream Wissowatium recognita atque emendata...*, Stauropolis [i.e. Amsterdam] 1680 (= Cat.2). In general I have quoted from this considerably expanded third edition and only go back to the first Latin edition, Rakow 1609 (= Cat.1), where it is necessary to demonstrate the development of Socinianism. Cf. Fock, *Socinianismus* (n.14), 183ff.

42. Cat.2, *Praefatio*, p.2. This preface is not in Cat.1, but appears for the first time in the second Polish edition (also used by Harnack) which was published

after the expulsion of the Socinians from Poland: *Irenopolis...post annum domini 1659.*

43. Otherwise this preface contains an acknowledgment of freedom and tolerance, of which Harnack says that no Protestant Christian can read it 'without being moved and involved' (*Lehrbuch* [n.17], 765). I quote a section here because at the same time it is characteristic of the spirit of Socinianism: 'In writing a catechism we are not prescribing anything for anyone; it is not our intention to oppress anyone. Each person should judge freely in religious questions: it is allowed to us only to express our conviction without harming or persecuting anyone. For that is the golden prophetic freedom which the Holy Scriptures of the New Testament impress so deeply on us and in which the early church of the apostles has borne the torch before us... Or do you alone have the key of wisdom, so that nothing is closed or sealed to you in Holy Scripture; so that what it discloses to you no one could conceal and what it conceals no one could disclose? Why do you not think that only one is our master to whom this is allowed, namely Christ, and that we are all brothers, to none of whom is given power and dominion over the conscience of others' (Cat.2, *Praefatio*, p.2). The preface is the only place in the whole catechism which has a degree of solemnity, and that is certainly no coincidence; underlying it are experiences which we need to take into account if we are to understand the motive force behind Socinianism. Here, moreover, the Socinians join company with the Arminians, whose aims Episcopius defines in very similar fashion in his great peroration to the Synod of Dordrecht: 'We did not intend, desire or seek anything other than to preserve that golden freedom which lies between slavery and libertinism' (C.Sepp, *Het godgeleerd onderwijs in Nederland gedurende de 16e en 17e eeuw*, Vol.2, Leiden 1874, 282).

44. The idea of continuing and completing Luther's Reformation 'is the starting point for the Socinian criticism of orthodox dogma'. In this context Gensichen (*Wittenberger* [n.13], 41) quotes a characteristic verse from the tradition: 'Old Babylon is falling: Luther destroyed the roofs, Calvin the walls, but Socinus the foundations.'

45. Stegman, *Brevis disquisitio*, 22.

46. Cat.1, p.1; Cat.2, which has made considerable progress in rationalization, no longer speaks of a 'manifest way of divinity' but of a 'way shown from God through Jesus Christ', Cat.2, p.1. For the relationship of Old and New Testaments see Diestel, 'Socinianische Anschauung' (n.6), 734ff.

47. *Praelectiones theologicae (Bibliotheca fratrum Polonorum, quos Unitarios vocant...*, Irenopolis [i.e. Amsterdam] post annum Domini 1656, I, 537ff.). Cf. Fock, *Socinianismus* (n.14), 307ff. For this problem cf. also W.J.Kühler, *Het Socinianisme in Nederland*, Leiden 1912, 230ff.

48. Cat.1, 18. In Cat.2 (p.9) *cognoscere* is replaced with *invenire*, which still leaves upon the possibility of natural knowledge.

49. Even if the catechism does not explicitly adopt a position on this, it is beyond question that the Socinians assumed an inspiration of scripture, but this only extended to the 'things necessary for salvation'. Cf. the Preface to Cat.2, xx, and Fock, *Socinianismus* (n.14), 328ff. (who also provides evidence from Socinian writings).

50. Cf. above, 23f.

51. Cat.1, p.7; Cat.2, p.3.

52. Cat.2, pp.3ff.

53. Cat.2, pp.4ff.

54. *De sacrae scripturae autoritate libellus* (*Bibliotheca fratrum Polonorum* I, p. 279). Cf. Fock, *Socinianismus*, 344ff.

55. Cat.1, p.14.

56. As one example of many see P.van Mastricht, *Novitatum Cartesianarum gangraena*, Amsterdam 1677, 60: 'The Socinians think that reason and scripture are the principle of theology...', and the further quotations there. Similarly P.Poiret, *Fides et ratio collatae*, Amsterdam 1708, 10: '..and Socinianism emerged, claiming that innermost divine light but in fact commending nothing other than human reason, its ideas and operations, to which indeed faith itself must be subject and by which the sacred scriptures are to be interpreted.'

57. Cat.2, p.xx.

58. Cat.2, p.8.

59. Cat.2, pp.8f. For this see also Diestel, 'Socinianische Anschauung' (n.6), 740f.

60. Cat.2, pp.8f., point 4; Fock, *Socinianismus* (n.14), 363f.

61. Diestel, 'Socinianische Anschauung' (n.6), 768; cf. also Harnack, *Lehrbuch* (n.17), 790: 'Here [in scriptural proof against dogma] the Socinians did sterling work and freed exegesis from the spell of dogma. Their discussions, exegetical and polemical, are largely irrefutable.'

62. Anonymus [J.Stegman Sr], *De iudice et norma controversiarum fidei libri* II, Eleutheropolis (i.e. Amsterdam) 1644 [UB Leiden. MF] I, ch.3. On this cf. also the quotation from Crell in Fock, *Socinianismus* (n.14), 383 n.13.

63. Fock, *Socinianismus* (n.14), 384. Cf. also the section on Socinian exegesis in Baur, *Dreieinigkeit* (n.9), 165ff.

64. *Brevis disquisitio*, 33.

65. Ibid., 34f.

66. The most important Socinian works on the theme are given in Fock, *Socinianismus* (n.14), 456 n.71.

67. Ibid., 464.

68. Ibid., 473.

69. Cat.2, 15.

70. Cat.2, 16.

71. Cf. *RE* III, 45.45ff.

72. Above, n.61. Cf. also Fock, *Socinianismus* (n.14), 458ff.

73. S.von Dunin-Borkowski, SJ, *Spinoza IV* (Aus den Tagen Spinozas, Part 3), 1936, 114.

74. Ibid.

75. Fock, *Socinianismus* (n.14), 384f., here follows the *Religio rationalis* by A.Wissowatius, which appeared in 1685, probably in Amsterdam, after his death in 1678. For details see Kühler, *Socinianisme* (n.47), 230 n.2, and Wilbur, *History* (n.1), 572. This work, which is probably influenced by philosophical developments in the second half of the seventeenth century, marks a conclusion to the rationalization of Socinianism and in some respects was already out of date when it appeared. See also Schramm, *Antitrinitarier* (n.9), 490ff.

76. Baur, *Dreieinigkeit* (n.9), 166.

77. See Kühler, *Socinianisme* (n.47), 234ff.

78. Ibid., 235.

79. Ibid., 144. Cf. also the lapidary formula in *RGG*³ VI, 1024 ('Trinität II'):

'It is generally agreed that there is no doctrine of the Trinity in the New Testament.'
80. Ibid., 30ff.

3. The Credibility of the Biblical Picture of the World: I. Copernicus and the Consequences

1. For the intrinsic connection between world-view and faith see also E.Hirsch, *Geschichte der neuern evangelischen Theologie* I, 1952, 117ff. H.Blumenberg, *Die kopernikanische Wende*, 1965, has recently with justification stressed the particular significance of astronomy for the development of the modern picture of the world: '...for the self-understanding of modern times, until well into the nineteenth century, astronomy was to become something like the *model process* which the human spirit had to develop for the investigation and confirmation of its capacity for knowledge and its universal objectification of nature. Only in this way could Copernicus achieve a paradigmatic significance for modernity which could not be justified through the purely theoretical content of his astronomical reform and its scope, which was soon seen to be partial', ibid. 11.

2. Here for the sake of brevity I refer to the accounts in Elert, *Morphologie des Luthertums* I, ²1958, 366ff., and H.Bornkamm, 'Kopernikus im Urteil der Reformatoren', *AfRG* 40, 1943, 171ff., here quoted from the reprint in *Das Jahrhundert der Reformation*, 1961, 177-85. For the whole question see also A.Titius, 'Naturwissenschaft und Theologie', *RE* 24, 195ff., and Blumenberg, *Kopernikanische Wende* (n.1), 100-21: 'Reformation und Kopernikanismus'.

3. Cf. the text and notes in Elert, *Morphologie* (n.2), 367ff., and Bornkamm, 'Kopernikus' (n.2), especially 184f.

4. Ibid., 364. Hirsch, who takes a similar position, is here largely dependent on Elert, cf. Hirsch, *Geschichte* I (n.1), 115 n.1.

5. WA Tischreden 4, no.4638, 412f.

6. Bornkamm, 'Kopernikus' (n.2), 178.

7. Elert, *Morphologie* (n.2), 221.

8. Ibid., 364. Elert's thesis has largely been taken up by the literature. Cf. Hirsch, *Geschichte* I (n.1), 114f., and J.Baur, *Die Vernunft zwischen Ontologie und Offenbarung. Eine Untersuchung zur Theologie J.A.Quenstedts*, 1962, 127ff.

9. Elert, *Morphologie* (n.2), 220f. n.2.

10. L.Günther, *Kepler und die Theologie. Ein Stück Religions- und Sittengeschichte aus dem XVI und XVII Jahrhunderten*, 1905. He says of Kepler's work *De sacra coena domini* of 1599 that it was 'directed against individual parts of the Formula of Concord, above all the... doctrine of the ubiquity of the body and blood of Christ' (82ff.) For Kepler's understanding of the eucharist see his *Unterricht vom Heiligen Sakrament des Leibes und des Blutes Jesu Christi, unseres Erlösers*, Prague 1617, 89ff. esp.96.

11. *CR* 13, cols.213ff.

12. Elert, *Morphologie* (n.2), 368; similarly Bornkamm, 'Kopernikus' (n.2), 182.

13. *CR* 13, cols.216f. Elert, *Morphologie* (n.2), quotes the last sentence as evidence for his view, with the comment: 'So scriptural proof is meant to be a deterrent against bringing the liberal arts into disorder.' However, that is certainly not what it says. Rather, here scriptural proof is clearly claimed as a guarantee of the truth of the old picture of the world as against all new 'illusions'.

It is all very well writing 'No one can claim that this "scriptural proof" penetrated anywhere close to the centre of Protestant theology' (Elert, *Morphologie*, n.2), but Lutheran theologians passionately defended this scriptural proof for more than a century and probably regarded it as central, even if for understandable reasons it is no longer so for a Lutheran systematic theologian in the twentieth century (cf. also Titius, *RE* 24, p.196, 56ff.). Following E.Wohlwill ('Melanchthon und Copernicus', in *Mitteilungen zur Geschichte der Medizin und der Naturwissenschaften* 3, 1904, 260-7), H.Blumenberg has pointed out that 'the second edition of the *Initia* which appeared only a year later (1550), while in other respects the same as the first, shows quite considerable changes in the comments on Copernicus' (ibid., 108). A closer comparison of both editions, however, leads him to conclude that Melanchthon did not depart from his basic conviction in this question: 'So in fact not even a small step is taken towards Copernicus' (ibid., 112).

14. Nuremberg 1543, from J.Petreius.

15. E.Hirsch, *Die Theologie des Andreas Osiander und ihre geschichtliche Voraussetzungen*, 1919, 118f.

16. The preface is printed in Hirsch, *Osiander* (n.15), 290. For the whole question see also Blumenberg, *Kopernikanische Wende* (n.1), 41ff., 92ff.

17. P.Gassendi, *Nicolai Copernici vita*, The Hague 1655, 310f. Quoted from A.von Humboldt, *Kosmos. Entwurf einer physischen Weltbeschreibung* II, Stuttgart and Augsburg 1847, 498f. n.24.

18. Hirsch, *Osiander* (n.16), 120.

19. E.J.Dijksterhuis, *Die Mechanisierung des Weltbildes* (1950), German 1956, 330. Cf. also M.Born, *Die Relativitätstheorie Einsteins*, [3]1922, 251: 'Thus the return to the Ptolemaic position of the "resting earth" becomes a possibility; it would mean the use of a system of reference firmly bound to the earth... From Einstein's lofty position, Ptolemy and Copernicus are equally right; both standpoints provide the same natural laws... Which standpoint one chooses cannot be decided on in principle but is a matter of convenience. However, for the mechanics of the planetary system Copernicus' view is the more convenient.' See Blumenberg, *Kopernikanische Wende* (n.1), 45f., who comes to the conclusion: 'Osiander's disloyalty was supported by historical consequences but opposed by historical truth' (ibid., 47).

20. To be read with Hirsch as an emendation of *unus*.

21. Bornkamm, 'Kopernikus' (n.2), 180.

22. Cf. the extended demonstration in A.C.Crombie, *Augustine to Galileo, The History of Natural Science, AD 400-1650*, London 1952, and the reference to Johannes Buridan in Blumenberg, *Kopernikanische Wende* (n.1), 13. There is a good parallel to Osiander, say, in A.Nifo (1473-1546), who came from the Padua school. In *De caelo et mundo commentaria*, Venice 1553, he writes this on the evaluation of astronomical hypotheses: 'In a good argument the effect necessarily follows from the cause assumed and this must be assumed to be necessary with respect to the observed effect. If one assumes eccentricities and epicycles, it is certain that the appearance will be confirmed. But the reverse is not necessarily the case, that if the phenomena are given, the eccentricities and epicycles must exist. That is only provisionally the case until a better explanation is found which both necessitates the phenomena and also is required for them. Thus all those are in error who decide for a single cause.' So Rheticus is not, as

Bornkamm, 'Kopernikus', evidently thinks, the author of the concept of the hypothesis. Cf. also Blumenberg, *Kopernikanische Wende* (n.1), 87f.

23. Galilei, *Opere*, Edizione nazionale, XII, 171. Cf. Dijksterhuis, *Mechanisierung* (n.19), 429.

24. Bornkamm, 'Kopernikus' (n.2), 181.

25. S.Maresius, *De abusu philosophiae Cartesianae, surrepente et vitando in rebus theologicis et fidei dissertatio theologica*, Groningen 1670 [UB Erl.], 26f.

26. Dijksterhuis, *Mechanisierung* (n.19), 333.

27. Elert, *Morphologie* (n.2), 369ff; Bornkamm, 'Kopernikus' (n.2), esp. 184f.

28. Elert, *Morphologie* (n.2), 371. Similarly Hirsch, *Geschichte* I (n.1), 115: 'Copernicus' theory owes its first publication and its first circulation entirely to the renewal of science as a result of the Lutheran Reformation.'

29. It is perhaps not superfluous to point out that here we are initially concerned only with the specific problem of Copernicus' discovery. The general question of the relationship between the Reformation and modern natural science is extremely difficult to understand in view of the complexity of both terms. It is certain that Elert's Lutheran provincialism has not taken into account its European dimensions. I must limit myself here to referring to at least the most important current literature. R.Hoykaas, 'Science and Reformation', *Cahiers d'histoire mondiale* III.1, 1956, 109-39 (the short bibliography on 139 is important) has pointed to the connections between Calvinism and scientific development and stressed e.g. the significance of Calvin's exegetical treatment of Genesis: 'Consequently, it is to Calvin's great credit that he recognized the discrepancy between the scientific world system of his days and the biblical text, and secondly, that he did not repudiate the results of scientific research on that account' (136). R.H.Bainton, ibid., 140f., has added 'Critical Comments' with the question: 'The examples are taken from England and Holland, but what of Catholic Germany, Catholic France, Italy and Spain?' Hoykaas' answer (in *Cahiers d'histoire mondiale* III.3, 1957, 781-4) does not take things substantially further. But the contribution by F.Russo SJ, 'Rôle respectif du Catholicisme et du Protestantisme dans le développement des sciences aux XVIᵉ et XVIIᵉ siècles' (ibid., III.4, 853-80) is interesting. Russo attacks the statistical method of J.Pelseneer, 'L'origine Protestante de la science moderne', in *Lychnos*, 1946-47, 246, which had established a very marked numerical preponderance of Protestant scientists in the sixteenth and seventeenth centuries (cf. also Hoykaas, 'Science', 109f.). According to Russo, no certain correlation can be established between confession and scientific tendencies: 'There is no really certain evidence that the activity of Catholic or Protestant countries is bound up with their religious attitudes. In any case, it would be necessary to take account of cultural and economic factors, which are at least just as important' (879f.).

S.F.Mason, 'The Scientific Revolution and the Protestant Reformation', in *Annals of Science* 8, 1952, 64-87, 154-75, evaluates the natural philosophical aspect, which is generally noted far too ltitle; he similarly refers to Pelseneer (64f.). I would not venture a verdict given the present state of discussion. The one thing that is certain is that the one-sided claim for Luther and Lutheranism as influences on the development of modern natural science is not tenable in that form.

30. Thus e.g. Hirsch, *Geschichte* I (n.1), 135: 'For the relationship between the European spirit and Christianity has been blighted by the fact that at this

very moment the Roman church made a desperate attempt by means of the instruments of its inquisition and censorship to eliminate the new doctrine, which had finally been consolidated by facts, and to stress as an unassailable dogmatic principle the connection between Christian thought and the old picture of the world, which in fact is grounded in history.'

31. Hooykaas, 'Science' (n.29), 136. Ignorant of these facts, Elert, *Morphologie* (n.2), 377, makes the 'incursion of an unevangelical biblicism' responsible for the theological intolerance of the seventeenth century towards the astronomers. As things are, it is very much more probable that the extension and consolidation of the Copernican theory sparked off the general theological polemic. Otherwise we would have to conclude that until about 1630 the Roman and Reformed churches (the former contented itself in 1616 with a warning to Galileo) had an evangelical Lutheran understanding of scripture which made it possible for them to tolerate the new doctrine.

32. Cf. Dijksterhuis, *Mechanisierung* (n.19), 343, 426.

33. J.Kepler, *Opera omnia*, ed. C.Frisch, Frankfurt 1854ff., I, 95ff.

34. Venice 1610, here quoted from the edition by M.T.Cardini, Florence 1948.

35. '*Mathemata mathematicis scribuntur.*' Cf. Dijksterhuis, *Mechanisierung* (n.19), 331.

36. On 11 June 1598, Kepler wrote to Maestlin in connection with a letter of M.Hafenreffer (see n.43 below): 'What shall we do? The whole of astronomy is not worth causing offence to one of Christ's little ones. Since the majority of doctors do not ascend to the heights of astronomy (as it would seem) in their intellect: act the Pythagorean or at least let us also imitate their practice. Let us communicate candidly our view to anyone who approaches us privately. In public let us keep silent. Why should we destroy astronomy by astronomy?' (*Opera* I, 38).

37. For its rapid circulation see e.g. R.Laemmel, *Galileo Galilei und sein Zeitalter*, 1942, 95ff.

38. Dijksterhuis, *Mechanisierung* (n.19), 425.

39. *Astronomia nova*, αἰτιολόγητος, *seuphysica coelestis tradita commentariis de motibus stellae Martis*, Prague 1609 (*Opera omnia* III, 136). On this see 453 n.15.

40. There is already a sharp refutation of Osiander by Kepler in the *Apologia Tychonis contra Ursum* of 1599 (*Opera* I, 236ff..., esp.245ff.).

41. *Opera* III, 153-6.

42. Ibid., 153. Cf. also the work *Tertius interveniens* of 1610 directed against Feselius, *Opera* I, 547ff., esp.594: 'It is indeed the case that whenever D.Feselius and others are in a dilemma they resort to Holy Scripture. It is as if the Holy Spirit taught astronomy or physics in scripture and did not rather have a higher intent for which he made use not only of their words and language, communicated to men formerly, but also their popular knowledge of natural things to which they attain with eyes and outward senses? But one could overturn all science and specially also geography simply from the book of Job if no one understood scripture rightly, but only Feselius and his followers.'

43. *Opera* I, 37f. Cf. also the *Vita Joannis Kepleri*, Opera VIII, 978f. To read out of this letter 'that Tübingen theology also wanted to preserve freedom of science' and that Hafenreffer here recognizes 'the autonomy of scientific research' (Elert, *Morphologie*, n.2, 376f.) is somewhat absurd. On the contrary,

Hafenreffer will in no circumstances allow this 'autonomy' which exerts pressure towards the reality of phenomena, for biblical theological reasons. Moreover terms like 'freedom' and 'autonomy of the sciences' are *a priori* questionable for the sixteenth century.

44. *Opera* III, 153.

45. *Opera* III, 154f.

46. Cf. also the fine exegesis of Gen.1.1 (*Opera* III, 154): 'In the beginning, Moses says, God created heaven and earth, because these two parts are more obvious to the sense of the eyes. As if Moses were to say to man: God created all the structure of the world which you see, bright above and dark and stretched out wide below, on which you stand and with which you are covered.'

47. Aristotle's saying, which was well known at that time, ran: 'Socrates is a friend, Plato is a friend, but the truth is a greater friend.' Cf. C.Louise Thijssen-Schoute, *Nederlands Cartesianisme*, Verhandelingen d. Kon.Ned.Akad. van Wetenschapen, Afd.Letterkunde, NR LX, Amsterdam 1954, 475 n.2.

48. *Opera* I, 36.

49. *Opera* I, 40. The editor adds: 'It appears from these letters that the opinions of Copernicus were no more approved of by men in Italy who observed the Catholic faith than they were at that time by the Lutherans in Germany, as evidence for which we have Hafenreffer' (41).

50. *Opera* I, 42.

51. 'Lettera di Madama Cristina di Lorena, Granduchessa di Toscana' [1615]: *Opere di Galileo*, Edizione nazionale V, 1895, 307-48.

52. We have this work only in a Latin translation: *Epistola... circa Pythagoricorum, et Copernici opinionem de mobilitate terrae, et stabilitate solis: et de novo systemate seu constitutione mundi: in qua sacrae scripturae autoritates, et theologicae propositiones, communiter adversus hanc opinonem adductae conciliantur... ex Italica in Latinam linguam perspicue et fideliter nunc conversa. Iuxta editionem Neapoli... anno 1615.* It also appears, along with the section from Kepler's preface to the *Astronomia* which we have already met, in the appendix to the (first?) Latin translation of Galileo's *Dialogo sopra i due massimi sistemi del mondo*: *Dialogus de systemate mundi, autore Galilaeo Galilaei*, Augustae Treboc. (Strassburg) 1635. Bonaventure and A.Elzevir supervised the printing from Leiden. The translator and editor is the Strassburg philologist, historian and mathematician M.Bernegger (1582-1640), a close friend of Kepler's and one of the most important cultural go-betweens of his time. During the Thirty Years' War his house 'was an information centre for the cultural elite of Germany and beyond as a result of his wide-ranging correspondence' (*NDB* 2,106f.). The only Latin translation of Galileo's letter to Grand Duchess Christina known to us comes from the same group: *Nov-antiqua sanctissimorum patrum, et probatorum theologorum doctrina, de sacrae scripturae testimoniis, in conclusionibus mere naturabilis, qua sensata experientia, et necessariis demonstrationibus evinci possunt temere non usurpandis: in gratiam serenissimae Christianae Lotharginae... privatim ante complures annos, Italico idiomate conscripta a Galilaeo Galilaei*, Strassburg 1636. The editor and translator of the bilingual edition is R.Robertin (1600-1648), a friend and pupil of Bernegger and a much travelled man, who later became the admired centre of a poetic circle in his home town of Königsberg (see *ADB* 28, 722ff., and *RE* IV, 14ff.). In the preface addressed to Bernegger he writes of 'a discourse not previously, so far as I know, published, but sought after with curiosity by many, seen, taken

by me some fifteen years ago and diligently kept among my valuable possessions from Italy...' We do not know whether these publications had any effect in Germany.

53. The page references in the text refer to *Opera* V, 432ff.

54. There is a complete English translation of the letter in S.Drake, *Discoveries and Opinions of Galileo*, New York 1957 (n.22), 432ff.

55. See above, 48f.

56. On this see J.Moltmann, *Theology of Hope*, London and New York 1967, 293.

57. To begin with he explicitly states (314f.) that he would like to see his work torn up and put in the flames if anything is found in it contrary to church and piety. We cannot venture to decide how serious he was.

58. In view of this work, and in comparison with Kepler, Galileo's contribution to the theological sphere seems rather more than 'modest' (against Hirsch, *Geschichte* [n.1], I, 205).

59. Dijksterhuis, *Mechanisierung* (n.19), 357.

60. For this much disputed question, which is of great significance for the later trial, cf. Laemmel, 'Galileo' (n.37), 163.

61. Ibid., 161.

62. The letter is reprinted in *Opere di Galilei*, Edizione nazionale XII, 171f. Evidently Bellarmine was wrongly informed here about Copernicus' view. The view put forward by Dijksterhuis (*Mechanisierung*, n.19, 429), that Bellarmine was the only wise man in the Galileo controversy, certainly cannot be maintained in that form. As early as 1908 P.Huhem, 'Essai sur la notion de théorie physique de Platon et Galilei', in *Annales de philosophie chrétienne* 8, 1908, 584f., 588, thought that recent developments in physics had shown logic to be on the side of Osiander, Bellarmine and Urban VIII and not on the side of Kepler and Galileo, as the former had recognized the real significance of the experimental method and the latter had misunderstood it, in that one can argue from a theory only to possibility and not to the reality of particular processes. This view, which recurs in Hirsch as possibly an 'extremely modern scientific theory' (*Geschichte* I [n.1], 120) and still in Moltmann (*Die Theologie in der Welt der modernen Wissenschaften*, 1963, 4), fails to note that at any rate for the seventeenth century truth was clearly on Kepler's and Galileo's side. They understood the argumentation *ex suppositione* for what it was at the time: an expedient which was intolerable in the long run because it was dishonourable.

63. *Dialogo di Galileo Galilei... sopra i due massimi sistemi del mondo Tolemaico e Copernicano*, Florence 1632. 'Save... that I do not feel, nor have I ever felt, that I should give praise to others for this fantastic view which I myself deny to it. I would hardly object if it were described as an empty chimaera, as a monstrous paradox'. Similarly 271, 372, etc. The work was the direct occasion for the intervention of the Inquisition.

4. The Credibility of the Biblical Picture of the World: II. The Problem of World History

1. E.J.Dijksterhuis, *Die Mechanisierung des Weltbildes* (1950), German 1956, 319.

2. Thus e.g. H. von Srbik, *Geist und Geschichte vom deutschen Humanismus bis zur Gegenwart* I, 1950, 114. So too, with qualifications, W.Kaegi in his fine

article 'Voltaire und der Zerfall des christlichen Geschichtsbildes', in *Historische Meditationen* I, Zurich 1942, 223ff.; F.Meinecke, *Die Entstehung des Historismus*, Werke III, 1959, 73ff.

3. A.Borst, *Der Turmbau von Babel. Geschichte der Meinungen über Ursprung und Vielfalt der Sprachen und Völker* III, 1, 1960, gives an unusually impressive picture of the slow alteration to conceptions of universal history. This is no place to provide a detailed evaluation of this 'world history of a single detail' (ibid., vi), but that is all the more reason for stressing it here. The bibliography in Vol.IV, 1963, 2119ff., is also important.

4. Kaegi, 'Voltaire' (n.2), 229, has referred to 'the small crack in the royal building', namely the uncertainty in chronology, which was 'to deepen within a few decades and was to contribute to the collapse'.

5. A.Klempt, *Die Säkularisierung der universalhistorischen Auffassung. Zum Wandel des Geschichtsdenkens im 16. und 17. Jahrhundert*, Göttinger Bausteine zur Geschichtswissenschaft 31, 1960, 12.

6. On this cf. K.Kretschmer, *Geschichte der Geographie*, 1923, especially the section on 'Geography in the time of the Great Discoveries up to the Middle of the Seventeenth Century', 69ff.

7. E.Hassinger, *Das Werden des neuzeitlichen Europa 1300 bis 1600*, 1959, 1-6, recalls the (extreme) case of a French account of the world from the second half of the sixteenth century 'which does not mention America at all'! This is 'a striking warning not to overestimate the rate at which people took note of the "New World"'.

8. Kaegi, who in his dating is largely dependent on Hazard, even wants to put it a century later: 'Only towards the end of the seventeenth and beginning of the eighteenth century did descriptions by missionaries, colonial officials and officers, and also simple travel accounts, flood so abundantly into Europe that they first gave the educated public a concrete, reliable picture of foreign cultures and secondly made the value of these cultures a problem' ('Voltaire' [n.2], 242).

9. *Bibliotheca fratrum Polonorum* I, 538. The *Praelectiones* were probably written around 1600 but only published after Sozzini's death in 1604: O.Fock, *Der Socinianismus nach seiner Stellung in der Gesamtentwicklung der christlichen Geistes, nach seinem historischen Verlauf und nach seinem Lehrbegriff*, 1 Abt., Kiel 1847, 170. Cf. also L.Strauss, *Die Religionskritik Spinozas als Grundlage seiner Bibelwissenschaft. Untersuchungen zu Spinozas Theologisch-Politischem Traktat*, Veröffentlichungen der Akademie für die Wissenschaft des Judentums, Philosophische Sektion II, 1930, 35 n.40.

10. *Praelectiones theologicae* (n.9).

11. See below, 82ff.

12. Kaegi, 'Voltaire' (n.2), 225f.

13. This account of world history, which was widespread at the time of the Reformation, appeared for the first time in German in 1532. For Melanchthon's authorship cf. E.Menke-Glückert, *Die Geschichtsschreibung der Reformation und Gegenreformation. Bodin und die Begründung der Geschichtsmethodologie durch Bartolomäus Keckermann*, 1912, 23ff. For the person of J.Carion and the source analysis of the chronicles see ibid., 136ff., 143ff. I quote here from the Latin version, to some extent the last, which Melanchthon published in 1558 along with lectures on the same subject. It is in *CR* XII, 711ff.

14. *CR* XII, 714.

15. After its first appearance in 1541 this short work, which Luther himself

describes in the preface expressly as a 'private occasional piece', had a considerable circulation. The Latin text is in *WA* 53, 22ff. For the history of the text and the composition see ibid., 1ff. Here I follow the German translation of J.Aurifaber Vratislaviensis, *Chronica des Ehrnwirdigen Herrn D.Mart.Luther Deudsch*, Wittenberg 1550. This translation had gone through three further editions by 1559.

16. Ibid., preface, unpaginated (a ij and end). Flacius makes quite similar comments in his *Clavis scripturae sacrae* of 1567 (ed. J.Musaeus, Jena 1674, I, 90). There, in connection with the discussions of the problems of chronology, we read: 'But if you notice other differences in numbering, beyond doubt there are certain reasons for them; and it is important to be open to them... But we have followed (as far as possible) the authority of scripture, to which we know it is safest to adhere.' See also G.Moldaenke, *Schriftverständnis und Schriftdeutung im Zeitalter der Reformation* I, *Matthaeus Flacius Illyricus*, FzKGG 9, 1936, 208, esp n.125.

17. The address 'Young Ones', which occasionally appears in the *Chronicon Carionis*, recalls the contemporaneous lecture of Melanchthon, Menke-Glückert, *Geschichtsschreibung* (n.13), 37.

18. Apries, an Egyptian Pharaoh of the Twenty-Sixth Dynasty, ruled from 588 to 570 BC. The Hebrew form of the name is Hophra. The prophecy in Jer.44.30 refers to him.

19. *CR* XII, 714.

20. *CR* XII, 714.

21. On this see *RE* II, 512.9ff.

22. However, that does not apply to all. One exception is S.Franck, *Chronika, Zeitbuch und Geschichtsbibel von Anbeginn bis 1531*, the material in which is largely dependent on Schedel. But the *Historiarum et chronicorum totius mundi epitome* of the Augsburg doctor and historian A.P.Gasser (1533; I used the third edition of 1538) is still divided according to the ages of the world. For Gasser (1505-1577), the first Protestant historian of Augsburg and friend of Flacius, cf. *NDB* 6, 79ff.

23. *CR* XII, 717. The saying appears in Talmud Sanhedrin 97a/97b and Aboda Zara 9a.

24. P.v.Burgos (Paulus a.S.Maria), a rabbinically trained Jew who later went over to Christianity and died around 1435 as Archbishop of Burgos (*RGG*³ V, 190). The quotation comes from *Scrutinium scripturarum*, Paris 1434, I, dist.3, Cap.4. Cf. also *WA* 53, 11ff.

25. The *Coniecturae* were intended as a preliminary study for a chronicle of the world and appeared in Latin in Nuremberg in 1544, and in Germany a year later. Cf. E.Hirsch, *Die Theologie des Andreas Osiander und ihre geschichtlichen Voraussetzungen*, 1919, 129.

26. Ibid., 132f.

27. *CR* XII, 717. For Melanchthon's view of history see also Klempt, *Säkularisierung* (n.5), 17ff.

28. *CR* XII, 718.

29. *CR* XII, 719.

30. *CR* XII, 713.

31. Ibid., unpaginated (A, ij f). Later Aurifaber becomes even clearer: 'And in sum contempt for such scripture and recollection of histories and their order is not only a coarse Tartar and Cyclopean barbarism but a devilish madness...'

Cf. also the quotation from the notes of a lecture by Melanchthon cited by Menke-Glückert, *Geschichtsschreibung* (n.13), 37: 'He is a coarse sow who does not delight in the knowledge of histories.'

32. Ibid. (A, iii).

33. For Bibliander cf. *RE* III, 185ff.

34. T.Bibliander, *De ratione temporum, christianis rebus et cognoscendis et explicandis accomodate liber unus*, Basel 1551, Epistola, unpaginated (a 2 v).

35. For Bodin see *Dictionnaire de Biographie Française* 6, 1954, cols. 758f. The information in *RGG*³ I, 1339, is quite inadequate. Cf. also Borst, *Turmbau* (n.3), III.1, 1244ff.

36. Up to 1650 I have discovered no fewer than twelve editions: Paris 1566 quarto; ibid., 1572 octavo: Basel 1576 octavo: the reprint in *Artis historicae penus*, Basel 1573 and ²1579, circulated widely; Lyons 1583 octavo; Heidelberg 1583 octavo; Geneva 1595 octavo: Strassburg 1599 16mo; Strassburg 1607 16mo; Geneva 1610 octavo; Amsterdam 1650 12mo. The list is certainly incomplete.

37. The page numbers in the text refer to the first edition, Paris 1566.

38. For the significance of the *Heptaplomeres* see E.Benz, 'Der Toleranz-Gedanke in der Religionswissenschaft', *DVfLG* 12, 1934, 540-71, which also lists the earlier literature.

39. 'Because no fruits of history are riper than those which can be gathered about the status of republics...' Preface, unpaginated (** a ij v).

40. For the following cf. Methodus, Cap.VII: 'A refutation of those who posit four monarchies and ages of gold', ibid., 346ff.

41. Unpaginated (** a v).

42. Cap. VIII: *De temporis universi ratione*.

43. However, it certainly not possible to universalize this into a 'marked lack of critical sense', as Menke-Glückert, *Geschichtsschreibung* (n.13), 118, attempts.

44. *La Démonomanie des sorciers*, Paris 1578, etc.; in Latin under the title *De magorum daemonomania*, Basel 1581, etc.; in German under the title *De magorum daemonomania. vom ausgelassnen wütigen Teuffelsheer, allerhand Zauberen, Hexen und Hexenmeistern, Unholden usw.*, translated by J.Fischart, 1586. Cf. also *RE* VIII, 35.

45. Cf. e.g. E.Feist, *Weltbild und Staatsidee bei Jean Bodin*, Marburg philosophical dissertation 1930 (partially printed), 14ff.

46. Ibid., 238.

47. Ibid., 239.

48. This compendium of the chronological knowledge of the time appeared for the first time in Herborn in 1628. I quote from the fourth edition, Herborn 1650. The quotation comes from p.7. The *Thesaurus* contains almost sixty different 'chronologies', from the *Chronologia Epocharum*, about the chronologies of all the great states, ruling houses, languages, discoveries (from 'God created heaven and earth' and 'Adam invented the names of things' to 'Johannes Guttenberg invented the art of typography', 266-70), schools, popes, schisms, famous theologians, philosophers, physicians and poets, alchemy, the philosophy of comets and so on up to the chronology of the Bohemian-German war, then from the year 1617 to 1650. For Alsted cf. *RE* I, 390f.; Borst, *Turmbau* (n.3), III.1, 1351ff. For the whole complex of chronology cf. P.Hazard, *La Crise de la Conscience Européenne (1680-1715)*, I, Paris 1935, 67ff.; Kaegi, 'Voltaire' (n.2), 239ff.; Klempt, *Säkularisierung* (n.5), 81ff.

49. *Supputatio*, ed. Aurifaber, preface (unpaginated).

50. This is the numbering of the so-called Alfonsine tables which Alfonso X of Castile had prepared in 1248-52.

51. Bibliander, *De ratione temporum* (n.34), 125f.

52. Alsted, *Thesaurus Chronologiae* (n.48), 36.

53. According to Kaegi, 'Voltaire' (n.2), 240.

54. According to Klempt, *Säkularisierung* (n.5), 85.

55. Alsted, *Thesaurus* (n.48), 219.

56. Hazard, *Crise* (n.48), 69f.

57. Bibliander, *De ratione* (n.34), *Epistola*, unpaginated (av v).

58. For what follows cf. K.Kretschmer, *Die Entdeckung Amerikas in ihrer Bedeutung für die Geschichte des Weltbildes*, Berlin 1892, esp.91ff.

59. Ibid., 93.

60. Ibid., 100f.

61. Ibid., 106.

62. Cf. Kretschmer, *Entdeckung Amerikas* (n.38), Atlas, plate III.

63. Kaegi, 'Voltaire' (n.2), 241. Cf. also E.Sieber, *Kolonialgeschichte der Neuzeit. Die Epochen der europäischen Ausbreitung über die Erde*, who points out that the decisive fact for historical developments remains 'that the impetus for this expansion came from Europe and that it was maintained by Europe' (7).

64. The complete title runs: *Epitome trium terrae partium, Asiae, Africae et Europae compendiariam locorum descriptionem continens, praecipue autem quorum in Actis Lucas, passim autem Evangelistae et Apostoli meminere*, Zurich 1534.

65. W.Näf, *Vadian und seine Stadt St Gallen* I, St Gallen 1944, 263ff.

66. Ibid., 265.

67. Ibid., 276f.

68. For J.Camers cf. ibid., 171ff. He had edited the late-Latin polymath historian Solinus and in this connection had taken up methods and results of Vadian. Vadian defended himself with *Loca aliquot e Pomponianis commentariis repetita indicataque in quibus censendis et aestimandis Joanni Camerti... suis in Solinum enarrationibus cum Joachimo Vadiano non admodum convenit*, Basel 1522 (as a supplement to the second edition of Pomponius Mela). Unfortunately this work was not available anywhere, so I am dependent here on the reference in Näf, *Vadian* (n.65), 274ff.

69. Quoted according to O.Peschel, *Geschichte des Zeitalters der Entdeckungen*, Stuttgart and Augsburg 1858, 679 n.5.

70. Näf, *Vadian* (n.65), I, 275.

71. Ibid., 276.

72. W.Näf, *Vadian II*, St Gallen 1957, 372ff.

73. *Epitome*, ibid., 29f.

74. Ibid., 20.

75. Ibid., 389.

76. Cf. D.R.McKee, 'Isaac de la Peyrère, A Precursor of Eighteenth-Century Critical Deists', in *Publications of the Modern Language Association of America*, Vol.LIX, 1944, 456-85: 456ff. For La Peyrère see also Borst, *Turmbau* (n.2), III.1, 1276ff.

77. Things are not wholly clear and probably can no longer be clarified. Cf. McKee, 'Isaac de la Peyrère' (n.76), 458f.

78. References in ibid., 459f. On the basis of the material McKee comes to the conclusion: 'It is evident that La Peyrère's retraction was never taken seriously by his contemporaries.'

79. E.Amann, *DTC* 12.2, 'Préadamites', col.2798.

80. The work was published simultaneously in two different formats, in octavo and in 12mo. I quote from the octavo edition. A second part of the 'System' never appeared.

81. Apart from the articles mentioned, accounts of La Peyrère's 'System' can be found in G.W.Frank, *Geschichte der protestantischen Theologie*, 2.Teil, Leipzig 1865, 67-75; L.Strauss, *Die Religionskritik Spinozas als Grundlage seiner Bibelwissenschaft. Untersuchungen zu Spinozas Theologisch-Politischem Traktat*, Veröffentlichungen der Akademie für die Wissenschaft des Judentums, Philosophische Sektion II, 1930, 45-64; Klempt, *Säkularisierung* (n.5), 89-96.

82. The reference is probably to the successful voyages of discovery by the Dutchman A.Tasman in 1642 and 1644. Cf. Kretschmer, *Geographie* (n.58), p.95, and O.Zöckler, 'Peyrère's Präadamiten-Hypothese nach ihren Beziehungen zu den anthropologischen Fragen der Gegenwart', *Zeitschrift für die gesamte lutherische Theologie und Kirche* 39, 1878, 28-48, here see esp. 29f. and n.1.

83. The page references in the text refer to the edition of the Pre-Adamites mentioned above. I have also quoted the 'System' by book and chapter.

84. Cf. also *Exercitatio*, Chap.VIII, 24f., the text of which is quoted on p.88 below: a highly remarkable and characteristic passage! See also below, 88.

85. Cf. H.-J.Kraus, *Geschichte der Historisch-Kritischen Erforschung der Alten Testaments von der Reformation bis zur Gegenwart*, 1956, 53f. I cannot see that La Peyrère's work as a whole is 'a significant document for literary criticism which with increasing intensity finds its way into the Pentateuch', as Kraus (ibid., 55) thinks. The role which these ideas play here is all too modest for that. Klempt, *Säkularisierung* (n.5), 101ff., has drawn attention to the connections between La Peyrère and R.Simon.

86. Ibid., 457. Unfortunately I have not succeeded in discovering the bibliographical details of these editions.

87. Cf. Zöckler, 'Präadamiten-Hypothese' (n.82), 434f. Cf. also Frank, *Geschichte* (n.81), 73f.; McKee, 'La Peyrère' (n.76), 458f. To mention some names of Catholic authors: E.Romanus (Philipp de Prieur), H.Bignonius, I.Bullialdus, J.Launonius (Jean de Launoy). Lutherans: Micraelius, the Rostock theologians Eobabus, Schomer and Schelwig, Hilpert of Helmstadt, Dannhauer of Strassburg, J.H.Ursinus of Speyer, later Calov and Quenstedt of Wittenberg, and Felgenhauer, Bechmann, Engelke and Grapius. Reformed: F.Spanheim Jr, A.Hulsius, Maresius, J.Pythius, Schotanus, etc. There are some bibliographical details in Zöckler, 'Präadamiten'. Among others I consulted Ursinus, *Novus Prometheus Praeadamitarum plastes ad Causam relegatus et religatus schediasma*, Frankfurt 1656.

88. Frank, *Geschichte* (n.81), 74.

89. For the influence of La Peyrère's theories above all in England and France up to the time of Voltaire, cf. McKee, 'La Peyrère' (n.76), 471ff. The verdict of Hirsch, *Geschichte der neuern evangelischen Theologie* I [n.1], 217, that the 'biblical framework of world history' had 'still hardly been attacked in the seventeenth century', evidently needs to be corrected in view of La Peyrère's book and its effect.

5. Theology, Philosophy and the Problem of Double Truth

1. *Exercitatio* VIII, 24f.

2. *Conciliare* already appears with the same meaning in Hafenreffer's letter to Kepler (*istas hypotheses cum scriptura sacra conciliare*, see above 56) and in the Latin title of Foscarini's work (*Epistola...in qua sacrae scripturae autoritates, et theologicae propositiones, communiter adversus hanc opinionem [sc. Copernici] adducate conciliantur...*' (see above, 158 n.52).

3. J.Stegman, *Brevis disquisitio*, p.34, see above p.22 and n.45; p.39.

4. The end of the preface to Copernicus, *De revolutionibus* (E.Hirsch, *Die Theologie des Andreas Osiander und ihre geschichtlichen Voraussetzungen*, 1919, 290, see above 52).

5. J.Kepler, *Astronomia nova*, Opera III, 156; see above, 58.

6. De la Peyrère, 'System' (see p.164 n.80 above), Preface, 64.

7. See above, 62.

8. For what follows cf. K.Heim, 'Zur Geschichte des Satzes von der doppelten Wahrheit', in *Studien zur systematischen Theologie, Theodor von Häring... dargebracht*, ed. F.Traub, 1918, 1ff.; W.Betzendörfer, *Glauben und Wissen bei den grossen Denkern des Mittelalters. Ein Beitrag zur Geschichte des Zentralproblems der Scholastik*, 1931, esp.185ff. (which lists the earlier literature); now above all A.Maier, *Studien zur Naturphilosophie der Spätscholastik*, I, *Die Vorläufer Galileis im 14. Jahrhundert*, Storia e lettatura 22, Rome 1949; II. *Zwei Grundprobleme der scholastischen Naturphilosophie*, ibid. 37, ²1951; III. *An der Grenze von Scholastik und Naturwissenschaft*, ibid. 41, ²1952; IV. *Metaphysische Hintergründe der spätscholastischen Naturphilosophie*, ibid. 52, 1955; *Zwischen Philosophie und Mechanik*, ibid. 69, 1958. Here cited as Maier I-V. For further literature see below in the text.

9. H.Denifle, *Chartularium Universitatis Parisiensis* I, Paris 1889, no.471, 541; letter of 18 January 1277.

10. Cf. ibid., no.473, p.543.

11. Cf. C.Colpe, 'Averroismus', *RGG³* I, 796f.

12. On this see F.Van Steenberghen in *RGG³* VI,31, though in contrast to Colpe he does not want to include Siger among the Averroists, but describes his system as 'heterodox Aristotelianism'. The conflict becomes redundant if with M.Grabmann, *Mittelalterliches Geistesleben* II, 1936, 289, one understands 'by Latin Averroism not merely the doctrines of Averroes in so far as they were also held by professors in the faculty of arts in their opposition to the Christian world-view, but that philosophical Aristotelianism advocated generally in the faculty of arts which under the influence of Arabic philosophy attempted to discuss and to resolve all questions even to do with world-view merely "according to the philosophical way" without practical recourse to the doctrines of faith and church theology'.

13. Van Steenberghen, *RGG³* VI, 31.

14. Cf. Betzendörfer, *Glauben und Wissen* (n.8); he discusses the question and answers in the affirmative, against M.Grabmann, *Neuaufgefundene Werke des Siger v.Brabant und Boetius von Dacien*, SAM 1924, second edition, 21).

15. Denifle, *Chartularium* (n.9), I, 548, prop.90.

16. Ibid., 553.

17. Ibid., 550. In view of these formulations, Ebeling's comment on the Averroistic controversy (*RGG³* VI, 803), probably following Gilson, *Études de philosophie médiévale*, 1921, 68, etc.) is hardly tenable: 'as a so-called "doctrine"

of a double, i.e. contradictory truth nonsensical and probably never seriously advocated'.

18. Prop.1: 'That God is not three and one since trinity is not consistent with complete simplicity. Where there is a real plurality, there necessarily is addition and composition. For example, a pile of stones' (ibid., 544).

19. Prop.252: 'That the discourses of theologians are based on fables' (552). Prop.174: 'That there are fables and falsehoods in the Christian law, as in others.'

20. Prop.37: 'That nothing is to be believed unless it is known of itself or can be declared from things which are known of themselves' (545). Also the rejection of authority, prop.150: 'That man should not be content with authority in having certainty over any question' (552).

21. *RGG*³ I, 797. This conviction, which is also expressed by Betzendörfer, *Glauben und Wissen* (n.8), 194, etc. in essentials goes back to P.Mandonnet, *Siger de Brabant et l'averroisme latin au XIIIᵉ siècle,* Paris ¹1899, ²1908/11.

22. *RGG*³ VI,31. Thus also more recent literature, e.g. J.P.Müller, 'Philosophie et foi chez Siger de Brabant. La théorie de la double vérité', in *Studia Anselmiana* VII-VIII, and Maier IV (n.8), 5: 'The validity and "correctness" that many of them [viz. the mediaeval thinkers] attributed to these theses which Aristotle and the Arab philosophers had established and derived merely by the means of natural reason, and which often were opposed to the doctrine of the Christian faith, were more a *probabilitas*, i.e. something that could be demonstrated, than a *veritas* in the strict sense of a truth about reality.'

23. Moreover it had already been preceded by a condemnation of the most important Averroistic principles (evidently ineffective) which is contained in a decree of Bishop Tempier of 10 December 1270 (Denifle, *Chartularium* [n.8], I, no.432, pp.486f.).

24. Maier IV (n.8), 3f. She refers to a passage in the *Physics* of Johannes Buridan which states: '...but all the masters when they begin in the arts swear that they will dispute no purely theological question, like the Trinity or the Incarnation; they also swear that if it happens that they dispute or determine any question which relates to faith and theology, they will determine it for the faith and demolish the arguments which are opposed to it as they seem necessary to be demolished' (*Physica* IV, qu.8, according to the 1509 Paris edition).

25. Grabmann, *Mittelalterliches Geistesleben* (n.12), II, 261f.; Maier I (n.8), 266ff.

26. Maier I (n.8), 253.

27. On this see prop.3 of the 1277 list (Denifle, *Chartularium* [n.8], I, 544): '*Quod Deus non cognoscit alia de se*'.

28. Maier I (n.8), 278.

29. Cf. ibid., 279ff.: 'The revocation of Blasius of Parma'.

30. Ibid., 285.

31. See above, 61.

32. Maier I (n.8), 286.

33. Ibid., 299.

34. Ibid., 251ff.

35. Maier IV (n.8), 12ff. is concerned to demonstrate this.

36. For Pomponiatus see *RGG*³ V, 459f.

37. Cf. W.Betzendörfer, *Die Lehre von der zweifachen Wahrheit bei Petrus*

Pomponiatus, philosophical dissertation Tübingen 1918 (Tübingen 1919), section IV, 89ff.

38. Denzinger-Schönmetzer, *Enchiridion Symbolorum* [32]1963, nos.1440, 1441.

39. Ebeling, *RGG*[3] VI, 799.

40. Ibid.

41. Cf. A.Dempf, 'Metaphysik des Mittelalters', *HPh*, 1930, 80ff.

42. Ibid., 81. Similarly Maier I (n.8), 299: Blasius of Parma 'represents a further link in the chain of a development which perhaps more than any other trend in the fourteenth century prepares for the coming revolution in world-view at the Renaissance and the rise of modern science'.

43. Maier IV (n.8), 397; V, 376ff. This principle also applies even if one follows Blumenberg in assuming an internal restructuring of scholastic natural philosophy as an answer to the question of the 'mere *possibility* of the Copernican shift. However, whether one can really say that 'Copernicus already entered on a freedom which the Middle Ages had finally achieved for itself against itself in the consistency of its controversies and in the toleration of its systematic tensions' (ibid., 40) seems to me doubtful in view of our questioning.

44. However, this formulation applies only if one keeps in mind the 'Averroistic' side. As is well known, the question of the possibility of proof was disputed in Scholasticism. Thus for example Raymond Lull held that the existence of God could be proved absolutely: 'God's being is necessary and can be demonstrated by a more compelling demonstration than any in mathematics' (*Articuli fidei sacrosanctae*, 1651 edition, 1965, quoted from Betzendörfer, *Glauben und Wissen* [n.8], 204). William of Ockham puts forward the opposite position: 'It cannot be proved by natural reason that God is the immediate effective cause of everything' (*Quodlibeta septem* II, q.1, Betzendörfer, p.243).

45. Maier IV (n.8), 6ff.

46. For this see e.g. G.Ebeling, *Luther: An Introduction to his Thought*, London 1972, 76ff.: B.Lohse, *Ratio und Fides. Eine Untersuchung über die ratio in der Theologie Luthers*, 1958, 24ff.

47. Ebeling, *Luther* (n.46), 79.

48. Lohse, *Ratio* (n.47), 7.

49. For the tradition cf. ibid., XVIIIff.; for the occasion, 1ff. The numbers in the text () in each instance give the numbers of the theses.

50. Cf.WA 39, II, 2 and B.Hägglund, *Theologie und Philosophie bei Luther und in der Occamistischen Tradition. Luthers Stellung zur Theorie von der doppelten Wahrheit*, Lunds Universitets Årsskrift, NF avd.1, 51.4, Lund 1955, 89 n.4.

51. Against Heim, 'Doppelte Wahrheit' (n.8), 1. Cf. also Hägglund (n.50), 94: '...a closer investigation shows that he [Luther] cannot be described as a representative of the theory of double truth'.

52. K.Heim, *Das Gewissheitsproblem in der systematischen Theologie bis zur Schleiermacher*, 1911, 237.

53. This misunderstanding can be observed for the first time in the 'Hofmann dispute' (E.Schlee, *Der Streit des Daniel Hoffmann über das Verhältnis der Philosophie zur Theologie*, Marburg 1862). The Helmstadt theologian Daniel Hoffmann had published 101 theses in 1598 which discussed the relationship between philosophy and theology. While thesis 12 contained a brilliant acknowledgment of philosophy in its own sphere, thesis 13 declared that it was

in the most marked contradiction with theology. Thesis 15 takes up Luther's remark against the Sorbonne and thesis 20 – referring to Luther and taking his line – calls for the complete exclusion of philosophical methods and concepts from theology: '(20) We therefore hold what Luther concludes: so we will have done right if dialectic or philosophy are left in their own sphere and we teach how to talk in new languages in the kingdom of faith outside every sphere. Otherwise we shall be putting new wine in old wineskins and will lose both, as the Sorbonne has done' (Schlee, 13f.). With insignificant stylistic differences this thesis literally reproduces theses 40 and 41 of our disputation. The philosophical faculty regarded Hofmann's theses as an attack on philosophy generally and on the basis of thesis 15 accused Hofmann of a doctrine of double truth (ibid., 16ff.). Jacob Martini was his chief opponent. After a long period in which tempers were heated by the dispute, Hofmann finally lost, not because he had not been able to make clear the distinction between incommensurability and contradiction, but because he himself had never fully understood it (Schlee, 56ff.).

54. The same notion appears in WA 39, I, 231.18ff. (dispute with Palladius and Tilemann in 1537 according to the Helmstadt manuscript): 'All words are made new when they are transferred from philosophy to theology, like man, will, reason... For when I ascend into theology I am speaking with new tongues'; ibid., 229.331ff.: 'If we want to use philosophical terms we must first take them to the bath; but we do not use them without danger.' Similarly WA 29, II, 94 (*Disputatio de divinitate et humanitate Christi* of 1540), thesis 21: 'For the creature by the use of old language and in other matters signifies something infinitely separated from the divinity'; thesis 22: 'To use new language signifies a matter inseparably joined to the divinity in the same person in ineffable ways.' See also Hägglund, *Theologie und Philosophie* (n.50), 102. Moreover Hofmann also seems to have concerned himself in greater detail with the idea. Cf. Schlee, *Daniel Hoffmann* (n.52), 44.

55. How little the sense and significance of this extraordinary formulation were understood is evident for example from the translation of these theses by E.F.Rambach from the year 1743 (*Luthers Sämtliche Schriften*, ed.J.G.Walch, X, Halle 1744, col.1400), where we find a statement which is harmless enough: 'For this truth, although it does not run contrary to reason, nevertheless quite incomprehensibly transcends all the concepts that can be understood in disputation.'

56. For the relationship of these theories to the Occamist tradition, which in some respects they seem to follow, cf. now Hägglund (n.50), *Theologie und Philosophie*, 41ff. and 82ff. Hägglund points out 'that Occamism in fact recognizes an undisrupted harmony between faith and rational knowledge', whereas for Luther, 'human reason is a hindrance to faith because of its corrupt state...' (86). 'At this point [viz. the relationship between philosophy and theology], therefore, Luther's conception represents a decisive break with the Occamite tradition' (54).

57. Moreover the *Disputatio contra scholasticam theologiam* of 1517 already puts forward the conviction: '47. No syllogistic form holds in divine terms. 48. However, it does not follow from this that the truth of the article of the Trinity is contrary to syllogistic forms. 49. If the syllogistic form holds in divine matters, the truth of the article of the Trinity will be known and not believed' (WA 1, 226). Two decades later we read: 'Philosophy and theology are different.

Philosophy is concerned with what is known by human reason. Theology is concerned with what is believed, that is, what we apprehend in faith' (WA 39, II, 6.22ff, 14.36ff., etc.).

58. From the marginal notes on Augustine and Peter Lombard of 1509/10 (WA 9, 66.9f.).

59. D.Jonas contra 4 (WA 39, II, 21.37ff.).

60. Ibid. 22.1ff. Copies B and C are very much shorter and have only the 'it is far different'.

61. See above, 85f.

62. In the *Responsio* according to C the sentence 'Three cannot be one' is explicitly described as 'a most certain demonstration: but outside theology' (WA 39, II, 22.30ff.).

63. WA 39, I, 229.4ff. (dispute with Palladius and Tilemann, 1537): 'theology is above human capacity: philosophy is sweet to the reason'.

64. WA Table Talk 4, no 4.638. See 47 above.

65. From the preface to the *Supputatio annorum mundi* in the translation by Aurifaber (n.15)), unpaginated. See above, 68.

66. K.Heim, *Gewissheitsproblem* (n.52), 237.

67. K.Holl, 'Luthers Bedeutung für den Fortschritt der Auslegungskunst', in *Gesammelte Aufsätze zur Kirchengeschichte* I, ⁷1948, 544-82.

68. Ibid., 546.

69. Ibid., 551.

70. Ibid., 552.

71. Cf. ibid., 559 n.4.

72. Ibid., 555ff.

73. E.Troeltsch, *Vernunft und Offenbarung bei Johann Gerhard und Melanchthon. Untersuchungen zur Geschichte der altprotestantischen Theologie*, Göttingen 1891; H.E.Weber, *Der Einfluss der protestantischen Schulphilosophie auf die orthodox-lutherische Dogmatik*, 1908; P.Althaus, *Die Prinzipien der deutschen reformierten Dogmatik im Zeitalter der aristotelischen Scholastik. Eine Untersuchung zur altprotestantische Theologie*,1914; J.Baur, *Die Vernunft zwischen Ontologie und Offenbarung. Eine Untersuchung zur Theologie J.A.Quenstedts*, 1962 (which has further literature); E.Bizer, *Frühorthodoxie und Rationalismus*, ThSt71, 1961.

74. As early as 1598, for example in Helmstedt, Martini refused his assent to Hofmann's thesis ' "that if philosophy is contrary to the word of God, then the latter must be believed", because he did not think such a contradiction possible' (Schlee, *Daniel Hofmann*, n.51, 20). The beginning of the Hofmann dispute also shows how much this view had already come to be taken for granted in Lutheranism.

75. Weber, *Einfluss* (n.73), 3.

76. For this section see the comments in ibid., 4ff.

77. Ibid.

78. Althaus, *Prinzipien* (n.73), 10f.; similarly Bizer, *Frühorthodoxie* (n.73), 17.

79. *Syntagma* (1610), ed. V.1624, 44; Althaus, *Prinzipien*, 14.

80. Ibid., 28.

81. Althaus, *Prinzipien* (n.73), 96ff.; Baur, *Vernunft* (n.73), 102f.

82. H.E.Weber, *Reformation, Orthodoxie und Rationalismus*, BFCT Theologie 2/35, 45, 1937ff.

83. Troeltsch, *Vernunft* (n.73), 10.
84. Ibid., 41ff.
85. Althaus, *Prinzipien* (n.73), 73ff.
86. Troeltsch, *Vernunft* (n.73), 9.
87. Baur, *Vernunft* (n.73), 21.
88. Ibid., 104f.
89. Ibid., 109-11, from which the following quotations are taken.

6. Cartesianism: Orthodox Opposition, Mediation and Radical Criticism

1. E.Hirsch, *Geschichte der neuern evangelischen Theologie im Zusammenhang mit den allgemeinen Bewegungen des europäischen Denkens* III, 217.
2. Quotations from the *Discourse on Method* and *Meditations* are taken from the Penguin Books edition, Harmondsworth 1968, translated by F.E.Sutcliffe; the classic French edition is by C.Adam and P.Tannery, Paris 1897ff.
3. 'The history of philosophical systems, ancient or modern, perhaps does not offer another example of a more prompt, stunning and universal triumph' (F.Boullier, *Histoire de la philosophie cartésienne*, Paris ³1868, I, 255).
4. P.Hazard, *La Crise de la Conscience Européenne (1680-1715)*, I, Paris 1935, 161f.
5. Quoted ibid, 163.
6. *Discourse* IV.1, pp.53f.
7. G.Krüger, 'Die Herkunft des philosophischen Selbstbewusstseins', *Logos* XXII, 1933, 232.
8. Ibid., 233.
9. *Discourse* II.7, p.41.
10. Krüger, 'Herkunft' (n.7), 237.
11. Cf. *Discourse* VI.1, p.77.
12. *Principles* III.4, 80f.
13. Feuerbach already observed that in a brilliant comparison of Descartes with Luther: 'While Descartes says "I think, I am," i.e. my thought is my being, Luther says "My faith is my being." Just as the former recognizes and posits as the principle of philosophy the unity of thought and being, Luther graps this unity of faith and being, and expresses it as religion' (*Geschichte der neueren Philosophie von Bacon v. Verulam bis Baruch Spinoza*, 1833, 219f.).
14. *Principles* I,25, 9.
15. *Discourse* II.11, p.41.
16. For the occasion and course of the controversy cf. A.C.Duker, *Gisbertus Voetius* I-III, Leiden 1897-1910; esp. II, 132-201; individual references in W.Goeters, *Die Vorbereitung des Pietismus in der reformierten Kirche der Niederlande bis zur labadistischen Krisis 1670*, Leiden and Utrecht 1911; C.Louise Thijssen-Schoute, *Nederlands Cartesianisme*, 1954, gives a comprehensive account. E.Bizer, 'Die reformierte Orthodoxie und der Cartesianismus', *ZTK* 55, 1958, 306-72, is particularly important. The monograph by J.Bohatec, *Die cartesianische Scholastik in der Philosophie und reformierten Dogmatik des 17.Jahrhunderts, I.Teil: Entstehung, Eigenart, Geschichte und philosophische Ausprägung der cartesianischen Scholastik*, 1912 (Part II never appeared. Cf. J.K.Egli, 'Josef Bohatec – der Mann und sein Werk', *Jahrbuch der Gesellschaft für die Geschichte des Protestantismus in Österreich* 71, 1955, 23ff.) attempts to demonstrate that the Cartesians often sought a balance between Aristotle and

Descartes. Descartes himself is claimed to have been largely a scholastic (Bohatec, 6f., 11). Now there is no doubt that Cartesianism has many scholastic elements, and Bohatec gives abundant examples of them. But its historical significance is not connected with that, but with the new beginning that it represents. Bohatec's principle of selection must necessarily distort his perspective on this more important side of Cartesianism.

17. For Mastricht see E.Bizer in Heppe-Bizer, *Die Dogmatik der evangelischen-reformierten Kirche*, 1958, LXXX; and *Nieuw Nederlandsch Biografisch Woordenboek*, 1911ff. [*NNBW*] X, 591f.

18. *Novitatum Cartesianarum Gangraena, nobiliores plerasque corporis theologici partes arrodens et excedens, seu Theologia Cartesiana detecta*, Amsterdam 1677, 7 [LB Stuttgart]. Cf. also Bizer, *ZTK* 55, 1958, 357ff.

19. Born 1634 in North Holland, a pupil of J.Alting in Groningen, from 1679 a Reformed pastor in Amsterdam, where he died in 1698, cf. *RGG*³ I, 1017.

20. *De Philosophia Cartesiana admonitio candida et sincera*, Wesel 1668, 114 [StB Mannheim]. Cf. also Thijssen-Schoute, *Nederlands Cartesianisme* (n.16).

21. Cf. also Boullier, *Histoire* (n.3), I, 255: '...it is in the Dutch universities, which are more open to new opinions than those in France, that one sees primarily Cartesian philosophy spreading and entering openly into a struggle with the old philosophy.'

22. Cf. also Thijssen-Schoute, *Cartesianisme* (n.16), 2: 'During Descartes' life and in the first decades after it the Netherlands was teeming with Cartesians, while conservative and anti-Cartesian became virtually synonymous.' Similarly 622.

23. Daniel Lipstorp, 1631-1684, was born in Lübeck; he was an astronomer, mathematician and jurist at the University of Uppsala, a passionate Cartesian and defender of the Copernican system. Cf. *ADB* 18, 746.

24. Lipstorp, *Specimina Philosophiae Cartesianae. Quibus accedit eiusdem authoris Copernicus redivivus seu de vero mundi systemate, liber singularis*, Leiden 1653 [UB Tübingen].

25. Ibid., *Praefatio* (unpaginated).

26. After his promotion in Tübingen Tepelius, who was born in 1649 in the Vogtland district of Saxony, became 'Informator' (i.e. teacher) in Reutlingen, a member of the order of Pegnitz and poet laureate. Otherwise little is known of him. Cf. *ADB* 37, 573.

27. Tobias Andreae, 1604-76, was born in Braunfels in the county of Solms. From 1635 he was professor of history and Greek in Groningen; he was one of the first followers of Descartes in Holland. Cf. *NNBW* I, 131f. and Thijssen-Schoute, *Cartesianisme* (n.16), s.v.

28. Andreae, *Historia Philosophiae Cartesianae*, Nuremberg 1674, 56f. [UB Tübingen]. In supposing that such expressions betrayed 'a complete lack of understanding of the most important tasks and goals of philosophy in the seventeenth century', S.v.Dunin-Borkowski, *Spinoza I, Der junge De Spinoza*, 1910, 316. Unattractive as this claim of modern science to infallibility may be to the Catholic author, it cannot be denied that it essentially helped to shape the modern mind. A systematic assessment is of course another matter, but that is not in question here.

29. For Roëll cf. *RE* XVII, 71-4; *RGG*³ V, 1137; Thijssen-Schoute, *Cartesianisme* (n.16), s.v.

30. Roëll, *Oratio inauguralis, de religione rationali*, Franeker 1686, 30 [LB

Stuttgart]. For G.W.F.Hegel see his inaugural lecture in Berlin on 22 October 1818 with its famous closing sentences: 'Courage for the truth, faith in the power of the Spirit, is the first condition of philosophical study; man should revere himself and think himself worthy of the highest. He cannot think greatly enough about the grandeur and power of the Spirit. The closed being of the universe has no power in itself which could resist the courage of knowledge: it must open itself to him, lay its riches and its depths before him and give it him to enjoy' ('Hegels Anrede an seine Zuhörer bei Eröffnung seiner Vorlesungen in Berlin', in *Hegels Vorreden*, ed. E.Metzke, 1969, 109-13).

31. Ludwig Meyer, 1629-1681. For Meyer's biography see now the information in Thijssen-Schoute, *Cartesianisme* (n.19), § 210-13, 353ff. This supersedes all earlier accounts.

32. Meyer, *Philosophia sanctae scripturae interpres. Exercitatio paradoxa*, Eleutheropolis [i.e. Amsterdam] 1666. Here quoted from the third edition edited by J.S.Semler, Halle 1776, 180. A quite literal translation of the difficult passage proved impossible. For the theological position and significance of the *Exercitatio* see below, 133ff.

33. C.Lentulus (Lentz) – his name is not in *ADB* – was confronted with Cartesianism at an early stage as a colleague of J.C.Clauberg and C.Wittich in Herborn in 1651 and 1652. He died as professor of church history and poetics in Marburg in 1678. Cf. S.Jöcher, *Allgemeines Gelehrten Lexicon* II, 1750, 2367f. and III, 1810, 1594. His bibliography is also there.

34. Lentulus, *Cartesius triumphatus et nova sapientia ineptiarum et blasphemiae convicta*, Frankfurt 1653, 85f. [StB Reutlingen]. The writing is, moreover, a blatant lampoon and does not hesitate to engage in falsification. Thus for example Lentulus reports the request for an opinion on Cartesian philosophy which Ludwig Heinrich of Nassau-Dillenberg gave to a series of Dutch universities and schools on 15 July 1651 because of the disputes at the High School in Herborn. He cites at length the negative replies of Leiden, Utrecht, Groningen and Harderwijk, but suppresses the positive responses of Franeker and Breda. (Some of the text of the opinion is also in Tepelius [ibid., 72ff] and more recently in the appendix to Bohatec, *Scholastik* [n.16], 155ff., according to the sources in the Wiesbaden state archive.)

35. This evidently refers to a passage in the *Discourse* (VI.2, p.78), where Descartes speaks of the possibility of a practical philosophy 'by which, knowing the power and the effects of fire, water, air, the stars, the heavens and all the other bodies which surround us, as distinctly as we know the various trades of our craftsmen, we might put them in the same way to all the uses for which they are appropriate, and thereby make ourselves, as it were, masters and possessors of nature'.

36. Lentulus, *Cartesius triumphatus* (n.34), 34f.

37. From 1646 du Bois was in Leiden; he died in 1661. Cf. *NNBW* IV, 193f.

38. Nicolaus Arnoldus was born in Lissa, Poland, in 1618 and died in Franeker in 1680. During his teaching activity of almost thirty years there Arnoldus primarily devoted himself to disputing against the Socinians and Cartesians. Cf. *RE* II, 129 and *NNBW* IV, 62f.

39. Arnoldus, *Dissertatiuncula de Theologiae supra Philosophiam dominio cum brevibus stricturis ad librum sub titulo Philosophia scripturae interpres*, Franeker 1667, 31 [UB Göttingen]. Maresius, *Valeriani Magni capuccini Methodus* ἀμέθοδος *et ignis fatuus, sive I.Examen theologicum novae methodi*

ab ipso nuper profusae ad retrahendos protestantes sub iugam pontificis. II, Brevis refutatio libelli alterius quem postea subtitulo Lucis in tenebris lucentis emisit, Groningen 1654, 8f., and M.Leydekker (*RE* XI, 427) in his *Fax veritatis, seu exercitationes ad nonnullas controversias quae hodie in Belgio potissimum moventur, multa ex parte Theologico-Philosophicae*, Leiden 1677 [UB Utrecht], argue similarly; in the latter, on *Controversia IV*, 'Is human reason no less certain than revealed truth?', we read 'Human reason is blind in matters of faith after the fall, weak and obscured in natural matters, particularly those relating to knowledge of God; which no one but Pelagius has denied' (15f.). For the *Fax veritatis* cf. also Bizer, *ZTK* 55, 1958, 363ff.

40. Mastricht, *Gangraena* (n.18), 37.

41. Ibid., 45f.

42. Arnoldus, *Dissertatiuncula* (n.39), 47.

43. N.Arnoldus, *Lux in tenebris, seu brevis et succincta vindicatio simul et conciliatio locorum Veteris et Novi Testamenti, quibus omnium sectarum adversarii ad stabiliendos errores abutuntur*, [²1662] Franeker 1665, Dedicatio (unpaginated) [UB Freiburg].

44. *Lux in Tenebris*, Dedicatio. Moreover the same or a similar argument occurs often in the orthodox literature. Cf. e.g. Leydekker, *RE* (n.39), 26: 'God can best bear witness to his work and his world; he is also attested to by his word; it is safer to believe the creator than our concepts, to reject blasphemous testimony as erroneous, such is our opinion, which in natural matters is most often wrong or led astray.' In fact on orthodox presuppositions it is hard to make any objection to the assertion that in the end the creator must know best.

45. *Lux in tenebris*, Dedicatio.

46. Ibid., 38.

47. Ibid., 39.

48. The orthodox are quite clear about the significance of philosophy in this connection. For example du Bois demonstrates this through Lipstorp, who as a Copernican still defended the authority of scripture, while as a Cartesian he wanted it to be limited: 'So much was Lipstorp the Cartesian changed from Lipstorp the pure Copernican. That [the limitation of the authority of scripture in principle] seems to be distinctively Cartesian' (*Veritas et authoritas sacra*, Praefatio [unpaginated], sub.IV).

49. Leydekker, *RE* (n.39), 24f.

50. So also Bizer, *ZTK* 55, 1958, 371: 'No one will fail to see that a legitimate theological interest is expressed in the remarks of these anti-Cartesians. They saw rightly that the scientific attitude which Descartes required is different from the attitude of faith required by the Bible.'

51. Du Bois, *Veritas et authoritas sacra*, Praefatio [unpaginated].

52. The opinion (see 172 n.34) above of 18 September 1651 refers back to a judgment which the Senate of the university had already made in March 1642. It runs: 'The professors of the academy reject that new philosophy: first, because it is opposed... to the old philosophy; then, because it turns the youth from old and sound philosophy... lastly because various false and absurd opinions in part follow from it and in part can be deduced by rash youth who will then fight with other disciplines and faculties and primarily with orthodox theology...', quoted from Lentulus, *Cartesius triumphatus* (n.34), 9f.

53. Born 1632 in Utrecht, as a theologian a representative of strict orthodoxy; he died in 1695, cf. *NNBW* III, 709f.; V, 301ff.

54. J. Koelman, *Het vergift van de Cartesiaansche Philosophie grondig entdekt. En meest historischer Wijze, uit de Schriften van des Cartes zelfs, en van andere Schrijvers, zo voor als tegen hem, getrouwelijk aangewezen. Op gestellt, tot een grondt van de Wederlegging van Bekkers Betover de Wereldt*, Amsterdam 1692, preface (unpaginated) [UB Amsterdam].

55. Ibid., 47.

56. Ibid., 60.

57. Ibid., 22.

58. Ibid., 30.

59. Bekker, *Admonitio*, 10 (the numbers in the text following relate to the pages in this edition).

60. Some further voices on this basic principle of the Cartesian centre party are: Petrus Allinga (from 1658 pastor in Wijdenes in North Holland, died 1692, *NNBW* IV, 37f.): 'Theology and philosophy rely on different principles, one nature or the light of nature, one scripture or divine revelation. Where disciplines differ so widely, one cannot say that one is the handmaid of the other', in *Illustrium erotematum, tam ex theologia, quam philosophia, decades duodecim, accuratis responsionibus (in quibus examinantur etiam, quae viri clarissimi, Witzius in Oeconomia et Diatribe, et Mastricht in Gangraena Cartesianismi protulere adversus cl. Cocceium et subtiliss. Cartesium*, Utrecht 1679 [UB Göttingen]). C. Wittich (see below, 124f.): 'Certainty is twofold, the one because it rests on evident demonstration and the other because it relies on clear revelation; each is equally great in its kind, nor may one certainty be called greater than the other...', *Theologia pacifica, in qua varias problemata theologica inter reformatos theologos agitari solita ventilantur, simul usus philosophia Cartesianae in diversis theologiae partibus demonstratur...* [1671], Leiden ³1683, CXXIV, pp. 10f. [BEvSt Tübingen] cf. also Bizer *ZTK* 55, 1958, 349 nn.2,3 and Titius, *RE* 24, 205,4ff. Lambert van Velthuysen (1622-1685), after study of theology, philosophy and medicine a doctor in his home town of Utrecht and one of the most influential champions of Cartesianism, *NNBW* IV, 1368ff.: 'Both philosophy and theology, considered objectively, are each in its way perfect, complete, certain and infallible; nor is one in that sense inferior to the other,' *Dissertatio de usu rationis in rebus theologicis et praesertim in interpretatione sanctae scripturae*, in *Opera omnia*, Rotterdam 1680, I, 102. The only copy in West Germany known to me is in BEvSt Tübingen.

61. Nor can anything more absurd be said than that 'one cannot theologize from philosophy'; for what is true in nature, cannot be false in theology, and with God the author of nature' (Petrus ab Andlo [presumably a pseudonym for the Utrecht philosopher Regnier de Mansfeld. See Duker, *Voetius* (n.16), III, 81 n.3, etc. and *NNBW* IX, 646f.], *Specimen confutationis dissertationibus quam Samuel Maresius edidit de abusu philosophiae Cartesianae*, Leiden 1670, 10 ([UB Erlangen]).

62. For Virgil, who died in 784, see *RE* XX, 695ff.

63. Du Bois speaks of the 'rein of the word of God' which must be imposed on philosophy and on its demand for freedom says: 'Let it be, but we must deny that it is unlimited...' (*Veritas et authoritas sacra*, Praefatio, unpaginated). The numerous prohibitions on Cartesian philosophy which were made by state bodies at the urging of the orthodox between 1640 and 1690 are the practical consequence of this conviction. They almost all remained without lasting effect.

64. I am not taking account here of the differences within the group because my main concern is to bring out the basic position.

65. Christoph Wittich was born in Brieg in Lower Silesia in 1625. After studying theology in Groningen and Leiden he became Professor in Herborn in 1651, in Duisburg in 1652, in Nymwegen in 1655, and in Leiden in 1671, where he died in 1687. In 1654 there appeared the *Dissertationes suae de sanctae scripturae in philosophicis usu*, with which the great controversy over the Bible and the new world view began. Wittich was the undisputed theological head of the Cartesian centre party. For biographical details cf. *ADB* 43, 631ff.: *NNBW* X, 1233f.; *RGG³* VI, 1786; C.Sepp, *Het godgeleerd onderwijs in Nederland gedurende de 16ᵉ en 17ᵉ eeuw, II,* Leiden 1874, 145ff., etc. For his work see Hirsch, *Geschichte* (n.1), 181-8, but he regards Wittich's posthumous *Anti-Spinoza* – probably with some justification, as his most significant work, and the evaluation of Wittich's work in Bizer, *ZTK* 55, 1958, 340ff., with which we largely agree.

66. The quotation appears in this form only in the *Duae dissertationes* of 1654, to which I had no access. Cf. Bizer, *ZTK* 55, 1958, 342 n.4. Later Wittich avoided this shift.

67. More recent literature on the accommodation theory still puts forward the theory of R.Hofmann, 'Accommodation', *RE* I, 127ff., who assigns it historically to the second half of the eighteenth century. 'A transition to the assumption that some of what is taught in the Bible is not to be understood as real (but by way of accommodation) was already formed by the treatise of Zachariä (*Theologische Erklärung der Herablassung Gottes zu den Menschen,* 1763)...', ibid. 129. Thus it seems to Karl Barth, 'Samuel Werenfels (1657-1740) und die Theologie seiner Zeit', *EvTh* 3, 1936, 196 n.33, worth mentioning that 'because of the "errors" in physics made by the biblical authors Werenfels preferred the so-called accommodation theory to later rationalistic exegesis'. C.Hartlich and W.Sachs, *Der Ursprung der Mythosbegriffes in der modernen Bibelwissenschaft,* 1952, 23 n.1, also refer to Hofmann's article in this connection. In *RGG³* I, 209, there is certainly a mention that this theory had 'already been put forward in the seventeenth century', but only Semler is mentioned. Similarly, G.Hornig, *Die Anfänge der historisch-kritischen Theologie. J.S.Semlers Schriftverständnis und seine Stellung zu Luther,* FSTR 8, Munich 1961, 212, comments: 'Although the accommodation theory had already been put forward in the seventeenth century in various forms, the dispute over this theory really came to a climax only in the decade between 1785 and 1795 [sic].' In his 'Discussion of the historical origin of the accommodation theory', Horning relies on S.J.Baumgarten (who is much better informed here than more recent literature) and Semler, without examining the source material himself. – All this seems to me to be an impressive example of the degree to which the seventeenth century is in fact *terra incognita.*

68. 'On the passages of scripture which seem to be contrary to the rotation of the earth and tend to oppose it, I would reply with a mode of language used by the Copernicans that in these passages scripture speaks according to the views of the common people and not according to assured truth...' (*Consensus veritatis in scriptura divine et infallibili revelatae cum veritate philosophica a Renato Des Cartes detecta,* Nymwegen 1659, Praefatio [unpaginated] [LB Stuttgart]).

69. *Dissertatiuncula* (n.39), 43.

70. Ibid., 17f.

71. Ibid., 26, see above, 52f.

72. Similarly Mastricht, *Gangraena* (n.18), 71f.; Leydekker, *RE* XI (n.39), 28: 'God would thus in fact have been misleading us and teaching us an error'.

73. Mastricht, *Gangraena* (n.18), 80.

74. J.A.Osiander, *Collegium considerationum in dogmata theologica Cartesianorum*, Stuttgart 1684, 24 [LB Stuttgart]. Osiander, born in Vaihingen in 1622, died in 1697 as the Chancellor of Tübingen University, where from 1660 he had a theological professorship. Cf. *RE* XIV, 513f, no 4. His *Collegium considerationum*, one of the few anti-Cartesian works to have been written in Germany, is an almost complete collection of all the orthodox arguments against Cartesianism and at the same time testimony to an increasing internal rationalizing of orthodoxy, which here prefers to use 'sound reason' in refutation. Cf. also the *Examen censurae Wittichianae quam praemisit commentario in Epistolam ad Romanos*, Tübingen 1688 [LB Stuttgart], an answer by Osiander to Wittich's attacks on the *Collegium considerationum*.

75. 'But if the heathen and the uneducated in scripture cherish erroneous opinions about those [viz. matters of faith], they should be banished from scripture, since it is its scope to convey what is to be believed, not erroneous thoughts about natural matters.' Quoted from the *Duae dissertationes* by du Bois, *Veritas et authoritas* (n.48), 18.

76. 'There can be no doubt that he [Wittich] took a decisive step beyond Wolzogen by introducing the concept of scope into the debate. He was the first to succeed in distinguishing between a picture of the world and theology and thus in showing a way out of the dilemma in which theology had become involved' (ibid., 347). Even if Wittich cannot be given priority here, his contribution nevertheless remains undoubtedly significant.

77. *Theologica pacifica*, Praefatio [unpaginated].

78. Ibid., XVII, 13f.

79. Ibid., XIX, 14f.

80. 'But with the mythical form of explanation... a view had appeared which on the basis of the insight into the universal and necessary character of the mythical form of conception and expression excluded erroneous and false conceptions in the Bible through accommodation...' (ibid., 73f.).

81. *Consensus veritatis*, § 813. Cf. Bizer, *ZTK* 55, 1958, 345.

82. That can also be demonstrated, for example, from Velthuysen, who for the sake of the authority of scripture wants to remove the internal and external contradictions: 'We think that equal divine authority is to be given to each and every book of Holy Scripture and the parts of them as received by the Reformed according to the canon; but they are to be regarded as holy scripture not according to the letters or the words, but according to their sense, lest here and there the sacred letters seem to contradict themselves' (*Demonstratio quietem solis ac motum terrae minime pugnare cum verbo dei*, Opera omnia, 1047).

83. L.Strauss, *Die Religionskritik Spinozas als Grundlage seiner Bibelwissenschaft. Untersuchungen zu Spinozas Theologisch-Politischem Traktat*, Veröffentlichungen der Akademie für die Wissenschaft des Judentums, Philosophische Sektion II, 1930, 163.

84. For Bekker, see above, 171 n.19 and especially the fine evaluation by Hirsch, *Geschichte* (n.1), 209ff.

85. In what follows I quote the first German translation, which appeared in 1693, the same year as the Dutch original: *Die bezauberte Welt: Oder Eine*

gründliche Untersuchung Des Allgemeinen Aberglaubens/ Betreffend/ die Art und das Vermögen/ Gewalt und Wirkung des Satans und der bösen Geister über den Menschen/ Und was diese durch derselben Krafft und Gemeinschafft thun: So aus natürlicher Vernunfft und Hl.Schrift in vier Bücher zu bewehren sich unternommen hat Balthasar Bekker, S.Theol.Doct. und Prediger zu Amsterdam, Amsterdam 1693 [BEvSt Tübingen]. I quote in the text by book, section and paragraph.

86. Ibid., 902-32, 933-84.

87. Thus for example Wittich explains that no one fought the anonymous author of the *Exercitatio paradoxa* better than did he and his friends (*Theologia pacifica*, Praefatio); so too does P.Allinga, *Fax dissidii extincta, seu exercitationes pacificae ad nonnullas quaestiones problematicas, quae hodie in Belgium potissimum moventur*, Amsterdam 1682, 18 [UB Freiburg]. For the opinion of the Leiden faculty cited here see Bizer, *ZTK* 55, 1958, 333. There is also a longer but more balanced discussion of the *Exercitatio paradoxa* in Velthuysen, *Opera omnia*, 148-59.

88. For the author and the work cf. above 172 nn.31, 32. I cite the above-mentioned edition in the text by page numbers or chapters and paragraphs.

89. *ZTK* 55, 1958, 329-33.

90. E.g. Roëll also expresses these ideas at length in his *Oratio inauguralis de religione rationali*, which in some respects is close to Meyer's *Exercitatio*. Ibid., 9f., etc.

91. Dunin-Borkowski, *Spinoza* I (n.28), 519.

92. Ibid., 115.

93. That Meyer himself was familiar with Socinian literature emerges from XVI.1, where he mentions and cites the Rakow Catechism, Smalcius *contra Frantzium disputatio de iustificatione*, the *Brevis disquisitio* of J.Stegman (ibid., 30 nn.45, 46) and Schlichting's treatise against Balthasar Meisner (*de Trinitate*).

94. *ZTK* 55, 1958, 333.

95. They relate to the concept of God, transubstantiation and the Trinity, which Meyer in each case interprets philosophically (VI.3).

96. I have not been able to discover the exact year in which it appeared. Hazard, *Crise* (n.4), 125, gives 1669; Baumgarten, *Geschichte der Religionspartheyen*, ed. J.S.Semler, Halle 1766, 118f., gives 1670. In any case it must have appeared before 1671, since in this year P.Jurieu had already published a work directed against it: *Examen du livre de la réunion du christianisme*, Orleans 1671 (*RE* IX, 639.49f.). Dunin-Borkowski wrongly thought 'what seems to be an utterly freethinking book' to be 'unfindable'; my copy came from the Bibliotheque Nationale in Paris [MF].

97. d'Huisseau's exact biographical dates are evidently unknown. At all events, the *Grande Encyclopédie* (20,383) simply says 'born in Paris at the beginning of the seventeenth century and died in England after 1685'. As well as the Réunion, d'Huisseau also produced a collection of Reformed church ordinances which went through several editions: *La Discipline des Église réformées de France...*, 1650, ²1660, ³1670. The charge in Baumgarten-Semler that d'Huisseau wrote his work 'to make himself popular with the Catholic Church and at the court' (119) seems quite incredible and might derive from Jurieu's polemic.

98. The page references in the text refer to the edition mentioned in n.96 above.

99. For this cf. Part Two of the *Réunion*: 'Des causes de la division qui est entre les Chrestiens', 60-101.

100. I shall just give some basic ideas of this complex work which are particularly important in this context. A complete account of the problem as a whole would have exceeded the limits of the present work.

101. The quotations from the *Tractatus* are taken from *A Theologico-Political Treatise*, translated by R.H.M.Elwes (London 1883), reissued New York 1951, to which the page numbering refers.

102, *Ep*.XX.

103. The Dutch original has 'aensien', the Latin transcription correctly *auctoritas*.

104. *Ep*.XXI.

105. The second edition of the *Tractatus* appeared in 1673 printed together with *Philosophia Sanctae Scripturae interpres*! Cf. Thijssen-Schoute, *Cartesianisme* (n.16), 394.

106. *Cogitationes metaphysicae* II, XII. They appear as an appendix to Spinoza's first printed work, the *Renati Des Cartes Principiorum Philosophiae Pars I et II, More Geometrico demonstratae*, published in 1663.

107. *Ep*.XXX. Cf. also the preface to the *Tractatus*, which deals at length with the terms 'superstition' and 'prejudice', 3-11.

108. Ch.XIV, 189.

109. Ibid., 189f.

110. Ch.XV, p.198.

111. In fact Spinoza is convinced that 'revelation' is necessary only for ordinary people. There is the possibility of becoming completely blessed through 'natural illumination'. That is even the higher form because it is associated with a clear concept (Ch.V, p.78).

112. Ch.I, 19; Ch.II, pp.27ff.

113. Ch.II, 33f.; Ch.VI, 93.

114. Ibid., p. 35.

115. Cf. the list of Spinoza's books left at his death in J.Freudenthal, *Die Lebensgeschichte Spinozas in Quellenschriften, Urkunden und nichtamtlichen Nachrichten*, Leipzig 1899, 166 no.54. There are comparative extracts from the Pre-Adamites in Dunin-Borkowski, *Spinoza* (n.28), 114.

116. Ch.VI, 86f.

117. Ch.VII, 99f.

118. Cf. C.Siegfried, *Spinoza als Kritiker und Ausleger des Alten Testaments. Ein Beitrag zur Geschichte der alttestamentlichen Kritik und Exegese*, Berlin 1867; H.J.Kraus, *Geschichte der Historisch-Kritischen Erforschung des Alten Testaments von der Reformation bis zur Gegenwart*, 1956, 55f. and the literature mentioned above 145 n.5.

Conclusion

1. Cf. K.Scholder, 'Herder und die Anfänge der historischen Theologie', *EvTh* 22, 1962, 425-40.

2. H.Liebing, *RGG*³ II, cols.601f.; K.Scholder, 'F.C.Baur als Historiker', *EvTh* 21, 1961. We still need a detailed account of this development.

ABBREVIATIONS

ADB	*Allgemeine Deutsche Biographie*
AfRG	*Archiv für Religionsgeschichte*
BEvST	Bibliothek des Evangelischen Stifts Tübingen
BFCT	Beiträge zur Förderung christlicher Theologie
CR	*Corpus Reformatorum*
DTC	*Dictionnaire de Théologie Catholique*
DVfLG	*Deutsche Vierteljahrsschrift für Literaturwissenschaft und Geistesgeschichte*
EvTh	Evangelische Theologie
FSTR	Forschungen zur systematischen Theologie und Religionsphilosophie
FzKGG	Forschungen zur Kirchen- und Geistesgeschichte
HPh	*Handbuch der Philosophie*
JdTh	*Jahrbuch der Theologie*
LB	Landesbibliothek
MF	Microfilm
NDB	*Neue deutsche Biographie*
NF	Neue Folge = New Series
NNBW	*Nieuw Nederlandsch Biografisch Woordenboek*
NR	Nieuwe Reeks = New Series
RE	*Realencyclopädie für protestantische Theologie und Kirche*
RGG	*Die Religion in Geschichte und Gegenwart*
StB	Stadtbibliothek
UB	Universitätsbibliothek
WA	Weimarer Ausgabe. The Weimar edition of Luther's works
ZTK	*Zeitschrift für Theologie und Kirche*

INDEX